Engineering the User Interface

Miguel Redondo • Crescencio Bravo • Manuel Ortega
Editors

Engineering the User Interface

From Research to Practice

 Springer

Editors

Miguel Redondo
College of Computer Science Engineering
Department of Information Systems
and Technologies
University of Castilla – La Mancha
Spain

Crescencio Bravo
College of Computer Science Engineering
Department of Information Systems
and Technologies
University of Castilla – La Mancha
Spain

Manuel Ortega
College of Computer Science Engineering
Department of Information Systems
and Technologies
University of Castilla – La Mancha
Spain

ISBN: 978-1-84996-735-8   e-ISBN: 978-1-84800-136-7
DOI 10.1007/978-1-84800-136-7

British Library Cataloguing in Publication Data
A catalogue record for this book is available from the British Library

Printed on acid-free paper

Springer Science+Business Media
springer.com

Contents

Creativity Support Tools: A Grand Challenge for HCI Researchers

Ben Shneiderman

Department of Computer Science, Human-Computer Interaction Laboratory & Institute for Advanced Computer Studies, University of Maryland, College Park, MD 20742
ben@cs.umd.edu

Abstract Human-computer interaction researchers can play a key role in designing, implementing, and evaluating a new generation of creativity support tools. Understanding creative processes, especially when mediated by user interfaces will remain a continuing challenge, especially in dealing with novice and expert users, across a variety of disciplines. The expected outcomes include (1) refined theories of technology-supported creative processes, (2) active discussion of user-oriented empirical research methods, (3) new software architectures, database management strategies, and networking technologies, and (4) improved user interfaces to support discover and innovation, especially in collaborative environments.

1 Introduction

During the past 40 years, computing professionals have been enormously successful in developing productivity support tools for many users, so that they can perform their work more rapidly, effectively, and with fewer errors. Now, computing professionals are turning their attention to developing creativity support tools, which enable users to explore, discover, imagine, innovate, compose, and collaborate [8].

The grand challenge for creativity support tool designers is to enable more people to be more creative more of the time [7, 12]. Creativity takes many forms, such as paintings, sculpture, symphonies, songs, poems, plays, and prose. Creativity is also part of the design culture in consumer products, graphics, and architecture, as well as through the innovations from engineering, software development, and user interface design. Finally, creativity manifests itself in the scientific discoveries of physicists, biologists, chemists, mathematicians, or computer scientists.

M. Redondo et al. (eds.), *Engineering the User Interface*,
DOI: 10.1007/978-1-84800-136-7_1, © Springer-Verlag London Limited 2009

2 Theory of Creativity

My concepts of creativity were strongly influenced by the psychologist Mihaly Csikszentmihalyi, whose books include the widely cited *Creativity* [2]. He describes three key components for understanding creativity:

1. **Domain**: "consists of a set of symbols, rules and procedures" (creative work is within a domain), e.g. mathematics or biology,
2. **Field:** "the individuals who act as gatekeepers to the domain... decide whether a new idea, performance, or product should be included" (creative work is social and must be judged by others)
3. **Individual:** creativity is "when a person... has a new idea or sees a new pattern, and when this novelty is selected by the appropriate field for inclusion in the relevant domain"

Creativity's role in economic growth is well-documented by Richard Florida [4] in his book *The Rise of the Creative Class and How It's Transforming Work, Leisure, Community and Everyday Life.* He emphasizes the 3 T's: Technology, Talent and Tolerance. Further evidence of the economic impact of creativity comes from the U.S. National Academy of Sciences report *Beyond Productivity: Information Technology, Innovation and Creativity* [6], which argues that the challenge for the 21st century is to "work smarter, not harder."

As user interface designers we have a grand opportunity to improve and extend current software tools such as drawing programs, word processors, and information visualization tools to more effectively support creativity. The strategies may vary across disciplines, but there are enough common principles that we can learn from different tools and from different disciplines [5].

3 Creative Processes

Creative projects often begin by building on previous work, so methods for searching previous work are needed. Google is a good place to start in finding previous work, but exploratory search methods including stronger tools to organize and filter search results would be helpful additions. Visualization tools that enable users to see hundreds or thousands of alternatives help trigger creative associations or form meaningful groupings [11]. Information visualization tools enable users to find patterns, clusters, trends, gaps, and outliers. A small treemap of the gene ontology reveals some interesting outliers and subtrees with elevated levels of activity (Fig. 1).

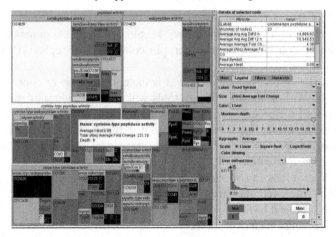

Fig. 1. Visualizations can help users make discoveries by presenting a large amount of information in a compact way that enables patterns and outliers to stand out. This small segment of the 14,000 genes represented in the gene ontology. Larger rectangles indicate increased activity, color shows significance by t-test.

For most creative projects users need to generate and review many alternatives. Large displays and software to organize many possibilities can be helpful to artists looking at hundreds of color schemes and biologists examining thousands of genes. Opportunistic discovery is appealing but systematic approaches to reviewing thousands or millions of alternatives are also valuable. The Hierarchical Clustering Explorer provides powerful methods to find features in high dimensional data sets such as found in genomics research (Fig. 2).

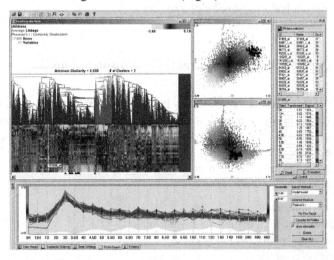

Fig. 2. The Hierarchical Clustering Explorer (http://www.cs.umd.edu/hcil/hce) enables users to find clusters, correlations, patterns, and outliers in high dimensional data sets, such as this example with gene expression data. This display shows a dendrogram in the upper left, parallel coordinates view on the bottom and two scattergrams towards the right hand side.

As part of the exploration process, users often have to backtrack to previous states, so effective tools provide history keeping and undo commands. Histories should also be convenient to save, send to colleagues, or replay in the form of macros.

A key part of most creative processes is the collaboration or consultation with other people. Well-designed software tools will enable sending of partial results, and help record the process of innovation during discussions. Finally, when work is completed innovators need better tools to disseminate their results. The balance of attention between individual and social creativity will ensure that both strategies get sufficient attention [3].

These descriptions can be summarized by eight creative activities that could be facilitated by improved interfaces [8]:
- searching and browsing digital libraries,
- visualizing data and processes,
- consulting with peers and mentors,
- thinking by free associations,
- exploring solutions, what-if tools,
- composing artifacts and performances,
- reviewing and replaying session histories, and
- disseminating results.

Researchers on creativity support tools will have to grapple with the methods for evaluating their products. Since quantitative metrics of creativity are difficult to obtain, observation and interaction with creative individuals and groups over weeks, months or years will be necessary [1, 10]. Case study research methods can provide feedback to refine creativity support tools and to develop a deeper understanding of what features were helpful to users.

4 Principles of Design for Creativity Support Tools

In June 2005, a workshop sponsored by the U.S. National Science Foundation met to discuss creativity support tools). The full report is available online (http://www.cs.umd.edu/hcil/CST), but the summary tells the story quite well [9]. The group came to support long term case studies as the preferred research method and proposed a set of user interface design principles that support rapid exploration and easy experimentation:

1. Support exploration
2. Low threshold, high ceiling, and wide walls
3. Support many paths and many styles
4. Support collaboration
5. Support open interchange
6. Make it as simple as possible - and maybe even simpler
7. Choose black boxes carefully

8. Invent things that you would want to use yourself
9. Balance user suggestions with observation and participatory processes
10. Iterate, iterate - then iterate again
11. Design for designers
12. Evaluate your tools

The participants also came to a consensus about these desirable future steps:

Accelerate research and education on creativity support tools by:
- Making the case for increased funding for creativity support tool research
- Encouraging investment in multi-dimensional indepth longitudinal case studies
- Proposing ways to create greater interest among researchers, educators, students, policymakers, and industrial developers.

Promote rigorous multidimensional evaluation methods by:
- Understanding the benefits and limits to controlled experimentation
- Developing observation strategies for indepth longitudinal case studies
- Collecting careful field study, survey, and deep ethnographical data

Rethink user interfaces to support creativity by offering principles for:
- Design tools for individuals and socio-technical environments for groups.
- Promote low floors, high ceilings, wide windows, and powerful history-keeping
- Support exploratory search, visualization, collaboration, and composition

5 Creativity and Cognition 2007 Conference

To help push this agenda forward, several of the organizers of the June 2005 workshop organized a major conference in June 2007 (http://www.cs.umd.edu/hcil/CC2007). We received 104 full-length paper submissions, from which the program committee chose 24 papers (23% acceptance rate) for presentation in the proceedings and at the conference. In addition to the papers, there were demonstrations and posters, plus two featured keynote speakers. Related events included 3 tutorials, 3 workshops, and a 3-month long art exhibit at the National Academies Building. An important event was our graduate student symposium that was funded by the U.S. National Science Foundation and the European EQUATOR project to bring 25 students from around the world. We believe that engaging students in these topics while they are still developing their research plans and performance projects could strongly influence the direction of their work.

More than 200 people participated in these activities producing comments such as:

> One of the best conferences I have attended. three days of intense inspiration.
> It was a fantastic experience for me… I've come away with renewed enthusiasm (though I am passionate about my work anyway), and filled with new ideas of how to progress.
> Very very extraordinary.
> I cannot begin to express my thanks and sincere appreciation to you and the organizing committee for the wonderful experience.
> It is a rare opportunity to be a part of a group of individuals that come together through a shared vision and that so passionately work to enhance the development of new knowledge in the arts and sciences.
> I benefited greatly from the student symposium, in particular from the diversity of project work and the inter-disciplinary dialogues established between people in the group, which have continued to develop since the event.
> Since I returned from Washington my feet have hardly touched the ground, thanks in no small part to the stimulation and encouragement I received from engaging with the other conference attendees.

These comments convey the enthusiasm from many participants. They expressed satisfaction with external confirmation of their research directions by the unique community of professionals and students who attended the conference. I have seen this sense of enthusiasm in the early days of the human-computer interaction field, when supportive feedback produced powerful confirmation of novel work. Creative researchers who cross domain boundaries with interdisciplinary work and those who boldly initiate new domains are understandably anxious, and therefore eager for confirmation of their efforts.

6 U. S. National Science Foundation Efforts

Further confirmation of the growing recognition of creativity research is the expansion of support from the U. S. National Science Foundation. Their program managers provided support for the 2005 workshop and the 2007 conference, plus they conducted several other workshops. During spring 2007, they announced the CreativeIT program (http://www.nsf.gov/publications/pub_summ.jsp?ods_key= nsf07562) to provide larger funding for research:

> The goal of the CreativeIT Program is to fund research that focuses on creativity to produce simultaneous advances in both computer science and creative cognition, creativity support tools, engineering design or science… A better understanding of creativity and its role in computer science research, encouraging creativity in education, and supporting creativity with new information technology will improve American competitiveness and innovation.

An even more ambitious effort is proposed to start in 2008 under the Cyber-Enabled Discovery and Innovation program which may have up to $1B over a five-year period (http://www.nsf.gov/news/news_summ.jsp?cntn_id=108366). This program's focus is on discovery and innovation in the sciences and engineering, which is appropriate considering the funding source. While the initial description focuses on technology aspects, we can hope that there will be sufficient attention to user requirements studies, early user prototype testing, observations of users, data logging of usage, empirical tests with users, and case study reporting.

7 Near-term Outcomes

Assuming that these and other funding efforts greatly expand research on discovery and innovation, what might we expect in the coming years? I believe that facing the challenges of creativity support tools could lead to at least these four near-term outcomes:

- **Refined theories of technology-supported creative processes**. The popular and scientific literature on creative processes in business, science, arts, etc. is huge, but the literature on how to design, manage, and use technology to accelerate discovery and innovation is modest. Cognitive theories of individuals make discoveries and the more challenging social psychology theories of small teams, larger groups, and broad communities will flourish. Researchers will study wikipedia.org to understand its remarkable success in bringing together hundreds of thousands of editors and writers to create a compelling resource. Similarly open source software communities, such as Linux, and information visualization communities, such as ManyEyes or Swivel, give an indication of much more ambitious collaborations that will emerge in the coming years. Understanding the determinants of success will be central. How important is lowering/raising barriers to entry, providing/limiting a hierarchy of administrators, or stability/change in content and interface? Other questions include the impact of rewarding active contributors, recognizing quality, and preventing malicious attacks?

- **Active discussion of user-oriented empirical research methods:** The traditional controlled experimental methods of perceptual or motor psychology are less effective for the complex cognitive, affective, and social processes involved in discovery and innovation that takes place over weeks and months. The shift to case study and ethnographic methods is well-underway, but many researchers still need convincing. Improved methods that ensure validity while promoting replicability and generalizability will be much sought after. Physicians and medical researchers have happily blended case study reports on small groups of individuals with carefully controlled clinical trials on thousands of patients over several years. Discovery and innovation researchers could follow this example, but major funding will be necessary for multi-year observation of large numbers of creativity support tool users.

- **New software architectures, database management strategies, and networking technologies:** The intense demands of discovery and innovation will cause designers of existing tools to revise their technology infrastructures to enable much improved search engines, larger and more diverse databases, and advanced networking to provide rapid synchronous and asynchronous collaboration. Google's impressive performance speed for their query responses sets a high standard for the more ambitious search requests that are desired for video, music, medical, and scientific databases.

- **Improved user interfaces to support discovery and innovation, especially in collaborative environments:** Many current user interfaces can be dramatically improved with better history keeping mechanisms that not only support undo, but allow capture of session histories as first-class objects. Histories should be constructed so that users can review, edit, send, and replay them. Moreover, histories should become the basis for programming-by-demonstration (sometimes called enduser programming), so that users can easily extend the functionality of their system to accommodate domain-specific needs and innovative applications. Science notebooks and document composition tools need improved versioning, annotation, and copying with linkbacks (so copied components point back to the source) will help promote collaboration while ensuring appropriate credit. Discovery and innovation tools that provide systematic yet flexible exploration, will guide users in their efforts over weeks and months. Such discovery management tools will also support partnerships by enabling large problems to be broken in to components that many people can work on simultaneously.

Of course, many other directions seem fruitful, but these four are a starting point for an expanded research agenda the focuses on discovery and innovation. These are high risk research directions with design, implementation, and evaluation challenges, but the payoffs could be remarkable.

References

1. Candy, L. and Edmonds, E. A. (1997) Supporting the creative user: A criteria based approach to interaction design. *Design Studies*, 18, 185-194
2. Csikszentmihalyi, M. (1996) *Creativity: Flow and the Psychology of Discovery and Invention*, HarperCollins, New York
3. Fischer, G., Giaccardi, E., Eden, H., Sugimoto, M., and Ye, Y. (2005) Beyond binary choices: Integrating individual and social creativity, *International Journal of Human-Computer Studies (IJHCS)* Special Issue on Creativity, E. Edmonds, L. Candy (Eds.), 482-512.
4. Florida, R. (2002) *The Rise of the Creative Class and How It's Transforming Work, Leisure, Community and Everyday Life*, Basic Books, New York
5. Hewett, T. (2005) Informing the design of computer-based environments to support creativity, *International Journal of Human-Computer Studies* 63, 4-5, Special Issue on Computer Support for Creativity, E. Edmonds, L. Candy (Eds.), , 383-409.
6. National Academy of Sciences (2003) *Beyond Productivity: Information Technology, Innovation and Creativity*, NAS Press, Washington, DC.

7. Shneiderman, B., (2000) Creating creativity: user interfaces for supporting innovation, *ACM Transactions on Computer-Human Interaction 7*, 1, March 2000. 114-138.

8. Shneiderman, B. (2002) *Leonardo's Laptop: Human Needs and the New Computing Technologies*, MIT Press, Cambridge, MA.

9. Shneiderman, B., Fischer, G., Czerwinski, M., Resnick, M., Myers, B. and 13 others (2006) Creativity Support Tools: Report From A U.S. National Science Foundation Sponsored Workshop, *International Journal of Human–Computer Interaction 20*, 2, 61–77.

10. Shneiderman, B. and Plaisant, C. (2006) Strategies for evaluating information visualiza-tion tools: Multi-dimensional In-depth Long-term Case Studies, In *Proc. Beyond time and errors: novel evaluation methods for Information Visualization, Workshop of the Advanced Visual Interfaces Conference*, Available in ACM Digital Library.

11. Terry, M., Mynatt, E. D., Nakakoji, K., and Yamamoto, Y. (2004) Variation in element and action: supporting simultaneous development of alternative solutions, *Proc. CHI 2004 Conference on Human Factors in Computing Systems*, ACM Press, New York 711-718.

12. von Hippel, E. (2005) *Democratizing Innovation*, MIT Press, Cambridge, MA

Integrating Learning Processes Across Boundaries of Media, Time and Group Scale

H. Ulrich Hoppe

Institute for Computer Science and Interactive Systems
University of Duisburg-Essen, 47048 Duisburg, Germany
hoppe@collide.info

Abstract   Recently, we have seen integration as a theme and purpose of educational media usage of its own right. The genuine value of integration is primarily characterised by improving the richness and directness of educational interactions. This article takes its starting point by looking at classroom activities. A good integration of interactive media in the classroom including groupware functions can already facilitate smooth "learning flows". Specific design principles can be extracted from the experience gathered in several recent projects. E.g., the "digital mimicry" principle refers to the extrapolation of expertise with conventional tools to similar computerised tools. The general issue of interoperability and connectivity includes aspects of software and hardware interfaces and even goes beyond technology in that it requires mental interfaces that allow users (teachers and learners) to realise and make use of the possible connections. These interfaces are conceived at design and provide implicit learning process support in the learning environment. In analogy to "business process modelling", there is also an explicit approach to integrating learning processes: The use of specific representations to describe and potentially operationalise the orchestration of learning scenarios. In Computer-Supported Collaborative Learning (CSCL), the integration of media and of group scales, e.g. between individual, classroom and community, relies essentially on mechanisms for handling emerging learning objects in terms of production, exchange, re-use and transformation. In the spirit of constructivist pedagogical approaches, we have to cope with "emerging learning objects" created by learners and learning groups in partly unanticipated ways. This assumption gives rise to specific new challenges for the indexing and retrieval of such learning objects (or products). Automatic indexing derived from the task-tool context and similarity based search allow for an asynchronous exchange of learning objects within larger anonymous learning communities. In this sense, objects of common interest may trigger social processes in learning communities.

M. Redondo et al. (eds.), *Engineering the User Interface*,
DOI: 10.1007/978-1-84800-136-7_2, © Springer-Verlag London Limited 2009

1 Introduction: Starting Point and First Orientation[1]

The understanding of the term "learning environment" (LE) is very significant for specific approaches in the area of technology enhanced learning. An LE is usually seen as a virtual or computational system that supports learning in a specific coherent way. There are domain oriented environments, sometimes called microworlds, which support specific semantic representations and processing mechanisms, but also general "learning platforms" that aim at organisational, communication and archiving support for learning communities. In spite of the differences between these approaches neither one challenges the conventional assumption of the LE residing on one or more computers. Particularly in the area of intelligent tutoring systems or ITS, we find a strong tendency to "understand" and control the ongoing learning processes to a maximum extent. This article is based on an alternative view of the learning environment.

The work of the COLLIDE group at the University of Duisburg-Essen (www.collide.info) was from its beginning in 1995 based on the assumption that the notion of "learning environment" should be given a much wider definition, including spatial and organisational surroundings, social constellations as well as external requirements on the learners beyond a singular learning experience. This implies that the system could never be in full control of the learning process. However it can enable or facilitate certain learning activities by providing interactive tools and materials. In both pre-computerised and computerised learning settings, we have seen discontinuities (or "gaps") between media based activities. We try to explore how technology can help to bridge such gaps. In this more integral view of LEs, we also consider different roles. In a classroom based learning environment the teacher is a central actor. Hence, technology can also be used to support the teacher and the teaching in terms, e.g., of taking over routine work, providing supervision support or helping to manage group formation processes. Often, this kind of support is seen as improvement of efficiency: reaching more students in a shorter period of time. However, there is an important potential benefit of integrating learning processes which is not identical with the acceleration of learning processes and the multiplication of effects by reaching a higher number of learners. *The value of integration is primarily characterised by improving the richness, directness and cohesion of educational interactions.* We can distinguish several aspects of integration: (1) the integration of media and processes to support a smooth and seamless information flow in both virtual and face- to-face classroom scenarios, (2) the use of ICT to bridge between different conditions of

---

[1] This article is based on a keynote speech given at the *8 International Conference on Intelligent Tutoring Systems* 2006 in Jhongli, Taiwan. The original talk was conceived as a synthesis of more or less recent developments of group learning environments centred around the notion of *integration* in several ways. The article maintains this perspective in which the concrete examples described in more or less detail are meant to illustrate certain aspects of the general theme of integration.

learning, such as individual, small group or large community activities as well as between synchronous and asynchronous settings, and recently (3) model-based integration using learning process modelling languages. All these aspects will be taken up on the following pages. Integrative types of technology potentially provide an added value also to grown learning scenarios such as the classroom. In a *computer-integrated classroom* (cf. [8]), a mixture of traditional (or natural) forms of communication and media may co-exist with digital media serving different functions which may be partly identical to traditional media use and in other parts actually qualitatively new. We have used the term "digital mimicry" to characterise interactive digital media functions which mimic traditional forms such as the use of a pen based big electronic display instead of a chalkboard (cf. [11]). Interactive simulations are a typical example of a genuine new media function which is bound to the digital modality. However, there is a general added value that we expect from combining digitised traditional media (e.g. scanned-in paper notes) with digital mimicry applications and real new media into a new form of digital information flow with specific forms of recording, re-use, re-enactment and extension/modification.

2 Media Integration in the Classroom

Traditional classroom scenarios suffer from discontinuities caused by incompatibilities of media and representations ("media gaps"). Often, e.g., results developed in small groups using paper and pencils are copied to the chalkboard, which is a redundant activity. The chalkboard, on the other hand, allows for flexible and spontaneous note taking and visualisation, but it has shortcomings in terms of persistence and re-use. Technology can help to bridge media breaks without introducing serious additional constraints. This is exemplified by the European project NIMIS (1998-2000) in primary school classrooms [19].

NIMIS has adopted ubiquitous computing technologies, particularly supporting pen and finger based interaction, for an early learning classroom and combined it with speech technology to support reading and writing. The NIMIS environment has been specially designed for the needs of learners who do not (yet) have full reading and writing skills by introducing a new visual desktop with very intuitive visual tools for archiving, sending messages and integration of peripherals (scanner, camera) to archiving. It has several groupware functions for synchronous and asynchronous cooperation.

The NIMIS software includes a special application for initial reading and writing ("Today's Talking Type-writer", see [26]). This application was designed in a participatory way together with the teachers. It was conceived as a computerised version of an existing phonetic approach to acquiring reading and writing skills ("reading through writing"). The flow of information and ownership of data were the major challenges in designing a computer-integrated classroom or CiC for early learners. As a child-oriented metaphor for handling and visualising data and different media we introduced the metaphor of a "companion" as a virtual representative of the child. The child logs in to the computer by *calling the companion*. The companion appears and shows the child's documents (results of previous learning episodes, multimedia messages from classmates etc.) in the form of small preview images. Data organisation for young children is supported by means of automatic arrangement and distribution in folders marked with icons. Later, children may create their own folders and use drag and drop operations to arrange their documents. Different from standard operating system conventions, two children can log in at the same time on one machine and work together at their desktop. When the child logs out, the companion disappears and *goes to sleep*. The companion also disappears in its original place, when a child logs in on a different machine. This feature, together with action logging, also allows for tracing distributed activities in the classroom.

Fig. 1. Scenes from the NIMIS classroom

Studies of classroom procedures and "educational workflows" have guided the design of the NIMIS tools, especially with respect to interoperability. The underlying requirements were formulated on different levels: (1) technology should not get in the way (with respect to established classroom processes), (2) technology should unify representations and interactions on a digital basis, (3) new workflows should be facilitated. As for (3), we have seen the use of the big interactive screen in a way unprecedented by the chalkboard (that is indeed rarely used in current primary education in our region): In phases of group reflection and looking back, kids would gather around the board, sitting on the floor, and revise and compare their learning results using asynchronous groupware functions. This is an example of a media facilitated transition between small group work and a whole classroom activity. Computer-integrated classrooms are a specific example of ubiquitous computing environments (cf. [27]) following the principle of functionally embedding interactive computerised devices with the physical environment. This embedment should be seamless and non disruptive. One strategy to achieve this is the above mentioned principle of "digital mimicry" [11], i.e. the introduction of digital device as a surrogate of a traditional one. In the consumer area this is the case with digital cameras and musical instruments. In the classroom, it is the case with pen based computing devices such as big interactive displays or tablets. Of course the digital device will provide added values, but, to start with, it can already be used in very much the same way as the analogue one. A very nice example of seamless integration is the usage of an analogue tool in conjunction with a digital device as shown in Fig. 2.

The scene shown in Fig. 2 stems from a computer-integrated classroom in Taiwan [21]. In this environment, tablet PCs are used as individual devices in combination with big interactive displays based on a wireless classroom network. The wireless platforms allows for more flexibility and portability of the whole environment.

Fig. 2. Digital-physical media integration in a Taiwanese classroom.

In the context of the EU project SEED (2001-2004), following up on NIMIS, the COLLIDE group has tried to create classroom innovation using interactive media together with a group of secondary school teachers. These teachers were introduced to the new types of hardware and software (mainly annotation and modelling tools) and were invited and supported in appropriating these for their own teaching. This has led to interesting software extensions and blueprints for teaching in areas as diverse as biology, mathematics and language studies (cf. [18]). The focus of these activities was clearly on representational tools, not so much on a general communication infrastructure. Indeed, we found that existing school intranets are still too poorly developed in terms of availability, maintenance and coherence to get the full added value out of the digital enrichment of the classroom in terms of organisational memory functions. Yet, we have explored the general feasibility of using new devices such as low cost graphics tablets for handwriting as well as big interactive displays, tablet PCs as well as PDAs in domain specific applications with a special focus on collaborative use.

We have also explored face-to-face learning scenarios integrating mobile devices. Our "Mobile Notes" [3] system supports classroom discussions by integrating PDAs with a big interactive screen. Following Liu and Kao [20], public interactive displays complement the lack of shared visual focus with smaller personal devices. In "Mobile Notes", the PDA is essentially only used as an input device to initially prepare and enter discussion contributions. When a contribution (either text-based or a hand-written sketch) is completed, it is sent to a database from which it can be retrieved and transferred to the public display application. This transfer can be controlled by a moderator. All plenary classroom discussions would be supported by and centred around the public display. This has turned out to be a very generally usable scenario. As opposed to scenarios with mobile devices only, this is an example of the "functional differentiation" principle: Based on an assessment of the strengths and weaknesses of available devices, specific functions are assigned to the adequate type of device in a blended scenario.

3 Process Integration and Explicit Learning Process Modelling

The NIMIS example demonstrates that a well designed integration of interactive media including groupware functions can already facilitate smooth "learning flows". This kind of implicit process integration comes as a result of the overall design. Tool interoperability is an important issue to achieve it.

In an analogy to "business process modelling", explicit approaches to integrating learning processes have been suggested: They are based on the provision and use of so-called "educational modelling languages" to specify and potentially operationalise the orchestration of learning scenarios. The most prominent representative of this line research and development is the educational modelling language EML, developed at the Dutch Open University, and its successor IMS Learning Design supported by the IMS Global Learning Consortium (cf. [16]).

IMS LD is typically used for designing and developing of web based learning environments. In this context, it allows for dynamically arranging predefined learning materials and adapting these to some extent to individual user characteristics. IMS LD is specified as an XML-based language. The top level structure reflects the metaphor of a theatrical play composed of acts. On lower levels it allows for specifying roles and activities, also the interaction between roles and activities. A general problem with IMS LD is that this quite complex definition is only precisely defined on a syntactic level. From a user perspective, a standardised diagrammatic representation would be desirable. Often UML diagrams are used to translate LD models into something easier to grasp and understand. However, these mappings are based on intuitive transformations which are not standardised.

From a CSCL perspective, we are e.g. interested in formulating "collaboration scripts" as learning process models [13]. These scripts are typically rich in role changes and in exchanging and re-using results (objects) generated on the fly between learning groups. The adaptation of IMS LD to these needs is not straightforward and leads to some additional requirements [22]. Hernandez et al. [6] showed that some aspects of complex collaborative designs (also called "collaborative learning patterns") are not represented properly in IMS/LD and extensions are necessary.

In our understanding, explicit learning process modelling has a great potential that goes much beyond the orchestration of web-based learning environments. If it had a clear conceptual basis and a representation readable also by teachers, it could be used as a tool for pedagogical design and engineering not only directly related to computerised learning environments but also, e.g., for lesson planning. To exploit the potential benefits of machine interpretable learning process specifications also in computer-integrated classroom environments, loosely coupled architectures for the interdependence of the learning environment and a process monitoring engine are needed. The COLLIDE group is working towards such an extended perspective on learning process modelling. The following section will elaborate on an approach to specify and capture specific classroom constellations from a CSCL perspective.

4 "Learning-Design by Example"

In the context of the SEED project, teachers had used our collaborative learning and modelling environment Cool Modes [23] to set up different group scenarios in their classrooms. These sessions involved several computers and required the setting up of a communication environment based on our MatchMaker communication server which allows for flexible workspace sharing and coupling. The setting up of the environment was time consuming and only the more experienced were able to do it on their own. Thus, there was a general demand for setting up classroom networks with flexible grouping and archiving/recording mechanisms with less additional time effort to be justified for a 45 or 90 minute lesson. This gave rise to the implementation of an "ad hoc session manager" [17].

Since we already used the collaborative modelling platform Cool Modes in schools for mathematical modelling, computer science lessons and graphical argumentation it was an obvious option for us to implement the session manager on this basis. So, the Cool Modes framework is used with two different intentions in our scenario: On the one hand, it is used by the students to perform their collaborative modelling task, and on the other hand, it is used by the teacher in order to specify and orchestrate the group work.

The graph-based visual language ("session manager") for the representation of the classroom networks was developed as an additional plug-in to the Cool Modes framework. The language consists of a specific set of nodes and edges: User nodes represent participants or clients. Visible indications on this type of node are the name of the user (or the partners, if students share one computer), the login name, the local host computer and the IP address of the host. Shared collaborative sessions are indicated by session nodes. At run time, the teacher has the possibility to model and control (start/stop) sessions, see how many clients currently are connected with the session and the unique name of the session. A database node allows the teacher to store the data of a connected session at a previously defined place. A *slot node* acts as a wildcard for clients which are not yet instantiated. This type of node allows the teacher to pre-define the different working groups before the students enter the classroom and log into the system. A *slot node* can be pre-configured in such a way as to automatically identify a specific student when he or she logs in. Then this slot node would be replaced by the client node representing the student. Alternatively, student names can be dragged on to the slot node.

Furthermore, the visual language provides three different types of edges. There are two types of edges that allow for connecting a slot node or a client node to a session. A *force edge* between a client and a session node results in an automatic join of the client to a session, whereas an *is allowed edge* just permits that a user might join a certain session. Another edge type connects sessions to database in order to store the session data in the previously defined place.

The only precondition to set up a classroom session from such a specification is that all machines have to be equipped with the Cool Modes software including a session manager client. The teacher's machine initiates the session and establishes the communication with the participant machines. The initial phase of setting up the topology as described in the session diagram relies on multicasting. Once the communication topology is set up, MatchMaker and Java RMI are used for workspace sharing and data transfer.

So far, the group management tool has been tested in a secondary school computer science courses with 12th graders in the area of modelling with UML. Our tool was not only used to administrate the group work but also to evaluate the work process and the results of different forms of group work. Each group work scenario can be classified by the degrees of freedom it offers students to structure their collaboration and their work on the task.

Our ongoing research work will have a closer look on the influences of these two dimensions on the learning process of students and its outcomes. Fig. 3 shows an example configuration. In this setting, two different groups worked on a UML class diagram. Whereas the second group was working on a common task, the first one was divided into two subgroups (1a and 1b) with a predefined division of labour. Additionally, in this group one student acted as a coach to merge and present the two component solutions. Fig. 3 shows the two sessions for group 1 with four respectively two students. Another student acting as a coach *is allowed* to join both sessions of group 1 and the final presentation session. The other students are *forced* to join the session of group 2. These different modes are indicated by differently coloured edges.

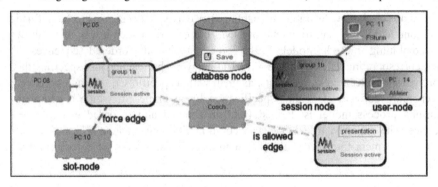

Fig. 3. Model representing the arrangement of computer based group work

The session manager diagrams capture the more static, structural elements of a specific group learning setting. Diagrams can be directly re-used on the basis of slot nodes (otherwise user nodes would have to be modified), and they can also be exchanged (e.g. between teachers) for documentation or replication purposes.

Elaborating on the exchange idea, the session manager tool has been extended to serve as an editor for collaborative learning designs with IMS/LD as output format. The teacher can specify the learning design "*by example*" creating a concrete visual model, instead of using the machine-level textual format of IMS/LD. We have defined the following mapping from our scenarios to an IMS/LD document:

- Each session within the classroom scenario is mapped onto an IMS/LD *learning-activity* (in our example "group 1a", "group 1b", "presentation", using the session's textual description for title and description of the activity).
- Each client node or slot node is mapped to an IMS/LD role of type *imsld:learner* (in our example "coach", "FSturm"). Since roles of a learning design are instantiated at runtime and not on beforehand, the client nodes are also abstracted to roles.
- The teacher who is implicitly present in the scenario (but not in the model) is represented in the learning design as a role of type *imsld:staff*.
- The whole classroom scenario graph of our visual language format is mapped onto an IMS/LD *act*.
- For each learner (client or slot node) an IMS/LD *role-part* is created within the act with the respective reference *role-ref*; this role-part includes a *learning-activity-ref* to the respective learning activity (a "session node" in the session manager specification) for each edge connecting the learner with the session node. In case of a "force edge", there is only one session available as *learning-activity-ref*. The *role-part* of the teacher includes every learning-activity to show the potential participation in every session.

Currently, we can only define single act scenarios directly using our Match-Maker/Cool Modes environment. More complex learning designs with sequences of acts are obviously desirable to enable richer classroom scenarios to be defined and conducted. We plan to extend our IMS/LD export in such a way as to allow for combining multiple models in the form of temporally ordered sequences of acts corresponding to a complete IMS LD "play". The teacher just specifies the configurations separately and connects them with a specific sequencing operation. Even more convenient is the "specification by example" in which a complete learning process model is derived from an enacted and recorded example sequence. The exported IMS/LD-format could additionally include a "learning objectives" element to enrich the design with more pedagogically oriented information.

5 Learning Objects and Learning Communities

The integration of media use across group scales in CSCL relies essentially on mechanisms for handling emerging learning objects in terms of production, exchange, re-use and transformation. In the spirit of constructivist pedagogical approaches and in contrast to standardised activities around pre-fabricated objects or materials, we assume that "emerging learning objects" be created by learners and learning groups in partly unanticipated ways. This assumption gives rise to specific new challenges for the indexing and retrieval of such learning objects (or products). In the absence of indexing through experts, learning object descriptions have to be derived from the learning situation with minimal input from the learners themselves. This constitutes a new challenge for intelligent support techniques, namely for the dynamic recognition and modelling of learning contexts on a semantic level. Contextualised indexing allows for an asynchronous exchange of learning objects within larger anonymous learning communities based on semantic similarities. In this sense, objects of common interest may trigger social processes in learning communities (cf. [12]).

Retrieval support for learning objects is usually associated with metadata standards like LOM or SCORM.

However, the use of metadata to facilitate the archiving and re-use of learning objects has not yet been widely discussed from a Computer-Supported Collaborative Learning (CSCL) perspective. The proceedings of CSCL 2003 contain just one article related to metadata issues [1], and also this contribution shows an early stage of conceptualisation. Given the relevance of metadata approaches in other fields of technology enhanced learning this may be surprising. A possible explanation is that learning objects in CSCL are typically conceived as emerging entities, i.e. as being created by the co-learners in the learning process. In contrast, most metadata approaches deal with predefined static learning objects, e.g. course materials. In the sequel, it will be explored how the CSCL perspective can be opened towards metadata, and vice versa how metadata techniques can be adapted to dealing with emerging learning objects.

6 Extending the Notion of "Communication through Artefacts" to Asynchronous Settings

"Communication through the artefact" is an essential principle used in a variety of shared workspace environments in CSCW and CSCL. Its basic function consists in complementing natural language communication through the creation and manipulation of shared objects. The typical shared activities are editing, brainstorming, co-construction and co-design. Several authors such as Hoppe and Plötzner (1999) or Suthers and Hundhausen [25] have characterised communicative and cognitive functions of interactively co-constructing and using shared representations. The latter distinguish the following support functions of interactively co-constructing and using shared representations: (1) initiation of negotiations of meaning, (2) provision of a representational proxy for gestural deixis and (3) basic support for implicitly shared awareness (external group memory).

The type of information communicated through a shared object or artefact depends on the nature of this object: It can be symbolic as in shared concept maps or argumentation graphs with textual nodes. Here, the semantic decoding relies essentially on the users' interpretation(s). Other representations such as Petri Nets or System Dynamics models come with an inherent operational interpretation on the machine which allows for dynamic simulation as well as for checking certain properties (e.g. deadlock detection in a Petri Net). Our experience with collaborative problem solving and model building is based on the multi-representational tool Cool Modes [24] which supports a spectrum of representations including hand written annotation, symbolic representations without machine semantics as well as representations with machine semantics and simulation capabilities. These tools are typically used in learning activities or "sessions" with smaller groups of 2-5 members over a time span of 30 to 90 minutes. A new challenge consists in relaxing these constraints in terms of time and group size while still maintaining essential features of "communication through the artefact".

The question is which of the support functions can be transferred to a situation of asynchronous use, and how this could be facilitated. Of course, we cannot expect a transfer of deictic reference support to the asynchronous case. Yet, negotiations of meaning may arise from exchanging variants and annotations. Also the external memory function can be redefined from - metaphorically speaking - short term to long term memory support. When using collaborative modelling environments such as Cool Modes in the classroom, we have experienced situations in which the sharing mechanism has been used to transfer information from small groups to the whole class, e.g. to display and discuss group results in the public. This is typically not a kind of "late re-use" but "immediate re-use". In a comparative study with a number of collaborative discussion and argumentation environments, we found a clear deficit with respect to their support for later re-use. This brought us to considering (and implementing) combinations of synchronous co-constructive environments with indexing and retrieval mechanisms [10]. Although this implied a relaxation of time constraints, it was not explicitly related to differences in group scale.

With respect to group size, there is a qualitative difference between groups in which members know each other and share context in terms of location, curricular content and institutional features (staff, teachers) and anonymous groups which may share an interest on the content level without sharing much context. Content oriented social relationships have been supported and studied with anonymous groups under the notion of "social navigation" (see [15]). Whereas social navigation relies mainly on process information in the form of "traces" left by other users or actors, we focus on the re-use of artefacts. We have recently described these objects used to exchange information in a larger learner community as "thematic objects" (cf. [12]). Asynchronous communication through thematic objects is, in first order, also asymmetric in the sense that the originator is not necessarily aware of the object's re-use. Yet, if a learning community is driven by common interests and disposes of rich means of communication, it is likely that object re-use can lead to social contact and interaction.

As with other predefined learning objects, semantic indexing and retrieval techniques are crucial to support the access to and re-use of emerging thematic objects. Given the fact, that learners are primarily motivated by the problems at hand, we cannot expect them to engage in time consuming indexing activities. To avoid this we extract as much contextual information as possible from the task/tool environment for the purpose of semantic indexing.

In the following section, the practical implementation of this approach in a European project will be described.

7 The COLDEX Project

The European project COLDEX ("Collaborative Learning and Distributed Experimentation", 2002-2005) has taken up issues and current challenges in the area of technology support for collaborative learning in science and technology with a special focus on learning based on both local and remote experimentation. The COLDEX user/learner community was conceived as being built up in a bottom-up way: Local teams in schools or a science centre have face-to-face interaction and a blend of hands-on and remote experiences in the general thematic area of "exploring space" with sub-themes such as "lunar cartography", "growing plants in space" (using small biospheres) and "robot vehicles". These local teams located in Sweden, Germany, Portugal, Chile and Colombia were encouraged to contribute to a global COLDEX Learning Object Repository (LOR). The LOR provided both group and community navigation tools as well as mechanisms to detect similarities of interests in terms of the produced objects or artefacts. The aim was to provide and explore exchange mechanisms between local communities in Europe and Latin America. In accordance with the general goals described above, the primary focus was on electronic support for the exchange of learning results and not on direct communication channels, e.g. via email contacts.

COLDEX relied on the already mentioned Cool Modes system as a general tool for model building and for the structured representation of scientific arguments. The tool supports synchronous cooperation by a shared workspace environment with full replication of the coupled objects. For the COLDEX purposes, Cool Modes has been equipped with an embedded interface to the LOR in two directions, (1) for uploading (with indexing support) and (2) for retrieval (exploiting similarities to the currently active workspace in the Cool Modes environment). These mechanisms will be explained in more detail.

In addition to the tool embedded LOR access, there is also a general web interface (for details, see [12]). Users of the LOR system can take multiple different roles which represent the different group scale they work in: *local group members* belong to the same (local) face-to-face learning group; *Cool Modes users* create models within the tool environment and upload them to the repository. *Community members* of a certain scientific domain may be interested in Cool Modes models. *Individual learners* can be members of all these groups, but also external visitors who are interested in the thematic content.

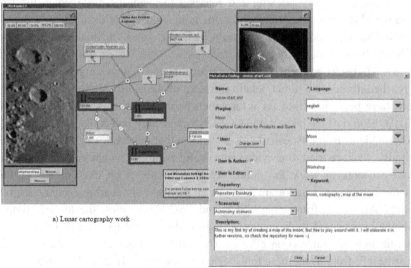

a) Lunar cartography work

b) Contextualised generation of metadata (for upload)

Fig 4. Archiving (uploading) lunar cartography work from COLDEX

8 Challenge-based Learning

The pedagogical approach of COLDEX is *challenge-based learning* (ChBL; [3]) –
a concept which is closely related to problem-based learning in that it implies
solving realistic, open-ended problems in authentic contexts. Challenge-based
learning has common aspects also with experiential, project-based and discovery-
based learning. The cognitive focus of ChBL lies in knowledge interpretation, in-
quiry, and knowledge construction. In a typical ChBL scenario, a student would
act as an active constructor, designer and researcher, usually supported by a
teacher as a coach, co-experimenter and co-designer in the creation of learning objects. The initial challenges are selected in such a way as to stimulate curiosity and
to be a source of rich experience. We assume challenges to be extra-curricular
problems which cannot be solved using routine skills or standard problem solving
strategies. In spite of the non-standard nature of the challenges COLDEX offers
packaged digital materials ("Digital Experimentation Toolkits" or DexTs) which
represent the initial challenge and computational tools for the tackling the central
problems.

The contextualised indexing and retrieval mechanisms provided in the Cool
Modes tool environment relieve the learners to some extent from entering detailed
specifications including formal parameters, yet some "manual" assignment of
keywords is still useful to support later re-use. Thus we are confronted with the
known "cold start problem": Before a critical mass of interesting thematic objects
is reached, there is no direct benefit in return of the effort. Similar trade-off situations have been discussed for information pooling scenarios with database tasks
[4]. At the end of the project, the COLDEX repository had about 400 learning objects (models, diagrams, calculation sheets) so that the break even point is passed.
Initially, we have tried to provide some useful examples on beforehand and to mo-
tivate students to work for future benefit. The focus on extra-curricular non-
standard problems is important to create an incentive for sharing concrete learning
results. As known from other CSCL and CSCW scenarios, the use of group or
community oriented tools comes with an additional cost (in terms of additional
coordination and interaction efforts). Thus, from a motivational point of view, a
clear benefit from using these tools should be expected. If, e.g., the explanation of
an experiment could be found in standard textbooks, it would be quite unlikely
that learners would engage in time consuming communications with people
around the world to better understand this experiment. In contrast, with problems
of non-standard and open-ended nature, there is an obvious incentive to engage in
such an exchange.

9 Contextualised Indexing and Retrieval

This section will describe the interface to the COLDEX Learning Object Repository (LOR) embedded in the Cool Modes tool environment. The basic idea is to maximise the use of contextual information to relieve the learner from the burden of generating metadata "by hand". The following relevant parameters are directly available in the tool environment:

- date/time of the activity;
- user id and potentially a user profile;
- potentially a reference to the original course material (e.g., from the metadata of a worksheet) and thus a reference to the course unit and theme;
- the set of visual languages used in the active workspace (i.e. the Cool Modes palettes used) as an indication of the problem type.

This information can be used during an upload to automatically instantiate some fields of the upload form (see Fig. 4). The user is then asked to add a semantic description in terms of keywords and potentially further comments.

The same type of description can also be used to generate a search query that would take the content of the currently active workspace as an example. Of course, in a query certain description parameters such as the user/author or the date would not make sense; usually we would expect that a learner is interested in similar learning objects created by *other users at any time*. Based on this idea, we have added tool embedded support for task contextualised queries: A user working within the Cool Modes environment has a menu option for asking "is there something in the LOR similar to what I am working on", without necessarily providing additional manual information. The generated query form corresponds to the upload format in Fig. 4, but it would not contain the attributes irrelevant to such a *similarity-oriented query*. This query form can still be modified. The result is a list of similar documents found in the LOR, ranked according to the number of attribute values shared with the example.

The same approach allows for a further step: Learners can take their current document as a query template, search for related content in the archive and not just the documents found but a ranked list of other users that created these documents. More technical details can be found in Pinkwart et al. [23].

The mechanism of generating contextual queries to find peers working on similar problems may lead to social interaction, e.g. to forming groups of similar interest. This links in with other current research on "communities of interest" (cf. [5]) based on the usage of document repositories. The specialty of our approach is the use of tool knowledge. The similarity oriented retrieval strategies can be used to personalise systems by a *"what's interesting?"* feature. Similarity queries could be used as a source of continuous information on themes of personal interest, considering additional constraints like language, time, and organisational proximity of persons. Similar functions are served by *recommender systems* (cf. [14]), but these rather based on information about usage processes and "traces" than on attributes of the objects themselves.

10 Summary and Perspectives

We have seen integration as a theme spanning over a wide range of topics in technology-enhanced learning. The guiding goal is enrichment rather than increasing efficiency. Integration is more than technical interoperability, but it may require certain types of technical connectivity. A first principle for facilitating educational workflows is to eliminate discontinuities in using different media and tools and thus support a seamless integration of media and processes. Unnecessary copying and re-coding of previous results should be avoided. Digital mimicry allows for a conceptual connection to existing expertise with conventional devices or tools. The added value of interactive and cooperative media, which comprises flexible re-use and sharing of results, can thus be gradually explored and appropriated in practical usage.

The *explicit representation and modelling of learning processes* allows for constraining interaction in a pedagogically purposeful way (e.g. with collaboration scripts) and can additionally support reflection and re-use on a process level. However, there is still a big challenge in providing learning process modelling tools which are both expressive enough as well as understandable and usable by the practitioner.

Bridging the gaps between small group and individual learning on the one side and learning communities on the other is another integration challenge. An important ingredient to achieve this is the provision of indexing and retrieval mechanisms for *emerging learning objects*. Typically, these emerging learning objects are constructed by learners in phases of individual or small group work. They are potentially discussed, compared or merged in whole classroom scenarios or even shared in broader anonymous learning communities. To support the sharing and re-use of emerging learning objects it is important to provide powerful semi-automatic indexing techniques as well as *similarity measures*. This draws on context information relating to user characteristics or to the task environment and goes beyond current applications of metadata standards in typical e-learning scenarios with predefined materials. The principles and ideas gathered so far are meant to be both a starting point and a signpost for further work. A research agenda to elaborate on the "integration challenge" for technology-enhanced learning would currently comprise the following goals:

- designing and providing conceptual/visual models and corresponding tools for learning process modelling on different levels of description and for a variety of purposes;

- developing "model-based classroom management tools" which would allow tracking classroom activities according to predefined models and/or recording activities in structured form to generate models ("learning design by example");
- extending conventional metadata methodologies and tools (e.g. existing platforms for learning object repositories) to allow for handling emerging learning objects and for serving different levels of scale between individual learning and exchange in a large and growing learning community.

In all these endeavours we should not only aim at serving the learners but also at enabling teachers and tutors to appropriate these technologies in their own professional practices. This will be an important factor for the spreading and dissemination of new value-adding technologies in the educational field.

References

1. Allert, H., Richter, C., Nejdl, W. (2003). Extending the scope of the current discussion on metadata towards situated models. In Proceedings of the International Conference on CSCL 2003. Dordrecht/Boston/London: Kluwer, 353-362.
2. Baloian, N., Hoeksema, K., Hoppe, H.U., Milrad, M. (2006). Technologies and educational activities for supporting and implementing challenge-based learning. In Proceedings of IFIP 19 World Computer Congress. Santiago (Chile), August 2006. Boston: Springer. 7-16.
3. Bollen, L., Juarez, G., Westermann, M. & Hoppe, H.U. (2006). PDAs as input devices in brainstorming and creative discussions. In Proceedings. of the IEEE Workshop on Wireless, Mobile and Ubiquitous Technologies in Education (WMUTE 2005). Athens (Greece), November 2006. 137-141.
4. Cress, U. & Hesse, F.W. (2004). Knowledge sharing in groups: Experimental findings of how to overcome a social dilemma. In Proceedings of ICLS 2004. Los Angeles: UCLA (June 2004), 150-157.
5. Francq, P., & Delchambre, A. (2005). Using Documents Assessments to Build Communities of Interest. In Proceedings of the International Symposium on Applications and the Internet, 237-333.
6. Hernandez, L.D., Perez, A.J., Dimitriadis, Y. (2004). IMS Learning Design support for the formalization of collaborative learning patterns. In Proceedings of IEEE ICALT 2004. IEEE Computer Society, Los Alamitos (CA).350-354.
7. Höök, K., Munro, A., and Benyon, D. (Eds.) (2002). Designing Information Spaces: The Social Navigation Approach. Berlin: Springer.
8. Hoppe, H. U., Baloian, N., Zhao, J. (1993). Computer-support for teacher-centered classroom interaction. Proceedings of ICCE 1993. Taipei (Taiwan), December 1993, pp. 211-217.
9. Hoppe, H. U., & Plötzner, R. (1999). Can analytic models support learning in groups? In Dillenbourg, P. (Ed) Collaborative Learning - Cognitive and Computational Approaches. Amsterdam: Elsevier, 147-168.
10. Hoppe, H. U., & Gassner, K. (2002). Integrating Collaborative Concept Mapping Tools with Group Memory and Retrieval Functions. In Proceedings of the International Conference on Computer Supported Collaborative Learning. New Jersey, Lawrence Erlbaum Associates, 716-725.
11. Hoppe, H. U. (2004). Collaborative mind tools. In Tokoro, M. & Steels, L. (Eds.): A Learning Zone of one's own - Sharing Representations and Flow in Collaborative Learning Environments. Amsterdam, IOS Press. 223-234.

12. Hoppe, H. U., Pinkwart, N., Oelinger, M., Zeini, S., Verdejo, F., Barros, B., Mayorga, J. I. (2005). Building Bridges within Learning Communities through Ontologies and "Thematic Objects". In Proceedings of CSCL 2005, Taipei (Taiwan), June 2005. Mahwah (NJ): Lawrence Erlbaum Associates.

13. Kollar, I., Fischer, F., Slotta, J.D. (2005). Internal and external collaboration scripts in web-based science learning at schools. In Proceedings of CSCL 2005, Taipei (Taiwan), June 2005. Mahwah (NJ): Lawrence Erlbaum Associates.

14. Konstan, J. A. & Riedl, J. (2002). Collaborative Filtering: Supporting social navigation in large, crowded infospaces. In

15. Höök, K., Munro, A., and Benyon, D. (Eds.) (2002). Designing Information Spaces: The Social Navigation Approach. Berlin: Springer, 43-81.

16. Koper, R. & Tattersall, C. (Eds) (2005). Learning Design. Berlin: Springer.

17. Kuhn, M, Hoppe, H.U., Lingnau, A, & Fendrich, M (2004). Evaluation of exploratory approaches in learning probability based on computational modelling and simulation. In Proceedings of the IADIS Conference of Cognition and Exploratory Learning in Digital Age (CELDA 2004), Lisbon (Portugal), November 2004.

18. Kuhn, M, Jansen, M, Harrer, A., Hoppe, H.U. (2005). A lightweight approach for flexible group management in the classroom. In Proceedings of CSCL 2005, Taipei (Taiwan), June 2005. Mahwah (NJ): Lawrence Erlbaum Associates.

19. Lingnau, A., Hoppe, H.U., Mannhaupt, G. (2003). Computer supported collaborative writing in an early learning classroom. JCAL 19, 186-194.

20. Liu, C. & Kao, L. (2005). Handheld devices with large shared display groupware: tools to facilitate group communication in one-to-one collaborative learning activities. In Proceedings. of the 3 IEEE Workshop on Wireless and Mobile Technologies in Education (WMTE 2005). Tokushima (Japan), November 2005. 128-135.

21. Liu, T.-C., Wang, H.-Y., Liang, J.-K., Chan, T.-W., Yang, J.-C. (2002). Applying wireless technologies to build a highly interactive learning environment. In Marcelo Milrad, M., Hoppe, H.U., Kinshuk (Eds.), Proceedings IEEE International Workshop on Wireless and Mobile Technologies in Education, August 29-30, 2002, Växjö, Sweden. IEEE Computer Society. 63-70.

22. Miao, Y., Hoeksema, K., Hoppe, H.U., Harrer, A.(2005). CSCL scripts: modeling features and potential use. In Proceedings of CSCL 2005, Taipei (Taiwan), June 2005. Mahwah (NJ): Lawrence Erlbaum Associates.

23. Pinkwart, N. (2003). A plug-in architecture for graph based collaborative modeling systems. In H.U. Hoppe, F. Verdejo & J. Kay (Eds) Proceedings of the 11 International Conference on Artificial Intelligence in Education Amsterdam: IOS Press, 535-536.

24. Pinkwart, N., Jansen, M., Oelinger, M., Korchounova, L., Hoppe, H. U. (2004). Partial generation of contextualized metadata in a collaborative modeling environment. In L. Aroyo and C. Tasso (Eds) Workshop proceedings of the 3rd International Conference on Adaptive Hypermedia. Eindhoven (NL): Technical University Eindhoven, 372-376.

25. Suthers, D., & Hundhausen, C. (2003). An experimental study on the effects of representational guidance on collaborative learning processes. Journal of the Learning Sciences, 12(2), 183-218.

26. Tewissen, F., Lingnau, A., Hoppe, H.U. (2000). "Today's Talking Typewriter" - Supporting early literacy in a classroom environment. In Gauthier, G., Frasson, C. & VanLehn, K.(Eds.), Proceedings of the 5th International Conference on Intelligent Tutoring Systems (ITS 2000), Montréal, Canada, June 19-23, 2000. Berlin: Springer LCNS. 252-261.

27. Weiser, M. (1991). The Computer for the 21st Century. Scientific American, September 1991, 94-104

Optimal Cost Haptic Devices for Driving Simulators

Elixabete Bengoechea, Emilio Sánchez, Joan Savall

CEIT, Pº de Manuel Lardizábal 15, 20018- San Sebastián, Spain

CEIT and TECNUN (Universidad de Navarra, Pº de Manuel Lardizábal 15, 20018-San Sebastián, Spain

Abstract Driving simulators reproduce actual driving conditions. The main purpose of these systems is to teach trainees how to drive under safe and controlled conditions. In order to have realistic training sessions, simulator manufacturers tend to use controls found in the actual vehicle under simulation. This paper presents two haptic devices that use force control to accurately reproduce the behaviour of a lever and gear shift. The presented devices are advantageous in their compact and versatile design, reaching an optimal balance between low cost and high performance. The devices have been tested by real drivers, and implemented in commercialized train, and bus/truck driving simulators.

1 Introduction

Training simulators constitute high immersion environments for learning and training in which novices can improve their skills as if they were interacting in real situations. There is a wide range of potential applications such as aerospace maintenance, salvage and driving [1] or medicine [2], etc. Training sessions with simulators deal with real situations but without risk. Taking advantage of this absence of danger, training sessions can simulate normal and extreme conditions alike. This applies to means of transport like airplanes [3], ships, trucks, trains (Fig. 1), motorbikes [4], and even space and underwater operations.

M. Redondo et al. (eds.), *Engineering the User Interface*,
DOI: 10.1007/978-1-84800-136-7_3, © Springer-Verlag London Limited 2009

Fig. 1. Examples of two driving simulators: truck simulator (left) and train simulator (right).

Training simulators should reproduce as closely as possible the sensory stimuli that users are subject to during real experiences. To achieve a highly immersive training session, most simulators exploit various forms of sensory-motor stimuli: visual, audio, proprioceptive or motion.

Another stimulus that augments the sensation of immersion is the tactile/force feedback that users encounter when they use vehicle gearshifts and levers. Some of these controls include real counterparts which are connected to train-gears or transmissions, such as gear shifts and hand brakes for cars, or reversers and regulator shafts in trains. These gears and transmissions do not exist in training simulators, so their mechanical behaviour is different.

To overcome this problem, haptic devices/levers have been designed to emulate the behaviour of real controls. The term *haptic* comes from the Greek αφή (*Haphe*), and refers to the sense of touch. And *haptic device* is the name given to a specific type of human-machine interface (HMI) that enables the user to 'touch' or interact with virtual reality. One of the advantages of haptic devices is that they can reproduce normal conditions as well as the malfunctioning of real counterparts.

Nowadays haptic devices are used to enhance the performance of simulators in many fields, such as surgical simulators [5] and driving simulators [6].

Moreover, haptic devices have a primary advantage; one device can simulate and substitute for a wide set of real manual operation controls, that is to say, one haptic actuator of 2 DoF (degrees of freedom) can behave as a manual, automatic or semi-automatic transmission by simply altering the running software (Fig. 2).

MANUAL GEARSHIFT | AUTOMATIC GEARSHIFT | TRUCK GEARSHIFT | SEQUENTIAL GEARSHIFT "SPEEDGEAR" | SEQUENTIAL GEARSHIFT "DURASHIFT" | TRAIN ACELARATION LEVER

Fig. 2. Classification of real gearshifts.

However, quality haptic devices are normally expensive solutions. And this high cost has impeded the implementation of haptic devices within simulators.

This paper presents two haptic levers (Fig. 3) that have been developed by reaching an optimal balance between low cost and high performance. These devices have been tested by real drivers, and implemented in commercialized train and bus/truck driving and training simulators.

Fig. 3. The two haptic devices presented in the paper: haptic gear-shift (left), haptic train lever (right).

The remaining sections are arranged as follows: first of all, the two developed haptic devices are described. Then, in section three and four respectively, the custom made control board prototype EOS and the overall system architecture are presented. Next is a brief review of contact models that are used in the controller of haptic levers. Finally, conclusions and experimental results are analysed.

2 Haptic Devices

Two haptic devices have been developed. The first device is a one rotational degree of freedom lever to emulate the behaviour of train and tram controls (Fig. 4). The second one is a two degree of freedom haptic device specially designed to simulate different gearshift behaviours (Fig. 5).

One of the main targets of the mechanical design has been to obtain a well-built, optimal-performing system at a feasible cost.

DC brushed motors with encoders transmit torque to linkages through pre-tensioned cable reductions. The use of cable transmissions allows for high mechanical performance. These kinds of mechanical transmissions present high reversibility, high stiffness, no backslash and near zero friction, allowing the system to reproduce realistic haptic sensations.

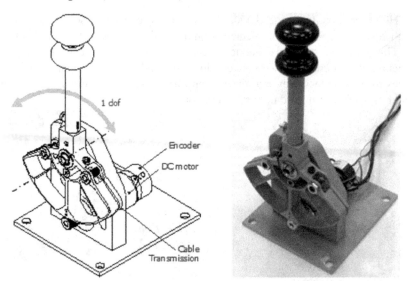

Fig. 4. One degree of freedom train/tram haptic lever.

The maximum rotation angle of the 1-DoF haptic lever is ±70 degrees. A Maxon DC motor is connected to the lever by means of a cable transmission with a reduction stage of 10. The maximum continuous torque is 0.184 Nm which corresponds to a force of 10.10N at the tip of the lever. Regarding the peak torque/force, the actuator torque is 0.736 Nm and the force, gauged at the tip of the lever, is 40 N.

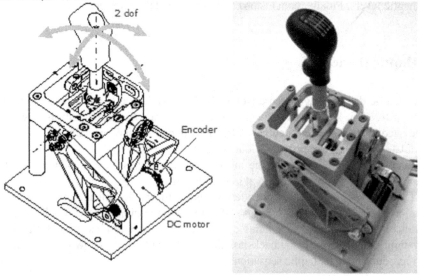

Fig. 5. Two degrees of freedom haptic gear-shift

The size of the workspace of the 2-DoF haptic device is similar to the one of a real manual gearshift with a workspace of ±60 mm in the X-axis and ±40 mm in the Y-axis.

In this case, the actuator strokes are 41 degrees for the first DoF and 55 degrees for the second DoF. The actuators in use are Maxon DC motors, with a maximum continuous torque of 0.184 Nm. In this case, a cable transmission is also used with two reductors of 17.33 and 16 for the 1st DoF and the 2nd DoF respectively. Hence, the maximum continuous torque capability of the device is 3.26 Nm for the 1st DoF and 3.01 Nm for the 2nd. Due to the type of application we can harness a peak force of 13.06 Nm for the 1st DoF and 12.06 Nm for the 2nd.

In both cases, relative encoders with a resolution of 5000 pulses per revolution (ppr) have been used. This resolution reaches 20000 ppr when a quadrature signal is used. Due to mechanical transmission, this resolution is enhanced by 0.0018 degrees in the cases of the haptic lever and the 2-DoF device; post-transmission resolutions are gauged at 0.001039 and 0.001125 degrees for each axis.

3 Control Board

In [6] the authors present a system architecture based on a commercial microcontroller board, model BL2600, manufactured by Zworld, Inc. This board represents a low cost solution compared to those commonly used at research laboratories, i.e. dSPACE acquisition boards. The use of such low cost solutions comes at the expense of reduced system performance. In many cases, this reduction does not aversely affect the user's perception when using haptic devices. However, this no longer holds true when complex models have to be used, as in the case of complex kinematics with two or more DoF or complex contact force models.

It is well known within the digital control theory framework that the stability of a system is highly dependent on the sampling time in the same way that a low sampling frequency can lead to system instability.

This inconvenience is due to common low cost microcontrollers which are slow at computing multiplications, trigonometric and exponential functions. This significant lag in computation time (ten milliseconds) provokes a decrease of the sampling frequency becoming the system unstable.

Thus, in these cases, a mathematic processor unit (MPU) must work in collaboration with the microcontroller.

In this paper, the solution adopted to overcome this problem is to develop a custom board (EOS). This board is based on a Spartan chip, an FPGA from Xilinx. The model that has been used is XC3S500-E and its main features are summarized in the following table:

Table 1. Specifications for the FPGA SPARTAN XC3S500-E

System Gates	500K
Logic Cells	10476
Dedicated Multipliers	20
Block RAM bits	360K
Distributed RAM Bits	73K
DCM (Digital Clock Mager)	4
Max Single Ended I/O Pairs	232
Max Differential I/O Pairs	92

One interesting feature of the Spartan family is that a customized processor can be programmed in the FPGA firmware. In this paper, a Microblaze microcontroller has been used. This microcontroller is also distributed by Xilinx. During trials, Microblaze implementation has been optimized for mathematical computation.

A simplified diagram of the board architecture is shown in Fig. 6. As shown, there are 6 encoder inputs, one USB port, one Ethernet port, two RS232 and two SPI modules to which several IO modules can be attached as needed. In this research, one module with six analog outputs and another with 48 digital configurable inputs/outputs were connected to SPI modules.

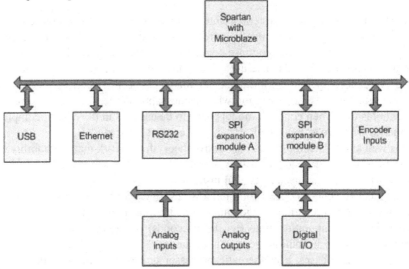

Fig. 6. Board architecture.

In order to analyse the performance of this board, the BL2600 board has been used as a point of reference. This acquisition board has been used previously, for research purposes at our labs in order to cut the price of haptic systems based on a dSpace solution. However, it does not fulfil all the needed requirements as a controller device. Table 2 shows the specifications for both solutions.

Table 2. Specifications for the tested solutions

Board	EOS	BL2600
Microprocessor	Microblaze, but changeable by FPGA configuration. 75MHz	Rabbit 3000, 44.2MHz
Flash memory	512K	512K expandable a 4-8-16 MB
Analog Inputs	8, (in an expansion module)	8
Analog Outputs	6, (in an expansion module)	4
Digital Input/Output	48 configurable, (in an expansion module)	16 inputs and 16 config.
Encoder Inputs	6	2
Ethernet	Yes	Yes
USB	Yes	No
Architecture	Stand alone	Stand alone
Sampling period/freq.	1ms/1kHz, upgradable	2.5ms/ 400Hz

The USB and Ethernet ports enable the system to be easily connectable to a PC directly or via a Standard Ethernet network. Then, a haptic device can be considered as a black box remotely configurable by that computer.

4 System Architecture

The proposed optimal-cost architecture can be seen in Fig.7

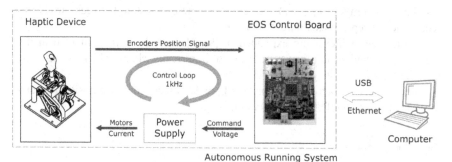

Fig. 7. Optimal cost architecture.

As can be seen, the haptic system is completely autonomous. On the left, there is a haptic device, either a 1-DoF lever or a 2-DoF gearshift. In the centre, the EOS board senses the encoder's positions and computes the control action at 1 kHz. The haptic system can be remotely configured by a computer via USB or Ethernet, depending on user requirements (on the right). Thus, this PC enables both tele-monitorization of the system and the changing of working modes (number of gears, normal behaviour, malfunctions, etc).

5 Force Contact Models

In this section, the programmed force contact models in the EOS board are presented. For reasons of clarity, the contact force models are classified according to the relative orientation of a plane tangent to the contact surface at the contact point. According to that classification we can find normal forces and tangent forces.

   As will be seen later, most of the used contact models compute a force based on a position or speed. These types of models are known as *impedance contact models* [21].

5.1 Normal Force Model

The penalty method is one of the most widely used methods to compute contact forces between two virtual objects. This method calculates virtual contact force as proportional to the penetration between the two objects in contact. Under the non-plastic-deformation hypothesis, the applied force can be expressed as the sum of two components Eq.1.

$$\mathbf{f}_n = \mathbf{f}_{el}(\mathbf{x}) + \mathbf{f}_v(\mathbf{x}, \dot{\mathbf{x}}) \tag{1}$$

   In equation 1 the normal contact force, $\mathbf{f}_e$, has two components: the elastic (or conservative) force, $\mathbf{f}_{el}$, and the viscous component (damping), $\mathbf{f}_v$. The vector $\mathbf{x}$ also has two components (x, y) and represents the penetration between virtual objects. The dot represents a time derivative[2].

   The models, which were explained in [9-13], have been implemented in the system presented in this paper in order to empirically check which is the most suitable for a low-cost system.

   The simplest contact model considers $\mathbf{f}_{el}$ and $\mathbf{f}_v$ linear, time and position invariant. This leads to the following equation:

$$\mathbf{f}_n = \mathbf{k}_n \mathbf{x} + \mathbf{B}_n \dot{\mathbf{x}} \tag{2}$$

   where $\mathbf{k}_n$ represents the stiffness of the elastic part, and $\mathbf{B}_n$, the damping. The sub index $\mathbf{n}$ refers to the fact that this corresponds to a normal contact model.

   Viscoelastic linear models have been used to model virtual walls that constrain the movement within the allowed trajectories when the user changes gears. These walls make an envelope that encloses the pattern of the gears. For example, a

---

[2] Notice that the bold letters appoints vectors and uppercase letters, matrices.

manual transmission has an H-shape and a train accelerator or reverser has an I-shape (**Fig. 10**). Elastic models have been used to enable an automatic shifting to neutral in the event that manual transmission is selected.

5.2 Tangential Force Models

By means of tangential models, friction and texture forces are computed. These forces are classified as either conservative or non-conservative.

5.2.1 Non-Conservative Tangent Force Models

Among the different models we can find in the bibliography, we have chosen Sal-cudean's model [14] with Adachi's simplification [15], due to its simplicity. This model considers dynamic rather than static (Coulomb) friction Eq.3.

$$\mathbf{f}_t = \mathbf{B}_t \mathbf{v}_t \tag{3}$$

In equation 3, $\mathbf{f}_t$ is the tangential force, $\mathbf{B}_t$ is the viscous damping and $\mathbf{v}_t$ is the tangential speed.

The viscous friction limits the mechanism speed when it is shifting to neutral in order to guarantee stability.

5.2.2 Conservative tangential force model

Minsky presents in [16] a force model based on the gradient of a function (a potential). Several research projects have used this model to render textures [17-20].

In this paper, Minsky's approach has also been used to create equilibrium points along the allowed path within the workspace of the haptic device. In this case, the potential function is defined by means of exponentials as follows:

$$u_{hi} = -e^{-(x-x_{0i})^2 - (y-y_{0i})^2} \tag{4}$$

where u_{hi} is a potential function, (x_{0i}, y_{0i}) is the point in the 2D space where potential origin is defined and (x, y) is the present position of the lever/gear shift.

This equation, Eq.4, creates a force field that is stable at the point (x_{0i}, y_{0i}), which will be felt as the *hard point* by the user. This hard point will constitute a desired resting point for the haptic device, such as a gear or in neutral. When more than one hard point is required, the superposition principle is applied as shown in Eq.5,

$$u_h = \sum_{i=1}^{n} -e^{-(x-x_{0i})^2-(y-y_{0i})^2} \tag{5}$$

where the points (x_{0i}, y_{0i}) are the equilibrium (or hard) points and u_h the total potential field due to hard points.

The force $\mathbf{f}_h$ is derived from the field u_h by computing the gradient:

$$\mathbf{f}_h = \nabla u_h = \left[\frac{\partial u_h}{\partial x} \quad \frac{\partial u_h}{\partial y} \quad \frac{\partial u_h}{\partial z} \right]^T \tag{6}$$

One advantage in using conservative fields lies in their definition of continuous and derivable functions. These characteristics lead to simpler control algorithms, since discontinuities can produce high force-peaks that can be a source of instabilities. Moreover, conservative field models can be easily expanded in the case of more than one degree of freedom.

5.3 Force Model to Render the Behaviour of Haptic Devices

The force model located in the haptic device controller is the summation of normal, tangential non-conservative and conservative forces.

Roughly speaking, all forces except the 'viscous forces', used in this paper are conservative. In order to easily visualize the composition of all of them, Fig.8-left shows a 3D representation of the complete potential field. The force at any given point will also be the slope at that point. Fig. 8-right is the summary of all force models used in this paper.

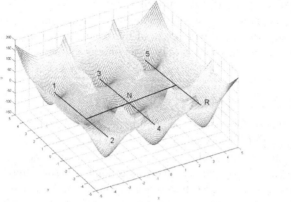

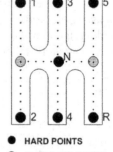

Fig. 8-left. Potential function in the case of a 5-gear manual transmission plus a reverse gear.

Fig 8-right Implemented force models.

6 Experimental Results

Several tests have been defined to empirically determine the critical values for stiffness and damping. These tests simulate the collision between the gearshift and virtual wall (see previous section).

Fig. 9 shows various tests for different levels of stiffness for both controller boards. The y-axis represents exerted force and the x-axis time. Instead of starting all tests from zero, an arbitrary 'time-shift' has been set between every two tests in order to maintain clear plots without overlapping among the different curves.

When it comes to stability, most conclude that critical stiffness is approximately 9kN/m for BL2600 and 18kN/m for the EOS Board. These values represent thresholds that would incur instability if breached. The optimum results obtained for the EOS Board are a direct consequence of the higher sampling frequency that this board can withstand.

The next issue of importance is that working with stiffness values slightly below critical ones leads to stable yet oscillatory conditions. (Fig. 9, right, K=9kN/m). From the user's point of view, this behaviour is undesirable because the virtual wall will be perceived as a vibrating spring, not as a stiff surface; when the user expects to continuously run up against a simple virtual flat surface. Consequently, the maximum usable stiffness is reduced to a level at which virtual contact is established with no oscillations or imperceptible oscillations to the users. Therefore, the maximum recommendable stiffness is 6kN/m for the BL2600 and 15kN/m for the EOS Board (see Fig. 9, left).

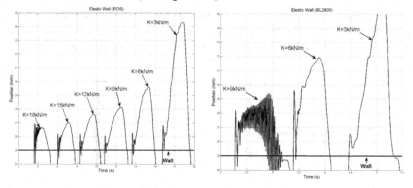

Fig. 9. Experimental tests for stiffness and damping for the viscoelastic model, EOS (left) and BL2600 (right).

Massie [22] says that humans perceive any stiffness greater than 2 kN/m as completely stiff surfaces. In both cases, therefore, such surfaces will be perceived as stiff ones. However, considering that humans exert a force of roughly 20N when they are handling these kinds of levers, and with a virtual stiffness close to 2kN/m, the haptic device will surpass the limits of the virtual wall by 10mm. This is detrimental to many applications because it reduces the precision and the believability of simulated tasks. A worst case scenario would be when a haptic device is used as a part of a surgical simulator. In the case of driving simulators, a slight over-extension (one millimetre approximately) would be perceived as a slash by the user and therefore be assumed with minimal detriment to the simulation experience.

To sum up, an increase in virtual stiffness is desirable. However, infinite virtual stiffness is worthless due to the limitation imposed by the saturation of our sense of touch: Tan [23] measured the maximum stiffness perceptible by human senses, limited by skin and muscle stiffness (boundary is between 15.3kN/m and 41.5kN/m). Thus, an optimal stiffness value can be found at the level of 33kN/m and only this value is given by the EOS based solution.

Other trials have been done with 10 users and different stiffness/damping values. In Table 3, a summary of the recommended parameters for the model of eq. 2 is presented.

Table 3. Empirical recommended values

Model	EOS	BL2600
Linear elastic	15kN/m	6kN/m
Linear viscoelastic	33kN/m and 150N•s/m	9kN/m and 40N•s/m

The second test was performed with 10 users who were between 25 and 45, had driver licenses and were accustomed to using manual transmissions. The test consisted of describing the perceived sensations when using the haptic gearshift under the control of the EOS compared to the BL2600. All users unanimously preferred the EOS board.

The following graphs present a selection of the most representative types of gearshifts, which have been implemented in the optimal cost system: manual transmission (Fig. 10, left); and automatic transmission (Fig. 10, right).

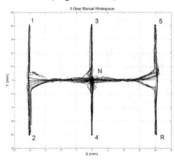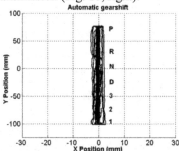

Fig. 10. Workspace: manual transmission with 5-gears (left) and automatic transmission (right).

The transmission workspaces are the envelopes of the plots depicted in previous figures. These plots have been drawn during several trials in which the user changed the gear many times randomly. It can be seen that the movements are constrained to the slots virtually created by the control algorithms.

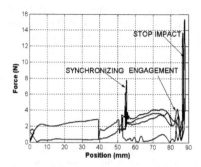

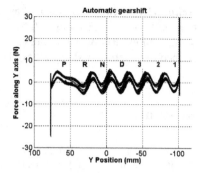

Fig. 11. Force vs. position, measured profile when the user engages the first gear in a simulated manual transmission.

Fig. 12. Force model for a simulated automatic transmission.

Fig. 11 shows the forces felt in the haptic session when a gear is engaged. This graph fits real profiles, such as the depicted ones in [8]. As is seen, both patterns are similar. In the case of the simulation the curve is sharper. In both cases the graphs depend on gearshift positions. There are several force peaks that correspond to moments in which the gear is engaged/synchronized or when the mechanism collides with an end-stroke. Despite the differences between the real and haptic plot, the sensation of shifting gears in the second one is realistic.

Fig. 12 depicts the forces felt in the Y-axis by a model for an automatic transmission (Fig. 10, right). The peaks, found at the beginning and at the end of the pattern, are linked to the force surge felt at the end-stroke of the gearshift. The local minimum values correspond to the gears of the transmission, i.e. the zones where a gear is engaged. The hysteresis shown in the figure is due to friction.

7 Conclusions

In this paper, two haptic levers are presented. These devices are used in driving simulators in order to emulate the behaviour of actuators. In order to cut of prices of haptic systems, but without reducing the overall performance, the prototype EOS card has also been developed and presented. This leads to a versatile optimal cost haptic architecture.

The main conclusions, obtained from experiments, confirm that it is possible to develop a cost effective haptic device that can be used for cars, trains, trucks, etc. with a capacity to render forces equivalent to the forces exhibited by real controls.

One of the advantages of using the EOS instead of the BL2600 is the possibility of introducing more complex haptic models than the one depicted in Fig.8-left. This leads to the possibility of malfunction simulation such as preventing the engagement/shifting of a gear when the clutch is not pressed or the transmission of engine vibrations.

Acknowledgments   This work has been financially supported by Lander Simulation and Training Solutions (http://www.landersimulation.com). This company manufactures driving simulators (bus, truck, train,) and the haptic devices described in the presented paper have been installed in a number of them.

References

1. Woon-Sung Lee, J.-H. Kim, and J.-H. Cho. (1998) A Driving Simulator as a Virtual Reality Tool. in IEEE International Conference on Robotics and Automation.. Leuven, Belgium.
2. Basdogan, C., et al., (2004) Haptics in Minimally Invasive Surgical Simulation and Training. IEEE Computer Graphics and Applications,. 24(2): p. 56-64.
3. Jorgensen, C., K. Wheeler, and S. Stepniewski. (2000) Bioelectric Control of a 757 Class High Fidelity Aircraft Simulation. in World Automation Congress.. Wailea Maui, Hawaii.
4. Ferrazzin, D., F. Salsedo, and M. Bergamasco. (1999) The MORIS Simulator. in Eighth International Workshop on Robot and Human Interactive Communication (RO-MAN '99).. Pisa, Italy: IEEE.
5. Madhani, A.J., G. Niemeyer, and J.K. Salisbury. (1998) The Black Falcon: A Teleoperated Surgical Instrument for Minimally Invasive Surgery. in International Conference on Intelligent Robots and Systems.. Victoria B.C., Canada: IEEE/RSJ.
6. Bengoechea, E., E. Sánchez, and J.J.Gil. (2006) Palanca Háptica de Bajo Coste para Simuladores de Conducción y Entrenamiento. in VII Congreso Internacional de Interacción Persona-Máquina.. Puertollano, Ciudad Real, Spain: Universidad Castilla la Mancha.
7. Angerilli, M., et al. (2001) Haptic Simulation of an Automotive Manual Gearshift. in International Workshop on Robot and Human Interactive Communication. 2001: IEEE.
8. Frisoli, A., C.A. Avizzano, and M. Bergamasco. Simulation of a Manual Gearshift with a 2 DOF Force-Feedback Joystick. in International Conference on Robotics & Automation.. Seoul, Korea: IEEE.
9. Brown, J.M. and J.E. Colgate. (1994) Physics-Based Approach to Haptic Display. in ISMRC 94, Topical Workshop on Virtual Reality.. Los Alamitos, Calofornia.
10. Hunt, K.H. and F.R.E. Crossley, (1975) Coefficient of Restitution Interpreted as Damping in Vibroimpact. ASME Journal of Applied Mechanics,: p. 440-445.
11. Hwang, J.D., M.D. Williams, and G. Niemeyer. (2004) Toward Event-Based Haptics: Rendering Contact Using Open-Loop Force Pulses. in Haptics Symposium 2004.. Chicago, Illinois.
12. Rosenberg, L.B. and B.D. Adelstein. (1993) Perceptual Decomposition of Virtual Haptic Surfaces. in Proceedings IEEE 1993 Symposium on Research Frontiers in Virtual Reality. San José CA.
13. Salcudean, S.E. and T.D. Vlaar, (1997) On the Emulation of Stiff Walls and Static Friction with a Magnetically Levitated Input/Output Device. ASME, Journal of Dynamic Systems, Measurement, and Control,. 119(1): p. 127-132.
14. Salcudean, S.E. and T.D. Vlaar, (1994) On the Emulation of Stiff Walls and Static Friction with a Magnetically Levitated Input/Output Device. ASME, Journal of Dynamic Systems, Measurement, and Control,. 119(1): p. 127-132.
15. Adachi, Y., T. Kumano, and K. Ogino. (1995) Intermediate Representation for Stiff Virtual Objects. in IEEE Virtual Reality Annual International Symposium..

16. Minsky, M., et al. (1990) Feeling and Seeing: Issues in Force Display. in 1990 Symposium on Interactive 3D graphics.. Snowbird, Utah, United States.

17. Basdogan, C., C.-H. Ho, and M.A. Srinivasan. (1997) A Ray-Based Haptic Rendering Technique for Displaying Shape and Texture of 3-D Objects in Virtual Environments. in ASME Dynamic Systems and Control Division.. Dallas, TX.

18. Kim, L., et al. (2002) An Implicit Based Haptic Rendering Technique. in IEEE/RSJ IROS..

19. Otaduy, M.A. and M.C. Lin. (2004) A Perceptually-Inspired Force Model for Haptic Texture Rendering. in 1st Symposium on Applied perception in graphics and visualization.. Los Angeles, California.

20. Otaduy, M.A., et al. (2004) Haptic Display of Interaction between Textured Models. in Visualization Conference.. Austin, Tx: IEEE.

21. Hogan, N., (1985) Impedance control: an approach to manipulation: Part I – theory, Part II – implementation, Part III – applications. Journal of Dynamic Systems, Measurement and Control.

22. Massie, T.H. and K. Salisbury. (1994) The PHANTOM Haptic Interface: A Device for Probing Virtual Objects. in ASME Winter Annual Meeting, Symposium on Haptic Interfaces for Virtual Environment and Teleoperator Systems.. Chicago, IL.

23. Tan, H., et al. (1994) Human Factors for the Design of Force Reflecting Haptic Interfaces. in ASME WAM.. New York.

Interference of Auditory Information with Haptic Perception of Stiffness in Virtual Reality

A. Reyes-Lecuona, F.J. Cañadas-Quesada

Departamento de Tecnología Electrónica, Universidad de Málaga, Málaga, España.
areyes@uma.es, fjcq@uma.es

Abstract: This paper describes an experimental study about how auditory stimuli interfere with haptic perception. Specifically, the interference of auditory stimulus duration with haptic perception of surface stiffness within a virtual environment is analysed. An experiment was performed in which subjects were asked to tap two virtual surfaces and to report which was stiffer. Our results show that there is an association between short auditory and stiff haptic stimuli, and between long auditory and soft haptic stimuli. Moreover, the influence of auditory information was stronger in the case of discriminating similar haptic stimuli when either facilitating or hindering this haptic discrimination.

1 Introduction

In the real world, when an object is manipulated, information coming from different sensorial modalities (haptic, visual, and auditory) is simultaneously received. This is what we call multimodality. Regarding multimodal interaction, perception of sensorial stimuli coming from one of these modalities can be affected by other sensorial stimuli coming from another modality, substituting complementing or interfering the former stimuli. Usually, this kind of information improves object manipulation performance. Previous works [9, 13, 19, 2] have established that the degree of realism [10] and the level of presence [18] experienced by a subject within a virtual environment (VE) can be increased if multimodal information is presented, as it occurs in the real world.

When manipulating objects, one of the basic properties to be taken into account is the stiffness of these objects, as it provides some cues about the nature of the object. Within a VE, all the information related to haptic sensation is provided by haptic devices (e.g. force feedback devices).

However, current haptic devices present a technological drawback related to the maximum stiffness which they can simulate within a VE. This drawback is due to the fact that haptic devices are unable to provide an infinite force. This is espe-

M. Redondo et al. (eds.), *Engineering the User Interface*,
DOI: 10.1007/978-1-84800-136-7_4, © Springer-Verlag London Limited 2009

cially problematic for force feedback devices based on an impedance control scheme, as most of them are (these devices provide a force against the movement as a function of their position within the VE). Hence, when simulating a rigid surface, a slight penetration into the simulated object and a force normal to the surface and proportional to this penetration are provided. This force must be kept under certain limits to avoid the feeling of 'live surfaces' or the presence of movements not caused by the user. This incoherence between virtual and real forces leads to some incongruities with the virtual objects that are being explored and manipulated [4]. A possible solution for improving the stiffness perception using force feedback devices could be the use of additional information coming from different modalities (e.g. auditory information that complements haptic information) as well as the use of perceptual illusions.

Many studies have been carried out about a combination of visual and haptic modalities, mostly related to the substitution of information coming from one modality by information coming from the other one. One of the first works in this scientific area was presented in 1964 by Rock and Victor [14]. It was a psychophysics study whose results showed that the perceptual experience of a person could be affected by interactions between different sensorial modalities. Specifically, this work pointed out that visual information may change the haptic perception of size, orientation and shape of an object.

In the Nineties, Klatzky showed that visual and haptic exploration are related with the material an object is made of [5]. Scultz and Petersik found out that adding visual information to haptic exploration of an object permitted greater accuracy [15]. Miner showed with his works that a visual stimulus as well as the combination of several stimuli may affect the haptic perception of an object. He also studied the complementary or redundancy effect that multimodal information provides, as well as the substitution effect [11].

Lécuyer showed through several studies that force feelings could be perceived using devices without force feedback by means of pseudohaptic feedback [8, 6]. In a later study he showed how subjects could perceive haptic information (e.g. macroscopic texture identification) adequately only when using visual information (through variations in the movement of a cursor) [7].

Poling, in one of his works, studied the role of visual-haptic multimodality in the perception of surface roughness. The obtained results pointed out that dominant sensorial information depended on the amplitude of simulated surface roughness and that the perception accuracy was greater in the case of using bimodal information. The haptic channel was the dominant one for low amplitude of surface roughness while, in the case of medium amplitude, subjects combined information from both modalities achieving higher performance [13].

On the other hand, there are far fewer studies tackling auditory-haptic multimodality than those devoted to visual-haptic multimodality. A study carried out by Peeva showed the existence of some correlation between surface roughness and some auditory properties (intensity and frequency) when rubbing the surface [12]. Subjects associated rougher surfaces with louder sounds and less rough surfaces with lower sounds. He also found a strong correlation between sound frequency and surface roughness. Bresciani showed that tactile perception when a subject's skin is tapped with a point can be modulated by a series of beeps. Specifically, his results showed that the nervous system tends to integrate haptic and auditory stimuli when they are administered at the same time [1].

Other studies have shown that, when a single visual flash is administered together with multiple beeps of irrelevant tasks, the visual flash is perceived as multiple flashes [16, 17].

DiFranco studied the influence of auditory stimuli in haptic perception of stiffness of virtual surfaces [4]. In this study, subjects were asked to tap different virtual surfaces. When tapping them, a pre-recorded sound accompanied the tapping. These sounds were recorded from the impacts of an instrument tapping surfaces of different materials as glass, metal, wood, etc. Obtained results showed that the sound played affected stiffness discrimination. When two haptic stimuli were identical, subjects sorted surface stiffness according to the sound heard. However, when different haptic stimuli were presented, only subjects less experienced with haptic devices were affected in their perception of stiffness by auditory stimuli.

In the real world, every mechanical impact between two objects is naturally associated with a sound. Therefore, it is interesting to study the relationship between haptic and auditory modalities in the task of tapping. This paper presents an experimental study about the interference of auditory information in haptic perception of stiffness. More specifically, how the duration of auditory stimuli affects haptic perception of stiffness of virtual surfaces is studied. Our goal is to obtain greater insight about the importance and credibility that subjects give to auditory information when trying to discriminate the stiffness of a virtual surface.

In section 2 the experimental design is presented. The results obtained appear in section 3. Section 4 is devoted to discussion of these results. Finally, in section 5, conclusions derived from the obtained results, as well as proposed future works to continue this research, are presented.

2 Method

2.1 Subjects

The experiment was performed with 25 subjects (20 males, 5 females). All of them were students of Telecommunication Engineering degree at the University of Málaga. They were aged between 16 and 25 (μ=18.88, σ =1.48). None of them suffered from any perception inhibiting. All except one were right handed. No payment was offered for their participation.

2.2 Material

Haptic stimuli were administered using a PHANToM Desktop (SensAble Technologies), a force feedback device with three degrees of freedom (3 DOF). This device was connected to a computer (Pentium 4, 3.2 GHz, 1GB RAM and a VNIDIA GeForce FX 5700LE graphics card with 256 MB).

Surface modelling was performed using OpenHaptics Toolkit (v1.0) Developer by Sensable Technologies for PHANToM. VEs were developed using Visual C++ programming environment, including OpenGL and OpenAL libraries to generate graphic scenes and auditory stimuli respectively. A slight static friction was added to virtual surfaces to avoid any slip over them when they were tapped by the user with the stylus. The tip of the virtual stylus was represented by a little blue sphere and a vertical shadow was added in order to provide depth information making it easier to tap the virtual surfaces.

When the virtual surface was tapped, an auditory stimulus consisting in a 1000Hz sinusoidal signal was generated. The characteristics of this sound were identical for all the trials, although its duration varied according to the experimental design, as is explained later on.

2.3 Procedure

The subjects were seated in front of the haptic device with the screen placed at the eye level. The haptic device was placed in the centre of the table aligned with the vertical symmetry axis of the subject in such a way that the subject held it with her/his dominant hand, as is shown in Fig. 1. The subjects wore headphones to hear auditory stimuli.

Fig. 1. Experimental setup

The subjects received all the necessary instructions at the beginning of the experiment. The experimental VE consisted of two white coloured square surfaces placed in the horizontal plane, one of them on the left side of the scenario and the other one on the right side (see fig. 2).

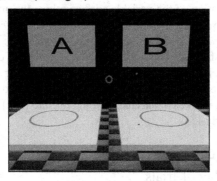

Fig. 2. The designed VE with the virtual surfaces used in the experiment

Both surfaces depicted a red circle to limit the area the subject should touch. The subjects were asked to tap each surface only once per trial starting always with the left one. Each time they tapped the surface the auditory stimulus was generated in a synchronous way with the tapping. After tapping the two surfaces, subjects should report, as quickly as possible, which surface was the stiffer one. To do so, the subject should press with the stylus one of the two buttons placed over the surfaces (labelled as A and B). When these buttons were pressed, they lit up for a short time and the trial was finished. There was no time limit for subject responses, although they were asked to respond as quickly as possible. The time between trials was three seconds.

The experiment was conducted in a research laboratory. The subjects were explicitly informed that the auditory stimulus was irrelevant for the task of determining which surface was the stiffer one. The experiment consisted of five blocks, with one minute between blocks to give subjects a break. Each block was composed of 25 trials. Therefore, each subject performed a total of 125 trials, which took approximately 30 minutes to complete. The first block was considered as training in the task and discarded for the analysis. After finishing the experiment a short questionnaire was administered to the subjects asking them about their previous experience with computers, 3D videogames, virtual environments and force feedback devices, as well as possible discomfort or boredom during the experiment.

For each trial, one of the two presented surfaces was considered as the reference surface. This was randomly chosen for each trial and was not known by the subject. The reference surface always had the same haptic and auditory characteristics: a stiffness value of 0.5 N/mm and an associated auditory stimulus 150 ms long. Then stiffness and sound duration for the other surface varied taking the following values: 0.3, 0.4, 0.5, 0.6, 0.7 N/mm as stiffness and 50, 100, 150, 200, 250 ms as sound duration. The combination of these values produces 25 different experimental conditions.

In the following, the stiffness value of the variable surface minus the stiffness value of the reference surface will be referred to as the *stiffness difference*. The auditory stimulus duration of the variable surface minus the auditory stimulus duration of the reference surface will be referred as the *sound duration difference*

Hence, the independent variables in this experiment were: stiffness difference (N/mm) and sound difference (ms). The dependent variables considered were the reaction time (RT), defined as the time spent between tapping on the right surface and pressing the chosen button; the contact time (CT), defined as the time the stylus point is in contact with each surface; and the hit rate (HR) when reporting the stiffer surface, defined as

$$HR = \frac{\text{Number of correct responses}}{\text{Number of trials}} \qquad (2.1)$$

The 25 trials of each block correspond to the 25 different experimental conditions. Therefore, the experiment uses a complete factorial design with two within subject factors (stiffness difference and sound duration difference) with five level for each factor (-0.2, -0.1, 0, 0.1, 0.2 N/mm for stiffness difference and -100, -50, 0, 50, 100 ms for sound duration difference). Hence, regarding the analysed data, each subject performed four trials for each experimental condition, one within each block, and the average of these four trials was computed for each dependent variable.

To avoid order effects, an incomplete counterbalanced design was applied within each block.

3 Results

A repeated measurement ANOVA was performed with the two factors and five levels per factor detailed above for the dependent variable Hit Rate. Significant differences were found for stiffness difference ($F_{4,96} = 54.48$, p<0.001). This is a logical result, because the more distinct the haptic stimuli are the easier it is to discriminate which surface is the stiffer one. Regarding sound duration no significant differences were found in the Hit Rate ($F_{4,96} = 1.41$, p = 0.383). However, a significant interaction between the two factors was found for the Hit Rate ($F_{16,384} = 4.12$, p<0.001). This result shows interference between auditory information and the haptic perception of stiffness. Our results also show an association between stiffer surfaces and shorter sounds, and vice versa.

In order to obtain more detail, a subset of two levels were considered for each factor (-0.1 N/mm and +0.1 N/mm as stiffness differences) and (-100 ms and +100 ms as sound duration differences). In this way, the influence of auditory stimuli, when haptic stiffness is similar in the two surfaces, can be studied. Results obtained using ANOVA also show a significant interaction between the two factors ($F_{1,24} = 16.81$, p<0.001); see Fig. 3 for more details.

A similar analysis was performed in the case of very different stiffness in the two surfaces (-0.2 N/mm and +0.2 N/mm as stiffness differences) and (-100 ms and +100 ms as sound duration differences). Significant interaction between the two factors were still found in this case ($F_{1,24} = 9.175$, p<0.01); see Fig. 4 for more details.

Figure 3 allows a detailed study of the Hit Rate variable. The data obtained show that it is more difficult to discriminate which surface is the stiffer one in the case of similar stiffness for the variable surface and the reference surface. So, it is reasonable that auditory interference is more important in these cases, as it provides new additional information to the haptic modality.

In the case of low stiffness differences, auditory modality could be considered as the dominant one. That is the case when auditory information improves the stiffness discrimination as well as when it worsens that discrimination, because the subjects give their responses more influenced by the auditory information than by the hapic information. Nevertheless, the interference caused by auditory stimuli is still present even in the case of high stiffness differences, as can be seen in Fig. 4.

These results also show that association between the haptic and the auditory stimuli can be coherent (the stiffer surface is associated to shorter sound or the softer surface is associated to longer sound) or incoherent (the stiffer surface is associated to longer sound or the softer surface is associated to shorter sound). When haptic and auditory stimuli are coherent the number of correct responses is greater than the number of correct responses obtained when they are non-coherent. On the other hand, when there is a haptic-auditory sensorial non-coherence the auditory stimulus misleads the subject perception and the number of correct responses is less.

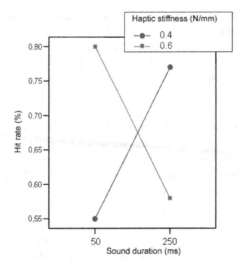

Fig. 3. Hit rate (percentage of correct responses) when haptic stimuli in the variable surface (0.4 and 0.6 N/mm) are similar to those in the reference surface (0.5 N/mm), while auditory stimuli in the variable surface (50 y 250 ms) are very different to those in the reference surface (150 ms). That is to say, low stiffness differences and high sound duration differences.

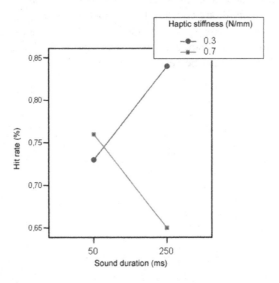

Fig. 4. Hit rate (percentage of correct responses) when haptic stimuli in the variable surface (0.3 and 0.7 N/mm) are far from those in the reference surface (0.5 N/mm), and auditory stimuli in the variable surface (50 y 250 ms) are very different to those in the reference surface (150 ms). That is to say, high stiffness differences and high sound duration differences.

Bivariate Spearman correlation analysis of the data collected with questionnaires showed no significant relationship with the dependent variables. This correlation was always lower than $\rho < 0.2$.

Regarding Reaction Time, pressing the left button (A labelled) takes more time than pressing the right one (B labelled) because the former is further from the right surface than the latter. Remember that the response was required as quickly as possible right after tapping the right surface. In order to avoid this effect, the measurement of RT was corrected removing the averaged extra time in the case of left button. Nevertheless, ANOVA results did not show any significant RT differences with neither stiffness differences nor sound duration differences. No interaction between stiffness differences and sound duration differences was found in the case of RT either.

Finally, ANOVA results for Contact Time showed significant differences for stiffness difference factor ($F_{1,24} = 8.996$, p<0.01 for low stiffness differences, as in the case of fig. 3; and $F_{1,24} = 23.916$, p<0.001 for high stiffness differences, as in the case of fig. 4). However, no significant differences were found for sound duration difference factor under the same conditions. No interaction between the two factors was found either.

4 Discussion

In accordance with previous works, we expected to find some interference between auditory stimulation and haptic perception. However, previous studies use auditory stimuli with more information. E.g. DiFranco [4] uses pre-recorded sounds which may affect the subject perception of haptic characteristics by evoking the real experience of tapping on different surfaces. On the contrary, auditory stimuli used in our experiment are synthetic sounds and therefore neutral. Our sounds give the subject much less information that pre-recorded tapping sounds and we have been able to control a very specific characteristic of the auditory stimuli: their duration.

Our results show that auditory information is more important when haptic stimuli are more similar. This is clearly because, in this case, subjects have less haptic information and so, auditory information is comparatively more valuable. Under these conditions, we can consider auditory information as the dominant factor. The presented experiment shows that auditory information interferes on stiffness haptic perception. Subjects perceive a coherence association (stiffer surfaces are associated to shorter sounds or softer surfaces are associated to longer sounds) and non-coherence association (stiffer surfaces are associated to longer sounds or softer surfaces are associated to shorter sounds) between the haptic stimulus and the auditory stimulus, as has been outlined in previous work [3].

In addition, as the contact time strongly depends on the surface stiffness, sound duration could be a cue interfering with the estimation of contact time that the subject realizes. Hence, sound duration could affect the haptic perception of stiffness through this mechanism. Something similar is presented in [1], where haptic perception is modulated by auditory stimuli, relating the number of perceived contacts with the number of emitted beeps. Therefore, Contact Time would be an intermediate variable in the interaction between sound duration and stiffness perception.

Regarding reaction times, it is important to say that, although our results have not found any significant result, it is possible that the proposed response mechanism has a negative influence. The use of the same haptic device to receive haptic stimuli and to provide the response might produce a strong contamination of response time variable by many other factors. Changes are therefore proposed in the interaction paradigm (e.g. providing the responses via the keyboard).

Moreover, the haptic properties of the left surface should be memorized in order to compare them with the haptic properties of the right surface. This unavoidable mechanism could affect reaction times, as the subjects have to recall haptic properties of the left surface to compare them with the other ones. This yields to propose changes in the experimental paradigm (e.g. asking the subjects for a sequential subjective evaluation of stiffness for each surface)

5 Conclusion

In this paper, a psychophysical experimental study to determine whether auditory information interferes with haptic perception is presented. The results show that auditory information interferes with stiffness haptic perception. The subjects perceive coherence between auditory and haptic stimuli when shorter auditory stimuli are associated with stiffer haptic stimuli and vice versa. This illusionary phenomenon could be used by designers of VEs in order to simulate stiffer materials with haptic devices.

As has been shown, a virtual surface can be perceived as more or less stiff as a function of the auditory stimulus simultaneously generated. That is to say, haptic perception of stiffness can be modulated by sound. This implies that haptic modality can be misled, under certain circumstances, by auditory modality.

Our results show that the more similar haptic stimuli are, the more difficult is for the subject to discriminate them, and so, the greater the influence from the auditory channel is.

Another interesting result has been the dependence found between contact time and surface stiffness. This is absolutely reasonable if we take into account how the haptic device works. Haptic device allows a slight penetration into the surface, and the provided force is computed as a linear function of this penetration and the stiffness. The stiffer the surface is, the stronger the provided force is. So, softer surfaces allow deeper penetrations and, therefore, the contact time is longer. This finding, together with the relationship found between sound duration and stiffness perception, suggests that the contact time unconsciously estimated by subjects may be an important factor in their perception of stiffness. Furthermore, the auditory stimuli could actually interfere with the contact time estimation and so, the haptic perception of stiffness.

Future work derived from these results could include the modelling of mechanisms of stiffness perception and their interaction with auditory information, including additional sound characteristics, as pitch, amplitude, delay and decay. Another future work proposal could be the development of a new experimental paradigm to avoid the masking of reaction times by the type of interaction mechanism used to provide subject responses.

Finally, it would be interesting to design new experiments to explore more in depth the importance of contact time and its perception by subjects in the surface stiffness assessment, as well as the interference of sound duration and contact time estimation by subjects.

Acknowledgments: We would like to thank Dr. Anatole Lécuyer and Dr. Marcos Ruiz-Soler for their valuable advice in the experiment design. We also thank the students that have participated as experimental subjects. This work has been partially supported by DIANA research group (TIC-171, Government of Andalusia).

References

1. Bresciani, J.P., M.O. Ernst, K. Drewing, G. Bouyer, V. Maury and A. Kheddar: (2005) Feeling what you hear: auditory signals can modulate tactile taps perception. Experimental Brain Research 162, 172-180,.
2. Campbell, C.S., Zhai, S., May, K.W., and Maglio, P.P. (1999) What You Feel Must Be What You See: Adding Tactile Feedback to the Trackpoint. INTERACT, 383-390,.
3. Cañadas-Quesada, F.J. and Reyes-Lecuona, A. (2006) "Improvement of Perceived Stiffness Using Auditory Stimuli in Haptic Virtual Reality". XIII Mediterranean Electrotechnical Conference, MELECON2006, Benalmádena (Málaga), May, 2006.
4. DiFranco, D., Beauregard, G.L., and Srinivasan, M.A. (1997) The effect of auditory cues on the haptic perception of stiffness in virtual environments. Proceedings of the ASME Dynamic Systems and Control Division, DSC-61, 17-22.
5. Klatzky, R. L., Lederman, S. J., and Matula, D. E. (1993) "Haptic exploration in the presence of vision", Journal of Experimental Psychology: Human Perception and Performance, Vol. 19, No. 4, pp. 726-743.
6. Lécuyer, A., Burkhardt, J.M., Coquillart, S., and Coiffet, P. (2001) "Boundary of Illusion": an Experiment of Sensory Integration with a Pseudo-Haptic System," presented at IEEE International Conference on Virtual Reality, Yokohama, Japan.
7. Lécuyer, A., Burkhardt, J.M., Etienne, L. (2004) "Feeling Bumps and Holes without a Haptic Interface: the Perception of Pseudo-Haptic Textures", ACM Conference in Human Factors in Computing Systems (ACM SIGCHI'04), Vienna, Austria, April 24-29.
8. Lécuyer, A., Coquillart, S., Kheddar, A., Richard, P., and Coiffet, P. (2000) Pseudo-Haptic Feedback: Can Isometric Input Devices Simulate Force Feedback? In Proc. of IEEE Int. Conf. on Virtual Reality, pages 83--90.

9. Lederman, S. J., Klatzky, R., Morgan, C. and Hamilton, C. (2002) Integrating multimodal information about surface texture via a probe: relative contributions of haptic and touch-produced sounds. Proceedings of the 10th International Symposium on Haptic Interfaces for Virtual Environment and Teleoperator Systems, 97-104.

10. McGee, M.R., Gray, P. and Brewster, S. (2001) Feeling rough: multimodal perception of virtual roughness. Proceedings of Eurohaptics 2001, 29-33.

11. Miner, N., Gillespie, B., and Caudell, T. (1996) Examining the Influence of Audio and Visual Stimuli on a Haptic Display. In Proc. of the IMAGE Conference.

12. Peeva, D., Baird, B., Izmirli, O. and Blevins, D. (2004) "Haptic and Sound Correlations: Pitch, Loudness and Texture," iv, pp. 659-664, Eighth International Conference on Information Visualisation (IV'04)

13. Poling, G.L., Weisenberger, J.M., and Kerwin, T. (2003) The role of multisensory feedback in haptic surface perception. Proceedings of the 11th International Symposium on Haptic Interfaces for Virtual Environment and Teleoperator Systems, 187-194.

14. Rock I, Victor J. (1964) Vision and touch: an experimentally created conflict between the two senses. Science, 143: 594–6.

15. Schultz, L. M. and Petersik, J. T. (1994) "Visual-haptic relations in a two-dimensional size matching task.", Perceptual and Motor Skills., Vol. 78, pp. 395-402.

16. Shams, L., Kamitani, Y., Shimojo, S. (2000) "What you see is what you hear", Nature 408:788,.

17. Shams L, Kamitani Y, Shimojo S, (2002) "Visual illusion induced by sound", Cognitive Brain Res 14:147–152.

18. Viciana Abad R., Reyes Lecuona A., Cañadas Quesada F.J. (2005) "Difficulties Using Passive Haptic Augmentation in the Interaction within a Virtual Environment", en Presence 2005, Londres, September 2005.

19. Weisenberger, J.M. and Poling, G.L. (2004) Multisensory roughness perception of virtual surfaces: effects of correlated cues. Proceedings of the 12th International Symposium on Haptic Interfaces for Virtual Environment and Teleoperator Systems,161-168.

Towards Implicit Interaction in Ambient Intelligence through Information Mosaic Roles

Ramón Hervás, Salvador W. Nava, Gabriel Chavira, Carlos Sánchez, José Bravo

Castilla-La Mancha University, Paseo de la Universidad, 13071 Ciudad Real, Spain
{ramon.hlucas, jose.bravo}@uclm.es.
Autonomous University of Tamaulipas, Tampico-Madero, México
{snava, gchavira}@uat.edu.mx
CCNT: Calidad Concertada Nuevas Tecnologías, 28037 Madrid, Spain.
carlos.barba@ccnt-spain.com

Abstract   Intelligent environments are responsive and sensitive to the presence of people. Users are integrated into a digital atmosphere which is adaptative to their needs, habits and emotions. Under the Ambient Intelligence vision, our main objective is to offer visualization of information services. They are integrated into a digital environment with contents adapted to the situation of the context at all times. These services are offered through a process of user identification by modelling the context around it (combining Near Fear Communication –NFC- and Radiofrequency Identification –RFID technologies). Moreover, by analyzing typical situations, we can define the "mosaic roles" that guide the generation process of Pervasive Display Systems.

Keywords: Ambient Intelligence, Context-Awareness, Information Visualization, Implicit Interaction.

1 Introduction

In the present work we seek services to aid users with their daily activities. People will be immersed in an intelligent environment. In it, the technology will become omnipresent and embedded, integrating microprocessors into everyday objects. Services will be present whenever we need them. In this sense, the interaction could be friendly and closer to the user.

The origin of Ambient Intelligence can be traced to Mark Weiser's proposals [1] that introduced Ubiquitous Computing as the third wave of computing, characterized by having many devices throughout the physical environment that are in-

M. Redondo et al. (eds.), *Engineering the User Interface*,
DOI: 10.1007/978-1-84800-136-7_5, © Springer-Verlag London Limited 2009

visible to the user who uses them without even thinking about their presence. In this way, Norman [2] proposes an application design that satisfies the task and attains a goal: "the tool has to become a part of the task". In this way, we can achieve an intuitive interaction with users centred on the task, not on the tool.

Only by understanding the world around us, the applications can be developed to make daily activities easier. The actions of a user could be predicted by an analysis of his or her situation. We have to consider that the same question can have several answers depending upon the context and the shared information. This is the main advantage of context-aware applications: They make several configurations and system adaptations possible in each situation.

In general, we can have an approximate and common vision of what the context means. However, it is a broad and ambiguous concept and it must be defined. There are several definitions of context. Anind K. Dey states: "Context is any information that can be used to characterize the situation of an entity. An entity is a person, place, or object that is considered relevant to the interaction between a user and an application, including the user and applications themselves". With regards to this idea, Dey defines Context-Aware application as "A system that uses context to provide relevant information and/or services to the user, where relevancy depends on the user's task" [3].

It is obvious that the concept of context is wide and complex. We need models to represent parts of the reality, or more precisely, to represent the context as an information source. In an initial analysis, there are five main aspects to consider, called the 5-W theory: Who, Where, When, What and Why [4], a theory applied to many fields, journalism and psychology among others.

We present a proposal for achieving a more natural interaction with the intelligent environment making it easier to access information and to adapt pervasive display services to the user context. The first section of the paper analyzes innovative approaches to user-intelligent environment interaction, looking for the implicit interaction by means of natural and simple inputs. We try to contribute to a better understanding of the schemas of interaction between users and Pervasive Display Systems (PDS, a fundamental part of Ambient Intelligence, as is explained in Section 3), i.e. embedding infrastructures into the environment and composing many multi-purpose and public displays.

The next sections show the key issues of these systems in general and ViMos (Visualization Mosaic) in detail: our experience in context-aware information visualization services. ViMos testing and experimentation allow us to identify several roles involved in the PDS and, therefore, to analyze the relationship between roles and interaction schemas.

2 Towards Implicit Interaction

To know the objectives of Ambient Intelligence, new ways of interaction are needed. The traditional human-computer interaction requires frequent user interventions in order to indicate every action to the computer. This vision is the opposite from the idea of invisible computing. Consequently, it is important to reach a more natural interaction making it implicit versus the traditional explicit dialogue with the computer. The decrease in user interaction will also reduce the user's attention.

In the upcoming years, we are going to think about Human-AmI interaction instead of Human-Computer interaction as a new perspective closer to human-human interaction [6]. Regarding human communication, there are three key issues: (a) Shared Knowledge between humans, an essential component to understand each other, but too extensive and not explicitly mentioned, (b) communication errors and recovery, including short term misunderstanding and ambiguities, and (c) situation and context [7]. We focus on the last one; the physical environment, the situation, the role of the user, their relation to others and the environment. Also, their goals and preferences are a good source of information. When a system is designed, we can change the current schemas of interaction using the above-mentioned information.

Albrecht Schmidt [9] introduces the concept Implicit Human-Computer interaction (iHCI) as "the interaction of a human with artifacts which is aimed to accomplish a goal. Within this process the system acquires implicit input from the user and may present implicit output to the user". An implicit input may be an action or behavior to achieve a goal and it is not primarily regarded as interaction with a computer, but captured and processed by a computer system as input. The system can perceive the human-AmI interaction and also predict the user goals. It is possible to provide support for the user task. The explicit user interactions are reduced; they are hold in the background and included as context information. Applications that make use of iHCI take the context into account as implicit input, and also, have an influence on the environment by implicit output. In this way, it is possible to increase the degree of satisfaction and reduce the learning curve.

Other proposals regarding the interaction styles have to be considered. Spontaneous interaction is introduced in the Digital Aura project [10]. This is a model in which things start to interact with others within physical proximity. A similar approach is persistent interaction, "providing continuous interaction moves computing from a localized tool to a constant presence" [11].

A possible evolution of implicit interaction is embedded interaction by Schmidt. In it, sensors and actuators are embedded in devices, tools and everyday objects and, also, interaction is embedded in the users' tasks [12].

3 Pervasive Display Systems

In the development of intelligent environments, we need devices designed to show information, amongst other infrastructures. Mainly, we handle public and large displays (in our case, 42-inch panels) that are distributed throughout the indoor space [13]. It is possible to recognize the spaces where display devices are placed, by analyzing the usual situations. In [14] four types of spaces are defined: transient spaces (e.g. walk-ways), social (e.g. coffee shops, bars), public/open (e.g. park) or informative spaces (e.g. notice boards). It is important to include a semi-public space: group rooms (e.g. conference hall, classroom). Group rooms are non-public spaces that may change into semi-public spaces depending upon the situation. For example, a classroom has a specific purpose during the class-time, however during the break it has a purpose similar to a social or an informative space. In this sense the pervasive display systems should change their services. Therefore, each display in a PDS should handle extra information in order to change its function, according to the space type and the rest of the context information.

A PDS should carry out three key principles [15]: (a) it should be made up of public displays, i. e. displays that are not under the control of a single user, which is the main difference between PDS and Distributed Displays Environment, (b) it has to be multi-purpose, and (c) a PDS is assumed to support coordination between multiple displays.

4 Interaction and Information Visualization Services

4.1 ViMos, our Information Visualization Service

ViMos is an information visualization service that applies context-awareness providing adapted information to the user through embedded devices in the environment. However, the real world is complex and people require higher mental processes to understand it. ViMos defines a model in which the complex real world is abstracted. As a result, computational systems may understand the world around them and act accordingly (similar to human behavior). For this reason, a key issue of ViMos is a formal ontology as a context model. In [16] the model is described thoroughly.

A mosaic of information is a set of information pieces that form a user interface. Initially we have a whole set of information pieces. A matching between the situation and the context model makes the selection of the best pieces possible. Each piece has several associated characteristics (e.g., optimum size, elasticity, etc.). These characteristics make the final generation process of the mosaic possible (Fig. 1).

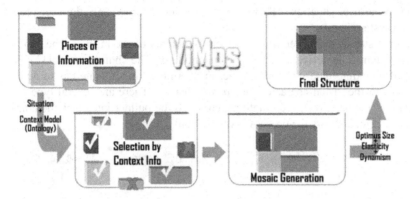

Fig. 1. Generation process of a mosaic starting from information pieces

The generation of information mosaics is carried out by adapting the user interface according to the situation. In this way, we can improve the dynamism, the adaptability and the content quality. Many applications and scenarios are possible. We have developed some prototypes in order to analyze and evaluate ViMos. The abstract and general information visualization service has been specified in services such as learning environments (e.g. classrooms, research labs and academic conferences), working environments (e.g. clinical session) and home environments.

4.2 Architecture and Implementation

ViMos has a context model that is represented by an ontology describing parts of the real world encompassing ViMos. The context information is obtained from sensors embedded into the environment (tags and RFID devices) and from the static system information (stored in Data Bases) and it is continuously inferred and selected according to the ontology rules. ViMos has three modules. The "analysis module" evaluates the situation changes and decides where this change prompts a modification in the information mosaics. There may be changes in the context information that are not significant for our system (e.g. a new user in the room may produce new information to show or not). The model decides which changes are important and which are not (one change could be significant or not depending on the rest of the context information at that moment). Additionally, the analysis module has the responsibility of keeping the data base consistency when the situation changes.

The "mosaic generation module" creates the XML mosaic description. The process consists of the generation of a representation of the situation at that moment, by means of the ViMos context model. The mosaic generates a module obtaining the visual interface. This contains the correct and optimum information according to the user situation. There are no user interactions, only the user presence as a system input.

The next step is the generation of specific contents of the mosaic. The visual aspect of the mosaic is fixed by the previous module. The "builder module" is in charge of including data into the mosaic. Furthermore, this module has to adapt the mosaic to the visual characteristics of the display. There are several types of information (pictures, text, presentations, etc.) and the builder integrates them appropriately. Fig. 2 shows the process in more detail.

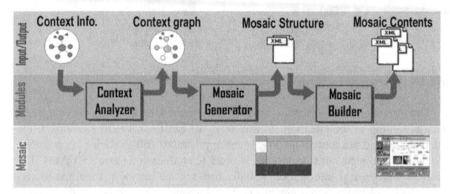

Fig. 2. Vimos Modular Architecture

4.3 Information Mosaics Roles & Interaction

ViMos has been tested in several scenarios generating diverse mosaics. In addition, different mosaics for every scenario have been created. We have analyzed frequent situations with similar characteristics. In them, the mosaic structure does not change and neither does the information, meaning the context information.

Table 1. Mosaic Roles

Mosaic Role	Situation	Schema of interaction	Users interacting with ViMos
Presentation	It includes one or several users showing selected information. The users have prepared this information previously (e. g. a presentation). The main goal is to share the information between present users.	Natural interaction + Implicit interaction	Low (1-2)
News	ViMos is located in a social space, such as a corridor, a common space or in a break room. The main goal is to show generic information.	Implicit interaction	High (1 – 12)
Groups coordination	A group of people with common objectives working on the same project.	Natural + implicit interaction + planning	Medium (1-6)

For example, when a teacher explains a lesson in the classroom, the mosaic generated keeps a similar structure, but the contents change (the current presentation, the information about the students present, etc.). In these cases, we identify a Mosaic Role, i.e. a mosaic structure with a specific functionality in a usual situation.

Mainly, we identify three key mosaic roles. They are shown in Table 1 and can be explained as follows:

a.   Presentation: The PDS has the main function of displaying presentations that have been previously prepared. The interface has to keep a main and outstanding space aside for the presentation. When the user is next to the screen, the situation information is generated and her/his presentation is shown (implicit interaction). In this mosaic role, a complement is required in order to interact with the presentation. We have focused on the approach to a more natural interaction; therefore several infrared sensors (Basic X24 Micro-controller that transmits through Bluetooth) have been integrated in ViMos. Fig. 3 (left) shows the components of the infrared complement. The user, by a sweep of his/her hand near the sensor, indicates to the system that he/she wants to advance or to go back in the pages of the presentation. The function of each sensor changes according to the situation and the user's preferences.

Fig. 3. Infrared Sensor, Micro-Controller and Bluetooth devices (left) and a mosaic for support in academic sessions (right)

Fig. 3 (right) shows a typical mosaic generated for an academic conference. The events based on conferences gather together a group of people who have similar needs and objectives. A PDS like ViMos can offer high-value information making the event more comfortable. During the contribution explanation, the greatest part of the mosaic is reserved for the presentation, but ViMos also offers adapted situation information such as authors' corporate information, research topics, session schedule and/or general event planning.

b.   News: Multiple users in a public area. The objective is to show general information that is of interest to users near the display (within more or less 1 metre). Since news mosaics have to adapt their contents to multiple users, issues such as privacy, dynamism and adaptability are especially important. We use a formal context model in order to cover these issues [16]. Explicit interaction with news mosaics should be reduced because there may be many users around of the display.

Fig. 4. Mosaics generated for offering information in a public display, specifically for an academic symposium (left) and for an information panel (right)

Regarding scenarios, we exemplify the role of news mosaics in academic conferences. The main goal is to provide information and assistance. In the break room, general information about the event is shown, e.g. area distribution, specific/personal notices and news, etc. An example of news for a workshop is shown in Fig. 4 (left). A similar approach, an information board for university faculties, can be seen in Fig. 4 (right).

c.   Group coordination: Several users who have common goals and collaborate frequently. Information flows exist between users; therefore the PDS must be very dynamic. The mosaic may be in two states. (a) When there are users in the room but nobody is near the display. The PDS should show information in order to support individual work as well as group work. (b) If one or more users are closer to the display, the PDS should show information on common work of these users. This situation requires previous planning. Fig. 5 shows a ViMos mosaic generated for coordinating a research group. It offers information about member location, the group schedule, to-do lists, etc. The rest of the mosaic contains specific information regarding the research group, e.g. academic event deadlines, news, notices, members' messages and shared documents. All information changes with the situation.

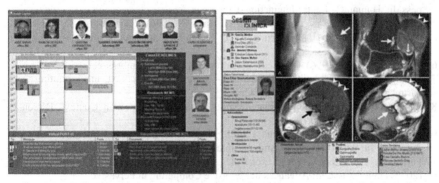

Fig. 5. Mosaic for coordination of research groups and mosaic for supporting clinical sessions

In Fig. 5 we also show another coordination mosaic. In this case, the mosaic supports physicians in a clinical session. Everyone has a software tool for planning the patient case. The plan consists of selecting patient proofs and, the system should include additional information (similar cases, patient affiliation, clinical records, etc.)

5 Conclusions

This paper presents an analysis of new interaction schemas that are necessary in order to achieve the ambient intelligence goals. We base our prototypes on diverse scenarios and situations, and it is possible to observe common characteristics. We use this analysis to identify roles and associated interaction schemas in Pervasive Display Systems. As a result, we can simplify the automatic generation of information mosaics. The better we select the information, the less explicit interaction will be necessary. These contributions bring us closer to disappearing interaction, in the same way that the new computing paradigms attempt to achieve invisible computing.

Acknowledgments   This work has been financed by a 2005-2006 SERVIDOR project (PBI-05-034) from Junta de Comunidades de Castilla-La Mancha and the Ministerio de Ciencia y Tecnología in Mosaic Learning project 2005-2007 (TSI2005-08225-C07-07).

References

1. Weiser M (1991) The computer of the twenty-first century. Scientific American September: 94-104.
2. Norman D.A (1998) The Invisible Computer. MIT Press, Cambridge.
3. Dey A.K (2001) Understanding and Using Context. Personal and Ubiquitous Computing. 5(1): 4-7.
4. Brooks K (2003) The Context Quintet: narrative elements applied to Context Awareness. In: Human Computer Interaction. Crete.
5. Bravo J, Hevás R, Sánchez I, Chavira G, Nava S (2006) Visualization Services in a Conference Context: An approach by RFID Technology. Journal of Universal Computer Science. 12(3): 270-283.
6. Reeves B, Nass C (1996) The Media Equation. C.U. Press. Cambridge.
7. Schmidt A (2002) Ubiquitous Computing - Computing in Context, in Computing Department. Lancaster University 1:294.
8. Schmidt A (2000) Implicit Human Computer Interaction Through Context. Personal Technologies. 4(2&3): 191-199.
9. Kawsar F, Fujinami K, Nakajima T (2005) Augmenting Everyday Life with Sentient Artefacts. In: Smart Objects & Ambient Intelligence (sOc-EUSAI). Grenoble.
10. Ferscha A, Hechinger M, Mayrhofer R, Dos Santos Rocha M, Franz M, . Oberhauser R (2004) Digital Aura. In: Advances in Pervasive Computing in Pervasive.
11. Abowd G, Mynatt ED (2000) Charting past, present and future research in ubiquitous computing. HCI in the new millennium 7(1):29-58.
12. Schmidt A, Kranz, M, Holleis P (2005) Interacting with the Ubiquitous Computing - Towards Embedding Interaction. In: Smart Objects & Ambient Intelligence (sOc-EuSAI). Grenoble.
13. Bravo J, Hervás R, Chavira G (2005) Ubiquitous Computing at classroom: An approach through identification process. Journal of Universal Computer Science 11(9):1494-1504.
14. Mitchell K, Race NJP (2006) Oi! Capturing User Attention Within Pervasive Display Environments. In: Workshop on Pervasive Display Infrastructures, Interfaces and Applications (at the Pervasive 2006) Dublin.
15. José R (2006) Beyond Application-Led Research in Pervasive Display Systems. In: Workshop on Pervasive Display Infrastructures, Interfaces and Applications (at the Pervasive 2006) Dublin.
16. Hervás R, Bravo J, Chavira G, Nava S (2006) Servicios de Visualización de Información Conscientes del Contexto: Modelo Semi-Formal y Escenarios (Spanish). In: Conferencia Ibérica de Sistemas y Tecnologías de la Información. Esposende.

Towards the Achievement of Natural Interaction

Javier Calle, Paloma Martínez, David del Valle, Dolores Cuadra

Computer Science Departament, Carlos III University of Madrid, Avda. Universidad 30, 28911 Leganés (Madrid, Spain)

Abstract The expansion of Information Technologies brings the need for systems providing Human-Computer Interaction which does not require previous technological training for users. Following this line, Natural Interaction (NI) research works aim at imitating human interactive behavior, as a well-known paradigm for every user. This work presents a complete Cognitive Architecture for Natural Interaction, focusing on two of its main components: Dialogue Management and Circumstance Modeling. First, through the description of the Threads Model, an Intentional Processing Dialogue Model that has been applied in several national and international research projects. Second, a Situation Model is introduced focusing on the material aspect of circumstance and supported by the Spatio-Temporal Databases paradigm. Finally, a description about the current implementation of the interaction system based on this proposal is provided.

1 Introduction

During the last few years, a growing interest within the Human Computer Interaction research has been targeting users who are not used to interacting with computers. This population of potential users brings the need for interaction systems that can work without the users' previous knowledge or technological ability from: the only requirement will be the user's ability to interact with other human beings. Interaction techniques involved in this research imply that (a) the system should behave and express itself in a way users can fully understand it with no extra effort from the one required for understanding a person, and that (b) the system interprets the users' interventions as they behave when interacting with other persons. In short, what is being pursued is to imitate human beings in their interactive behavior [2] processing "what comes naturally" [15]. Thus, this research line has been named Natural Interaction (or Natural Interactivity). The interaction paradigm does not only deal with non-technologically trained users, but it is also useful for overcoming other sorts of disabilities and for providing interaction alternatives to computer users.

M. Redondo et al. (eds.), *Engineering the User Interface*,
DOI: 10.1007/978-1-84800-136-7_6, © Springer-Verlag London Limited 2009

This field requires a strong support from several human sciences and knowledge engineering area within the area of AI. In developing Natural Interaction systems, two main trends are pointed out: the conversation and the discursive analysis. The first seeks an interactive behavior based upon the imitation of human behavior through similar cases [3] (establishing analogies between cases in its knowledge base and current circumstances). Such objective requires a huge knowledge base to produce a 'human-like enough' interaction. The later addresses the implementation of formal methods enabling flexible and coherent interactions with smaller corpus. To achieve this, knowledge-based reasoning for each intervention is sought for: interpreting users expressions and updating (the system's belief on) the interaction state, on the one hand and for generating the system's own interventions, on the other hand. Thus, interactive behavior is computed instead of being literally imitated through a case-based reasoning. Finally, a hybrid approach is possible for achieving a seemly natural Interaction from less amount of corpus.

A fundamental issue for discursive analysis is that knowledge supporting an intervention processing has different natures: purely interactive, circumstantial, emotional, operative, etc., and even further classification is possible within each of them. Discarding any of these factors, for its high complexity or cost, implies removing its effects on the interaction, thus reducing its natural quality and producing mechanical behavior (only for the aspect regarding the discarded knowledge).

Regarding knowledge modeling for dialogue management, Cohen [8] points out three types, highlighting those based on the 'joint action theories', because of their proximity to human interaction. Applied to language use [7], these theories define the interaction as a joint action between two (or more) participants where the support of a common ground and the commitment of both participants for each shared goal (as a prerequisite for its development) are key points in such activity. Traum and Allen's proposal of *obligations* can be found in this line [18].

Through these pages, a brief description of a Cognitive Approach to NI systems is provided, identifying different knowledge needs for such interactive paradigm [10]. Then, a Dialogue Model including some concepts of joint action will be explained. This Model proposes an intentional processing of dialogue, supporting techniques for shared goals commitment repair and reinforcement that will be applied when required, providing better understanding conditions for both participants. A section is dedicated to deal with another interactivity knowledge: the circumstantial knowledge. Finally, issues on current implementation are also included.

2 The Cognitive Approach

For achieving NI through the discursive focus, it is necessary to introduce any knowledge involving human interaction into the system. Since this knowledge is very complex and diverse, it should be split up into smaller specialized knowledge models. The study of the state of the art reveals several approaches, such as TRIPS' [5] or JASPIS [19]. On the one hand, TRIPS (The Rochester Interactive Planning System) is an interaction system composed of independent modules connected by message passing, which are divided into three functional areas (modality processing, dialogue management, and specialised reasoning). From the cognitive focus, these components are found to be grouped into three major areas: interpretation, behaviour, and generation. On the other hand, JASPIS implements a similar functional architecture over a multi-agent platform. This approach supports adaptivity and also concurrent interactions.

The Cognitive Architecture supporting this work has been applied in several national (IntegraTV4All FIT-350301-2004-2) and international (Advice IST 1999-11305, and VIP-Advisor IST 2001-32440) research projects, and it is the basis for another two ongoing ones, as detailed in section 6. It will be exposed as a global approach to NI and the framework for later description of two of its main models: dialogue and situation.

The specialized models gather structured knowledge and reasoning mechanisms that support both the interpretation of user's expressions and the production of system's interventions. A first classification of abilities distinguishes between three major parts of the interactive system: the interface, in charge of the expressive tasks (expression acquisition and emission); the interaction, for participating in a dialogue where the initiative, the tasks and the responsibilities are shared by the user and the system; and finally, the application, regarded as the set of the system's non interactive abilities that could be invoked during any dialogue.

This approach has a good functional value handling three sorts of entirely different problems that should be developed and evolved separately. The workflow starts at the interface with the semantic (literal) interpretation of the user's intervention, which is introduced later into the interaction components, which will perform a complete interpretation applying pragmatic knowledge [14]. Then the dialogue state is updated, and it is checked whether an external operation is required. In such case, proper inputs are arranged and provided to some application components that provide back the results of its performance. With such outputs, the interaction components update the dialogue state again, and generate the system's interventions that are finally delivered to the interface components for being expressed.

Communication between interaction and interface models involves the use of a tool capable of representing any semantic content within the Interaction Domain (both for user and system interventions). Such need is usually covered by semantic structures based on *Speech Acts* theories [1] [16]. On the other hand, connecting interaction and application components could be based either on an Agents Communication Language (a subset of any existing standard [9]) or on a suited set of commands (defined ad hoc). Consequently, the functions of interface and application components are strongly linked to the interaction model abilities and vice versa.

The present approach depends on a complex interaction model. Since its reasoning mechanisms and the knowledge supporting them are very diverse, it is appropriate to split it up into several knowledge models, thus shaping a more complete cognitive architecture. Figure 1 shows this approach, which includes:

- Dialogue Model: fixes the evolution of the interaction state and defines the system's interactive behavior.
- Session Model: organizes and handles contextual (static) information. Besides, it performs inheritance processes between contextual ambits and solves some types of deixis and anaphora.
- Situation Model: fixes the circumstance by observing five aspects: material (spatio-temporal situation), semiotic, operative, politic, and socio-cultural.
- User Model: gathers and manages knowledge on potential interlocutors.
- Ontology: handles the set of concepts (and their relations) susceptible of being referred to (through terms) within the Interaction Domain.
- Self-Model: arranges knowledge regarding the system, particularly its individual goals (either programmed or contracted).
- Emotional Model: processes short and long term emotional goals (emotional state and system's personality, respectively). It also provides mechanisms for interpreting and generating emotionally affected expressions.

Attached to the interface components, a Presentation Model should be set (Figure 1, left). Its purpose is to coordinate all input interface components in the acquiring phase and all output components in the generating phase, to produce complete and coherent interventions. In addition, it helps to manage turn-taking and handles some information about the interface state (activity events, timers, etc.).

Finally, for the dialogue management two different (though strongly related) sorts of knowledge are distinguished: the Dialogue Model (DM) supporting interpretation and evolution of interaction state; and the Discourse Generator, defining system's behavior anytime. The later handles the links between the interaction states and the tasks performed by the system (applications). This knowledge, along with how to build the inputs for these tasks and how to interpret their outputs, are gathered in a Task Model (within the Generator). In Figure 1, all these components are shown divided into the aforementioned three major knowledge areas, and focusing their relations with the Dialogue Model.

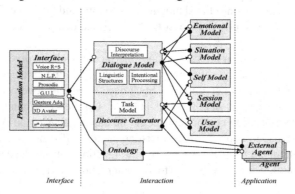

Fig. 1: Cognitive Architecture for a Natural Interaction System

3 Dialogue Model Role within Natural Interaction Systems

Classic dialogue modeling addresses 'handy' aspects of the interaction: formalizing an interaction domain so that corpus included dialogues can be reproduced. Trends in the area usually point to gaining flexibility and reusing of domain dependent knowledge. However, some features of human dialogues are more typical of reasoning than of the application of predefined cases. This is the case of the repair and reinforcement of shared goals.

Through human interaction, the involved participants usually take care of each subdialogue *health*. They check that their interlocutors have enough information for understanding and collaborating in the subdialogue development before making any progress on it. Besides, if any participant notices himself/herself lacking of information, he/she will surely make it clear to his/her interlocutor for fixing the problem. Hence, for the system behaving as a human in such interaction, it will be necessary to model a *common ground* for handling conjectures on dialogue shared goals and mutual knowledge, and to check potential problems in each subdialogue as a precondition for its development. There may be no current problem for that subdialogue but certain risk might appear, which also should be taken into account.

Anyway, in case of any problem/risk, the system will have to decide which corrective/preventive action (if any) to be performed in order either to fix the problem, avoid its occurrence or, in general, to reduce its influence on interaction success. Depending on the necessities of each particular case, diverse techniques could be applied with different interactive cost (from a minimum utterance or even a pause, to an entire discourse line interruption, that is, introducing a new subdialogue).

These procedures could also appear by using a more mechanical dialogue model approach (such as dialogue games, for example), but it should be observed that they occur mechanically. In other words, they are applied always at some interaction state, not because its execution is required to ensure interaction success, but because they were found in the corpus. For such procedure to be useful, a large corpus is required.

Consequently, the need for including this knowledge and reasoning mechanisms into the Dialogue Model arises. Carrying out these and other related processes will support interaction not only to be valid but also robust, flexible, comfortable, and in sum, more useful. The mentioned processed are those characterizing the joint action management [7], and the dialogue models observing them usually produce fluid, flexible, coherent and successful interaction supported by reduced extent of corpus (in comparison with other models that could produce similar behavior). Such dialogue modeling approach is quite appropriate for Natural Interaction paradigm, given that those referred features involve a clear way to human interactive behavior.

The following section offers a brief description of a Dialogue Model, which, among other features, includes the required knowledge for applying intentional repair and reinforcement when needed through any interaction.

4 Intentional Management and the Threads Model

The intentional dialogue management adds the benefits of intentional processing to classical approaches, discarding none of their positive features. This sort of model considers both the knowledge about intentions, which characterizes the dialogue segments that can be progressed within the interaction domain, and the structural knowledge that defines how to progress them (structural *form* of those segments). Together they validate produced dialogues against the collected corpus.

Therefore, the first issue in modeling a particular interaction domain is to acquire and analyze the corpus of interaction. This kind of modeling does not require a large corpus, but a significant covering of the interaction domain. The corpus analysis starts with dialogue segmentation (in the same way as other segment-based models, such as dialogue planning models). Posterior 'sequence identification' for each segment makes it possible to discover when and how the segment is started and when and how it is solved, as well as the steps that describe its evolution (its progress). Finally, each segment is characterized by a purpose or *intention*, which keeps a direct relation with the goals shared by both participants through the interaction. These are the shared goals included in the *common ground*, as the joint action theories explain.

4.1 Dialogue Manager Architecture

Functional architectures for Dialogue Systems usually show a separation between the components dedicated to interpret user expressions and those set to generate system expressions. The proposed architecture (figure 2) maintains this scope by including the *interpretation component* and the *discourse generator*. However, considering the architecture from the point of view of the interaction state could lead to detach each of the three different factors it observes: intentional, structural and contextual.

The mission of the interpretation component is to find out the interaction states went through during user expression (to create an interpretation framework, which is coordinated by all the knowledge models involved in this process). With these results, the state of the interaction is updated and the system is ready to perform new interventions as the realization of its turn. These interventions consist of expressions either built depending on the interaction states visited and the patterns inferred from the corpus, or formulated by the execution of the tasks related with the progress of the dialogue (*perlocution*). Knowledge about task execution (when, which inputs, and outputs consequences) is held at the Task Model.

This functionality is named 'cycle of interaction', and defined as the sequence of stages expanding a turn in the interaction. These phases are described as follow:

1. Last user intervention is introduced into the dialogue manager, in the form of communicative acts (CCAA), and it is interpreted in a coordinated way;
2. Understanding user expressions gives way to new interaction states, pending on being processed (and on revealing that they have been processed);
3. The generator decides which pending states should be processed. When doing so, it might call the execution of tasks (supported by the Task Model), or produce new expressions in terms of CCAA(in case);
4. If a task is executed, its result could modify the interaction state: by forcing state transitions, by introducing new context, by changing the focus (shared goal to be progressed), or even by introducing new system initiatives;
5. If any of these effects are produced, the newly reached state of interaction should be processed next by the generator (in the current cycle, before process any other pending states of the interaction);
6. The cycle ends when every pending state has been processed, or when currently analyzed state features denote that the floor should be handed over.

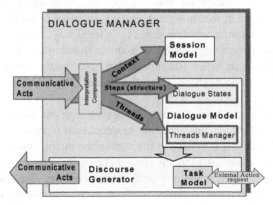

Fig. 2: Dialogue Manager Architecture.

It is important to point out that whenever several states are progressed, several elements could be generated (one or more discourses, each with one or more CCAA). Besides, some states processing might alter the set of CCAA generated till far (for current intervention): by altering their order, rescheduling or delaying its expression, or by removing pending discourses which have lost their relevance.

4.2 Intentional Processing in the Threads Model

A *thread* is the implementation of one segment of a dialogue (or a set of segments) obtained from the corpus. It is characterized by an intention (the purpose of
the segment) that identifies the thread. Opening and closing sequences, as well as
its development steps, should be learned during the corpus analysis. On the one
hand, the opening sequence of a thread is used for starting a new instance of this
thread during the interaction: to detect when the user is initiating the thread, or to
share with the user its initiative when the system does it. On the other hand, closing sequences are commonly used (by user and system) to solve the thread. Finally, the development describes the structure of the segment (the sequence of interaction states it goes through since its beginning till its end), and can be
formalized through grammars or automata.

   Each thread has a set of properties [6]. Among these properties the state stands
out, defining the point of development where the thread is at. Some states could
end up in sequences of communicative acts to be expressed; others could involve
the execution of external tasks; and others could have no effect. Eventually, the
result of any task execution could force the system to introduce an initiative (a
new thread) directly descendant from the focused thread (the thread instance that
was being developed at that moment). But an initiative could also be introduced
by the system in certain interaction states (in a fixed way, no need of a task execution). This could happen when such procedure is found in the corpus and the modeling of the dialogue reflects it (decomposition based on the corpus). Finally, users
can introduce initiatives anytime. Thus, the threads' organization seems to be tree-
like.

   Each entire dialogue from the corpus is itself a segment. Its formalization leads
to define the *base thread*, considered as the intentional representation of the whole
interaction: a thread that is created at the start of the interaction and is ended when
the interaction is solved. All threads started during the interaction are descendant
of the base thread, which is the root of the intentional tree-like structure. Because
of that, its context information can be accessed everywhere across the interaction.

   This intentional structure determines other kind (non intentional) of processing,
such as context management. During a dialogue, each instance of a thread has its
own contextual space for collecting any contextual information referred during the
subdialogue development. Filial links between parent-threads and their children
allow hierarchical process to take place between different contextual spaces. In
this way, a contextual information required during the development of a thread
could be accessed even if it is not available in its context, provided that it can be
located in a nearby contextual space (in the parent's thread, for instance). Two
kinds of inheritance processes are distinguished: top-down, accessing contextual
information from ancestors when required for a certain use; and bottom-up, providing relevant information to the parent when a thread is solved. Also two kinds
of contextual information are found: inheritable and non-inheritable information.

It is essential for any participant in the interaction to make sure which of the instantiated threads is being developed each time, and to decide which of them should be developed next, in case the thread in progress is solved. The Threads Model counts on a structure named *focus* that registers and organizes the references to the opened threads (those still unsolved), for supporting *attentional* processing (making sure which thread should be developed each time and also which thread the interlocutor probably expects to be developed). It is often implemented as a pile (FIFO) ordered by the last access. However, some attention management policies could point to place the focused thread on a predefined one (favorite), just by processing the intentional structure (the tree of threads). Finally, the focus management also may make use of an auxiliary structure named *focus history* that maintains pointers to every thread (including solved threads). In this structure, threads are chronologically ordered to enable establishing access probabilities (especially useful for already solved threads).

Other features of the threads are: age (turns since it starts), guide (participant who first initiate it), and a very important one: the commitment. This concept defines the degree of knowledge both participants have about the thread (about its existence and characteristics), and also the degree of agreement they establish for its progress. For a thread to progress with fluency, a high commitment is often required. On the other hand, if this commitment is undermined, the interaction becomes tedious and uncertain. In such case, the thread might end unsuccessfully.

Several interaction events might weaken a thread commitment, for example: unexpected changes in the focused thread (commitment variation should depend on the distance between currently pointed thread and the thread to receive the attention); succession of interruptions, that is, introduction of initiatives (variations should depend on the relationship between the new thread and the previously focused one); interventions neither matching an open thread nor opening a new one; and the progress of a user thread representing the his/her intention to communicate a lack of knowledge and/or his/her agreement about the previously pointed thread.

If the system decides to develop a low committed thread, it should first reinforce it. In order to do that, the system will introduce a new thread representing such intention that will probably procure this effect at certain point of its development. These threads are named *reinforcement threads* and the dialogs they produce employ different techniques to increase the commitment over a goal, achieving different results. From lower to higher effect, *announcement, redundancy, recompilation* or *interruption* could be applied, for example. The positive effect of any of these techniques (degree of reinforcement they produce), the negative effect on commitment of any other interaction event, and the thresholds for revealing the need of commitment reinforcement, are all parameters that can be obtained by applying training algorithms to the corpus (identifying previously every event and technique use). These parameters consequently depend on the corpus, but could also be influenced by the situation: a need for some normal reinforcement could be ignored under certain circumstances. On the other hand, if the system counts on a user model, some of the user features it provides could be used like modifiers to calculate more precise (and adapted) values for those parameters.

Since it is probably impossible to analyze a corpus for each situation and potential user, it is recommended to set the corpus acquired parameters as default values, and then apply some learning algorithm to refine them during the system's lifecycle.

Finally, *repair* is an extreme case of reinforcement usually applied to threads with very weak commitment that can only be repaired or given up. Typical repair techniques involve introducing new initiatives to fix the problem, which naturally implies a high interactive cost. Supporting dialogue healthcare at the intentional scope improve considerably the understanding between both participants, allowing them to agree attentionally and producing more agile interactions.

4.3 The Threads Model Components

To conclude the description of this model, it is important to enumerate the three main components of the system from the intentional processing perspective, due to its influence in the final design (in fact, current implementation is based on this characterization). The components and their relations are the following (figure 3):

1. User Thread: Organizes the knowledge taking part in interpreting user intentions. Its goal is to realize conjectures about the expressions of the user.
2. System Thread: Responsible of the knowledge controlling the introduction of system initiatives. It also processes the private pending states (not shared with other participants, as are the included in the Joint Thread).
3. Joint Thread: Implements the common ground; the knowledge about the progress of the dialogue as a shared activity (explained in the previous section)

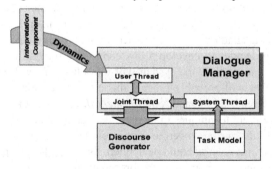

Fig. 3: Threads Model Components

It has been established that the System Thread offers the service of 'initiative introduction', used by the Task Model to introduce new threads when deemed appropriate. This service is not exclusively used by the Task Model, but by any component along the Cognitive Architecture. For example, User or Session models could include a strategy for solving their own services based on requesting initiative posing by the System Thread. Such procedure surely has a high interactive cost, but also it could end up in great results. However, it is not convenient to in-troduce too many interruptions during any interaction, because it increases the strain with the user revealing a very aggressive (impolite) interactive behavior. Therefore, each service request should include a value of criticism (measurement of the need of that service, often calculated over the number of existing possible alternatives). Thus, any interruption request is analyzed, based on the strain of the interaction and on the criticism value, for deciding if it should be achieved or not.

5 Knowledge on Circumstances: the Situation Model

Another representative knowledge type is the one supporting the circumstances management, hence including the system behavior reasoning regarding the inter-action situation. The circumstances having an effect on human's interactive be-havior influence are very diverse, but according to Gee [11], five main aspects for the situation should be observed: semiotic (signs in use), operative (task underly-ing the interaction), material (spatiotemporal), political (role of each interlocutor), and socio-cultural link. Some of these aspects might seem overlapped with other knowledge fields, as previously described in the cognitive architecture of the NI system. The operational range of the SM is well defined and dissociated: to fix the circumstances of any particular interaction.

Circumstance modeling has been long researched for context-aware systems [13], but with a slightly different focus. These systems seek to adapt their opera-tions to the current context, observing any element within the environment whose circumstances could influence the system behavior. For such systems, most of the interaction with the system is implicit, seeking a pervasive system able to under-stand the user's behavior and behave itself consequently. Situation Modeling, on the other hand, just focuses on the circumstance aspects of interaction itself, that is, the contextual parameters influencing the interaction situation and develop-ment.

Many interactive system requirements fix the circumstances so that they are well known, avoiding the need of situation modeling. Some others have some cir-cumstantial aspect modeled, fixing the rest. However, interaction systems rarely show different interactive behavior depending on reasoning mechanisms based on situational knowledge and on past, current and future predictions about the inter-locutor's positions. Hence, there is no complete implementation of any specific Situation Model for interaction by now, from which the interaction system could profit the power of the unification of the concept of 'situation'. This strength lies on three main abilities, which should be assumed by the SM: (a) to identify the circumstance, and to report it to other knowledge models so that they could leak their available knowledge to obtain 'circumstance relevant knowledge'; (b) to gen-erate events (and trigger their consequences) when a set of given circumstance conditions come true; and (c) to provide any information about situation: past positions, predictions about future situations, or strategies for moving from a starting situation (current, for example) to another one desired (goal).

The present proposal tackles the modeling of the material aspect as a starting point for situation management, given that this is one of the most significant aspects of interaction circumstances, and leaving the other aspects for further work.

5.1 Spatio-Temporal Database Paradigm

According to the description above on material knowledge, the spatio-temporal information handling appears to be the key for situation management. Two different elements should be observed to deal with: the location (through space and time) of the Natural Interaction System (NIS) and its users. Spatio-Temporal Databases are the suit tool to handle such elements, and provide mechanisms that will cover almost every situation modeling need. In this section, spatio-temporal concepts and objects concerning present proposal on situation modeling will be briefly glanced.

From the spatial perspective, a spatial object is always represented within a spatial reference system (for example, Cartesian coordinates) [3] and has an associated measure (meters, hectometers, etc.). This measure is named *spatial granularity*. Spatial elements are described in the OpenGis specification, and presented proposal is based on this standard. Figure 4 shows the geometry class description.

From the temporal scope, information (time) can be represented as an interval or *timestamp*, and characterized by three dimension type: valid time, transaction time or both [17]. The valid time considers the time during which a fact is true in the application domain. The transaction time represents when a fact is registered, for example, in a database system. According to this, the user position with valid time within a map determines the timestamp in which the user stays in this position during the marked time. The transaction time is when the user position is processed by a database system or other computer system. Apart from dimension and the way to represent time, it is important to define the temporal granularity,

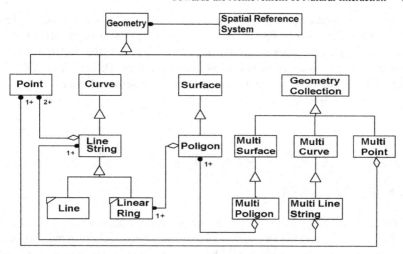

Fig. 4: Geometry description according to the OpenGis specification.

that is, the temporal measure unit such as minutes, hours, etc. The spatio-temporal multi-granularity concept joins both granularities. Multiple granularities, defined as a set of measuring units for space and time, are crucial in facilitating information management for applications such as air traffic control, meteorological forecast and so on [4] [12]. According to these properties, spatio-temporal objects can be classified into *topology evolution* and *position evolution*. The first one represents geometries and its changes over time. They are objects that represent, for example, the course evolution of rivers (as shown in figure 5, with century as temporal granularity), town planning evolution, etc. The second class, position evolution, observes the object movement (applied to *moving objects*), that is, the position changes of object (i.e., point) over time. For example, the car position changes in a highway.

Present Situation Model proposal is based on the material aspect through the STOR model [3]. This data model is an object-relational extension which gives support to the spatio-temporal properties explained above. Next, the NIS's location and its users will be described as spatio-temporal elements in the STOR model.

5.2 Situation Modeling proposal

The location is represented as a *net graph* composed by Nodes and Links between them, depicting the interaction system space. A Link describes the practicable way from a particular node to another one (direct graph). The representation of the interaction system space (*scenario* or context) is carried out through the spatio-temporal object type: *topology evolution*. Therefore, the scenario of interaction system is represented as a polygon or polygons collection where nodes represent interesting points within the Interaction Domain scenario or points where the crossing is required. Nodes are treated as points within a Spatial Reference System with an associated a measure as well as to be dynamics. This means that they can alter their position over time and even can add new points to the net.

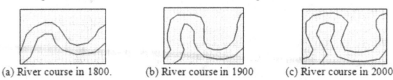

(a) River course in 1800.   (b) River course in 1900   (c) River course in 2000

Fig. 5. River course evolution

Thus, the topology evolution of the net graph is taken into account in the proposal. For example, if the Interaction Domain scenario describes a museum space, the interesting points or nodes could be the exposition rooms and the links could represent the different tracks to connect one room with another. In such scenario, this proposal could reflect when a room is closed and therefore, the net graph is modified. The geometry update storing is important because the NIS could use this information to provide explanations about current situation, for example when the user request explanations on the built plan, or asks why he/she can not perform a certain action.

Each user of the NIS is represented as a *moving object*. Using such approach, it is easy to manage the information about user position, and even to apply other user locations to resolve conflicts of interest between them. For example, the NIS's museum could track new ways if it detects traffic jam in some links between exposition rooms. Visiting other exposition room could also be proposed to the user depending on circumstances, his/her preferences, system's guidelines, etc.

Through the spatio-temporal proposal, several services to the Interaction System are supplied regarding the knowledge about material aspects. Three important directions are covered with the presented proposal:

1. The situation characterization provided by SMC is profited by the rest of the knowledge components across the cognitive architecture for filtering their own knowledge base (discarding non-relevant knowledge). Therefore, the NIS is more effective (overcoming some ambiguities) and efficient (dealing with reduced amount of relevant knowledge).
2. Event triggering enables to program consequence execution (set of actions to be taken) when some circumstances are reached. For example, the dialog component could initiate a sub-dialog as a consequence of some situation circumstance (e.g. for asking the user to change direction when guiding, or for informing him/her when a spatio-temporal situation is reached).
3. Circumstance knowledge based tasks such as providing knowledge related to the situation (past and current circumstances or predictions about future circumstances), or planning actions sequences to achieve a particular circumstance from another.

Next challenges to achieve involve the inclusion of more aspects into the model, such as the operative aspect (which task or set of tasks underlie interaction), with the same set of services (but, of course, extended to those aspects).

6 System Implementation

The presented approach has been developed and implemented in the course of several projects. A current version of this NI system is being developed under the auspice of the research consortium MAVIR (Improving Accessibility and Visibility of Multilingual Information in Internet for the Region of Madrid), supported by the Regional Government of Madrid (S-0505/TIC-0267), and some of its Models (Dialogue and Situation) are being improved within the SOPAT project (CIT-410000-2007-12), supported by the Spanish Ministry of Science and Education.

All previous implementations of the system were based on a sequential execution, where each of the task involved in the processing of the interaction was tackled in a concrete point of execution, with a predefined order. This fact hindered the system from applying the advantages of other paradigms, like the management of events or the resolution of problems using several strategies simultaneously in competition. For the present implementation, the system migrated from this sequential execution to a platform based on agents developed with ad hoc technology adapted to the specific requirements of this NI approach.

The implemented platform supports the existence of several agents and their message exchange in an environment named Ecosystem. Within Ecosystem, each agent is subscribed to an agency, which fixes the maximal and minimal number of simultaneous agents that can be registered in it. Ecosystem contains specific agents developed to supervise the number of agents of each agency inhabiting the environment in each moment, creating more of its agents when the load of the existing ones is too high or destroying some when it is too low, keeping the number of them limited to the predefined range.

In Ecosystem, agents provide services to the rest of the agents of the environment and, in the same way, they can request any service to the rest. Agencies register which services their agents provide and all agents subscribed to one agency must provide the services registered in its agency. Services registered by an agency are characterized by a function and a domain where the service can be solved. These domains restricting the application of a function are hierarchically organized (in a tree), so an agent can attend demands of services for any of its descendant domains.

In addition, the platform contains another kind of specific agent, the mediator or *Broker Agent*, in charge of receiving demands of services from the agents of the environment and deciding which agent or agents should attend them. Each broker defines the strategy she uses to select the agent assigned to receive each service demand. According to this strategy, the broker can consider parameters like the load of each agent, or how close the field of application of their functions to the requested one is. Hence, the brokers function is to get servers and requesters in touch depending on service features and servers state. If a service is requested to several agents, different results will be obtained from each one (this might occur for agents facing the service through different strategies). In such case, the applicant could choose the best response considering parameters as the value of certainty estimated by his/her provider.

The platform allows registering as many agencies as needed to provide one specific service, and also to include, delete, or suspend the functions that agencies offer during the interaction. Such flexibility of the platform is very useful for developing and evaluating purposes, enabling the comparison of the pros and cons of each strategy developed for a specific problem.

In order to apply this multi-agent approach on the implementation of a Natural Interaction system, a set of specific agents have been developed building the system named *Interactor*. These agents provide the main services described previously in the models of knowledge involved in the Cognitive Architecture.

The services provided by the agents within Interactor imply some communication performed by message exchange through a blackboard. The referred information includes the inputs and outputs, the session identifier (for storing the state of interaction within each model), and the service parameters representing the conditions of the service. Some of those basic parameters are briefly described next:

- Expiry-date: date/time from which any solution to a service is no longer useful.
- Need-before: date and time in which the (first) solution should be already set.
- Criticism: degree of the need for a solution (in order to apply a costly solution or not). If criticism is 100%, a solution is obliged or the session will collapse.
- Quality: percentage of the credibility (or correctness probability) of the response for a service. It is useful for defining what method to apply for obtaining a solution when several options (with different cost) are available.

The characteristics of each model of knowledge determine if it should be implemented through only one agent, or if it is appropriate to arrange several collaborating agents to assure the knowledge management. For instance, the Thread Model is composed of four autonomous and independent, but collaborative and coordinated, agents: the Interpretation Agent (including the User Thread), the Generation Agent (hosting the System Thread), the Common Ground Agent (comprising the Thread Joint) and the Presentation Manager Agent. The first provides services for the interpretation of user expressions; the second mainly provides services for the generation of user expressions and system initiatives introduction; the third represents the interaction state and the common ground management; and the last connects the interaction process with the acquisition and expression of the interventions (it coordinates the performance of the interface components, implemented through other agents, and it communicates the interface with interaction knowledge areas in the architecture).

The migration to such technology provides improvements in several aspects:

- It simplifies the system distribution over a LAN. It also enables the development of more complex systems in terms of computational load minimizing its influence to real time response. Hence, several expensive strategies (in terms of time) could be applied simultaneously to solve the same problem, taking advantage of the power of each without overload in response time with respect to the case of applying only one of these strategies.

- Any agent could provide a rough first reply according to the restrictions of the request (for instance, the value of the need-before parameter) and afterwards they could refine their result providing a new one as often as needed before the expiry date of the service. The requester can progress processing the first results, and when a refined one arrives, the system decides whether it is useful to discard previous results (and its processing) and apply a new one or not. This could even end up in a self interruption of the system: either by interrupting the currently uttered intervention, by discarding it informing the user (even expressing regret), or finally by expressing newly generated discourse. Such procedure reduces the response time (for first solutions) and also improves the fluency and usefulness of the interaction.

- As a proactive interaction system, each of its components is an independent process (composed by independent agents) and could subsequently decide to introduce a new initiative anytime, regardless of the state of the interaction and, thus, developing a strategy to solve its own services. However, to avoid continuous interruption of the discourse line, the user's thread has to decide whenever that need is worth the high interactive cost of an initiative (analyzing criticism and the interaction state).

- Agent technology lays the foundation for carrying out a dialogue management able to deal with overlapped turns and multi-user interaction.

7 Conclusions

Throughout this work, an intentional approach to Dialogue Modeling has been presented, along with a proposal for Situation Model for interaction. These are two of the most representative components of a Cognitive Architecture approaching a more natural interaction. However, NI depends on several types of knowledge, which forces to include all of them to ensure human-like interactivity behavior.

The described Dialogue Modeling, the Threads Model, empowers certain features typical in human interaction by enabling the application of some reasoning on some interaction eventualities. An example of this reasoning is the commitment handling within the *common ground*, using techniques of intentional repair and reinforcement (following joint action theories on interaction). Such processing is not always advantageous though since it might result in a less-fluent interaction for well technologically trained users. Hence, a careful analysis is required to decide where to apply this sort of model and the Natural Interaction paradigm.

A proposal on Situation Modeling has also been presented, empowering the Natural Interaction system abilities. The model is based upon Spatio-Temporal Databases technology for observing material aspects, leaving other circumstance aspects for further work.

Besides, intentional dialogue models have a long way to tackle some challenges for Natural Interaction, such as its extensions to interactions held by two or more participants, or to interaction domains with overlapped-turns dialogues. Such new issues require architectures based on independent and collaborative components, able to interpret interventions while they are happening and to act autonomously as required. The implementation of the referred cognitive architecture through a multi-agent platform is a valid way to undertake such challenges.

References

1. Austin, J.L. (1962) How to do things with words. Oxford Univ. Press, 1975.
2. Bernsen, N.O. What is Natural Interactivity? Procs. of 2nd Int Conference on Language Resources and Evaluation (LREC'2000). Ed. L. Dybkjær, pp.34-37.
3. Bertino E., Cuadra D., Martínez P. (2005) An Object-Relational Approach to the Representation of Multi-Granular Spatio-Temporal Data. In the proceedings of 17th International Conference CAiSE 2005. Porto, Portugal,.
4. Bittner, T, and Smith,B. (2001) A unified theory of granularity, vagueness and approximation. COSIT Ws on Spatial Vagueness, Uncertain and Granularity.
5. Blaylock,N., Allen,J., Ferguson, G. (2003) Managing Communicative Intentions with Collaborative Problem Solving. J.Kuppevelt and R.W. Smith (eds), Current and New Directions in Discourse and Dialogue, pp. 63-84. Kluwer A. Pubs.
6. Calle, J., García-Serrano, A., Martínez, P. (2006) Intentional Processing as a Key for Rational Behaviour through Natural Interaction. Interacting With Computers, vol. 18 (6) pp. 1419—1446. Elsevier Ltd.
7. Clark, H.H. (1996) Using Language. ©, Cambridge University Press
8. Cohen, P.R., (1997) Dialogue Modeling. In Survey of the state of the art in Human Language Technology; chap.6, pp. 204-209. Cambridge Univ. Press, 1998.
9. FIPA Communicative Act Library Spec. Foundation for Intelligent Physical Agents, 2000-2002. http://www.fipa.org/specs/fipa00037/SC00037J.pdf
10. Garcia,A., Calle, J. A (2002) Cognitive Architecture for the design of an Interaction Agent. Cooperative Information Agents VI. Eds. Klusch, Ossowski & Shehory. LNAI 2446, pp 82-89; Springer
11. Gee, J.P. (1999) Introduction to Discourse Analysis. Routledge,.
12. Katri, V., Ram, S., Snodgrass, R.T., and O'Brien, G. (2002) Supporting User Defined Granularities and Indeterminacy in a Spatiotemporal Conceptual Model. Special Issues of Annals of Mathematics and A.I. on Spatial and Temporal Granularity, 36(1-2) 195-232.
13. Meyer, S., Rakotonirainy, A. (2003) A survey of research on context-aware homes. In Procs. of the Australasian Information Security Ws on ACSW frontiers,.
14. Oishi, E. (2003) Semantic meaning and four types of speech act. Perspectives on Dialogue in the New Millennium. Eds Kühnlein, Rieser & Zeevat. John Benjamins Pubs. pp135-147

15.Oviatt,S.L., Cohen, P.R. (2000) Multimodal Interfaces That Process What Comes Naturally. Communications of the ACM 43(3): 45-53.

16.Searle J. R. (1969) Speech Acts. Cambridge University Press.

17.Snodgrass, R. T. (1999) Developing Time-Oriented Database Applications in SQL. Morgan Kaufmann Publishers, Inc., San Francisco, July 1999.

18.Traum, D.R., Allen, J.F. (1994) Discourse Obligations in Dialogue Processing. In the Proceedings of the 32nd Annual Meeting of the Association for Computational Linguistics (ACL 1994), pp 1--8.

19.Turunen, M., Hakulinen, J., Räihä, K. J., Salonen, E. P., Prusi, A. K., Prusi, P. (2005) An architecture and applications for speech-based accessibility systems. IBM Systems Journal, Vol. 44, No 3,

Science Learning in Blind Children through Audio-Based Games

Jaime Sánchez, Miguel Elías

Department of Computer Science, University of Chile. Blanco Encalada 2120, Santiago, Chile.
{jsanchez, melias}@dcc.uchile.cl

Abstract In this study we present AudioLink, an interactive audio-based virtual environment for children with visual disabilities to support their learning of science. AudioLink is a Role-Playing Game (RPG) for learning science concepts and scientific reasoning through audio. We analyzed how blind learners can learn science using audio as the main input/output interface and how to develop a challenging and engaging software. The usability of this software and a preliminary study of the cognitive impact were also evaluated. Results indicated that users considered the software was appealing, challenging and encouraging as a science learning tool. AudioLink promoted a free and independent interaction at the users' own paces. Evidence indicates that blind children developed scientific thinking skills to identify a problem, build a strategy to solve it, and understand when it was solved.

1 Introduction

Science learning is a process that uses mainly visual channels (charts, graphs, simulations, to name a few), therefore the difficulties that a child may have when learning science are stressed in children with visual impairments, since they have greater impediments to access information, to learn basic mathematics and science operations, and to solve problems [12, 0]. Computers are not just office tools to work with; rather, they are intellectual tools to strengthen a series of cognitive skills, and to solve problems creatively. Moreover, software –when properly utilized– can enhance learning. Another appealing way to support learning processes, is combining games and education (known as edutainment), so children can engage in learning situations playfully.

Most current software relies mainly on graphical interfaces, impeding the navigation of users without the benefit of sight. Therefore, it is evident that contemporary developments and approaches are unsuitable for visually impaired children who already have problems to access information through traditional sources of

M. Redondo et al. (eds.), *Engineering the User Interface*,
DOI: 10.1007/978-1-84800-136-7_7, © Springer-Verlag London Limited 2009

interaction such as Braille books, relief maps and schemes, and audio-tapes. Also there is a growing consensus that new designs and approaches should be considered [0].

A growing line of research in educational software for children with visual impairments is using audio as the preferred sensorial channel when assisting the construction knowledge and meaning making [0, 0, 0, 0]. These studies have shown that audio-based interfaces can be used to promote learning and cognition in blind children. They have also shown that virtual environments (represented through audio) are a powerful incentive for blind children to develop and train cognitive skills and to learn specific content. For instance, when virtual environments are represented through 3D sound interfaces they tend to enhance a series of cognitive processes [0] such as the development of general domain thinking skills such as tempo-spatial orientation, abstract and short-term memory, and haptic perception [0]. Although the literature describes software that supports the development of mathematics learning and problem-solving skills with significant results for blind children [0, 0], there is no relevant work in other science learning oriented software (such as Biology, Physics or Chemistry). A few attempts have been made but only with a rather limited user interaction, without providing interactive applications that encourage challenging and engaging them.

In this work we have designed, developed, and evaluated the usability of interactive audio-based multimedia software for learning science in blind children, using a gaming approach to enhance learning and cognition. We utilized a combination of incremental and evolutionary development, comprising the stages of analysis, design, development, and validation. They considered activities that take into account the particularities of developing educational software for blind children. We evaluated the usability of this game using evaluation instruments for end-users, experts and facilitators. A preliminary cognitive evaluation was also conducted to verify whether or not users developed abilities to identify problems, build strategies to solve them, and know when they have solved them.

2 Learning through games and simulations

Learning by using videogames is a new way of learning. Children enjoy the challenges and engagement of leaning with games. So, when having children as end-users it is important to provide software that is game-oriented, so they can learn playfully. As Kish et al. [0] stated one of the most important things when teaching a child is that he or she is actually willing to learn. Providing an enjoyable environment the learning experience can be most effective to construct knowledge and be open to new stimulus and actions.

When combining education and entertainment (edutainment) it is possible to provide a challenging and appealing learning experience, thus promoting effective learning. Playing is an appropriate way of achieving a higher level of commitment in learners as a consequence of the emotional attachment of the player with the game. Shaftel et al. [0] stated that games have an important effect on the acquisition of problem-solving skills, allowing learners to try new strategies, stimulating logical reasoning at the same time as also encouraging students to develop skills such as attention to task, social skills –including taking turns and courtesy, cooperation with others, leadership skills, and fine motor skills. Since learning sometimes involves being wrong, games are an appropriate and appealing way of practicing what was learned over and over again, without serious consequences. Furthermore, when a child finds something fun, it is likely that he or she repeats it over and over again.

Currently, there is a clear trend towards using games and simulations for learning purposes, which has an important impact on how formal and informal education can support each other to accelerate the learning process and the development of high-order cognitive abilities, strengthening skill-based learning [0]. Navigating a virtual representation of a real environment has an undeniable value and potential. Computer-generated simulations and virtual reality provide students with a unique opportunity to experiment and explore a wide range of environments, objects and phenomena inside their classrooms or at home. They can observe and manipulate objects, variables and processes in real time impossible to get by other means. It is the adeptness of this type of technologies that makes them appropriate instruments for the study of natural phenomena and abstract concepts [0]. They allow people to navigate a real environment that can be dangerous, hostile, or even unreachable, and to simulate realities for safe learning.

2.1 The AudioLink software

AudioLink is a Role-Playing-Game where users control a main character to carry out several quests or missions (Fig. 1). Each adventure is composed by sub-goals of lower complexity necessary to fulfill a main goal. The player navigates through connected scenarios that represent a virtual world with streets, houses, cities, and the like, and interacts with elements and characters. This way, the player receives information about the missions to be accomplished and the necessary clues. Each quest involves rewards, such as new objects, access to other quests or areas in the game, and so forth. Hence, it is possible to incorporate different science concepts in each quest so that each adventure considers the learning of one or more associated concepts. In addition, the accomplishment of side-quests results in different game endings. It is also possible to select between two levels of difficulty: normal or easy.

AudioLink includes a tutorial that teaches basic game interactions (keyboard, meaning of some audio cues, and others). The tutorial consists of a series of lessons grouped by the category to be learned –such as navigating and interacting with the non-playing characters, or taking and using items, for example– and provides a space to practice what was learned independently at the user's own pace.

Fig. 1. Interfaces of AudioLink

In this study we introduced a navigation model for virtual environment employed with great success in commercial videogames for sighted users that uses a third-person aerial projection. This navigation model was adjusted to blind users by adding 3D sound audio cues. AudioLink has also mini-games incorporated that break the main metaphor temporarily aimed to develop additional skills (such as improving coordination, spatial location, among others), and to become an additional incentive for software interaction. This leads to a more dynamic and attractive interaction, avoiding users to become tired and bored.

One of the mini-games developed is "Hammer Time" (Fig. 2-A), where the player has to hit a worm that appears in eight possible directions (ahead, back, right, left, and diagonals) and that quickly hides (besides of making fun of the player), hence the user must press the numerical keypad in the right direction and rapidly (before the worm hides). Another mini-game is the "Obstacle Race" (Fig. 2-B), where the metaphor shows a character running and avoiding obstacles (through lateral movements and jumps), while at the same time trying to take the emerging rewards.

As the embedded adventures are not trivial to solve (a sighted user that knows the plot can end this game in no less than 40 minutes), game saving is provided, so that players can keep their progresses and load them later. This function also leaves an automatic registry of times, used objects, and other behaviors to make further usability analyses such as how much time it takes users to complete a certain search and what zones were visited. To save the current game a menu is provided, which also lets users make volume adjustments (of the background music and sound effects).

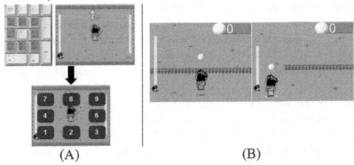

(A)   (B)

Fig. 2. The (A) Hammer-Time, and (B) Obstacle Race mini-games

Keyboard interaction was designed by considering keys already known by the users who evaluated the software, from which we expect to make a standard in the future. Blind users can detect the keys utilized rather easily by touching them and because of their spatial location. The 'F' and 'J' keys are also detected by touch since all keyboards have a notch in those keys, thus making references to the keys located besides them. To navigate through the environment, arrow keys are used. With the TAB key, the player can navigate through the equipment as in a circular list. The player can ask for a description of the current equipped item (with the 'D' key), or try to use it (the 'F' key). To know more about the current scenario, a description can be asked (SPACEBAR), or the player can use the Zily character, a fairy that follows the player, that can be sent to fly around the scene, indicating – visually and through 3D sound– the position of objects and characters. Another feat the player can take is through the action button (ENTER key), which activates a contextual action, depending on the position of the player (open a door, take an item, talk to a character). Finally, users can access a menu ('J' key) and save their progress, load another game previously saved, adjust the volume, or end the game.

2.2 Representing the environment

The representation of the fictional environments of the game was developed through a simple but highly representative model to retrieve and construct game scenarios and different logical connections (or plot) from an external file. This representation was described in a XML file with all attributes that characterize the scenes. This allowed the modification of any element and even the storyboard of the game just by editing the corresponding file without changing the source code. Therefore, adding new stages or levels was possible by modifying only an external file, with no changes whatsoever in the source code. From a different perspective, by using this model it is possible to have infinite different games using the same application. This can be done because the file, in addition to specifying how scenes are constructed, defines logical connections that compose the game plot or script, making it possible to modify the adventures of players through the external file, and thus helping to overcome the lack of educational software for people with visual impairments. AudioLink includes more than 150 different scenes to be explored. They are grouped in well-defined zones to promote long-term memory use, since users have to remember global points to locate scenes inside a bigger virtual world called the "Land of Imir" (Fig. 3). The software provides sequential, parallel, optional, and alternative stories.

The abstraction representation used conceives the virtual world as a composition of different scenes. There are also groups of scenes called "Zones", which relate the scenarios in a more abstract way, for instance, to associate different scenes of a city or forest. The model starts from an abstraction layer that describes the world as a combination of three main elements: Entities, Properties and Relationships.

Entities are all elements present in an environment that can be seen as self-contained pieces of data and that do not need to have a material existence. The combination of one or more entities to each other assembles the representation of the world. In a game environment, some entities could be the doors, the weapons that a character can pick up, other non-playing characters to whom the player can talk to, and the houses the player can enter, to name a few.

Entities can also be used to represent logical *Relationships* for embodying logical connections implicitly embedded in the represented world. For instance, in a classic gaming situation, the main character tries to enter to secret area, thus he or she has to pick up a certain key to unlock a secret door. In our model, there are several entities (a key, door, and character) related to each other (the character can grab the key and use it to open the door). Entities can also have a *state* to indicate variable contextual information; the door can be opened or closed, a light switch can be turned on or off, and so forth. Entities have different features and characteristics. For instance, each entity has its own size, location and shape. Similar patterns and features among related entities can be established, but the basic idea was that there should not be two identical elements in the same place at the same time. These characteristics that define the features of entities are denominated *Properties*.

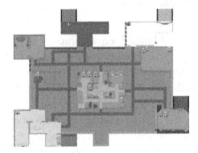

Fig. 3. The *"Land of Imir"*, the virtual environment built

Each scene is made up of different elements which define objects to be created in each scene, and the interaction with objects (elements to collide, to pick up, and others). These elements are: back, facades, solids, characters, entrances, items, doors, and points of use (Fig. 4).

Back corresponds to the background image that is used on the scene. It is the element that has the greater depth in the z-axis according to the graphical rank of layers and its function is just visual. *Facades* are surfaces placed over the back to give additional information of the scene where the user is placed. A facade is a visual aid, used to denote ways, footpaths, etc. But it also has a special sound associated. Thus a different sound is played if, for instance, the character is walking on the grass, to the sound played if the character is walking on plain ground or a wooden floor. *Solids* are all elements of the scene that the character can collide with. These elements span from small fences to houses, and they are used mainly to delimit the navigation through the scene. *Characters* are secondary characters or non-playing-characters (NPC) that may appear in one scene and with whom the user can interact. *Entrances and Doors* are elements of the scene used by the character to travel from one scene to another. They are invisible and facilitate leaving to another scene when interacting with them. *Items* are objects of the world that the player can pick up and use.

For the representation of logical connections the concept of *Dependencies* was created. Dependencies are actions the user has to take to cause different associated reactions, such as: picking up an object, using an object in a certain place (a point of use), speaking with a particular character, and visiting a specific scene. The reactions can be new dialogues of characters, getting access to new zones and new objects that can be taken.

Another crucial piece to achieve the script flexibility is the *Points of Use*, elements utilized to disrupt the logic of the game storyboard. A point of use is a special zone within a scene where a particular item can be used indicating whether the player loses or consumes that item. A point of use has an associated reaction that consists of a particular audio cue played when using the item. It can be a dialogue, an alert or anything that associates the fact of having used that item in such place. A point of use does not limit the possibility of using objects; rather, it limits the success or failure of using a specific object in a certain place. This is to say that the logic behind using most objects consists of verifying whether the player is at a point of use of the object to be used, so the corresponding reactions can occur. There are also special items that can be used in any place (like the map or compass items) and others whose logic is a bit more complex, such as the items used to access to the mini-games.

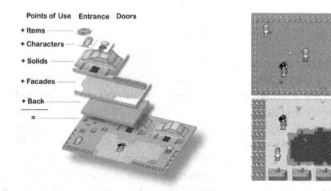

Fig. 4. A model for representing the fictional environment

3 Methodology

A suitable model and methodology for designing and developing audio-based games for blind children is proposed by [0]. The educational software model considers the representation of the world, the knowledge to be learned, and the learner. In this model (see Fig. 5), a combination of incremental and evolutionary development is proposed considering stages of analysis, design, development, and validation, stressing particular considerations when developing educational software for blind children. This model considers a prototyping approach that allows lowering the associated risk of failing to represent the user's mental map adjusted to potential unrevealed requirements at a low cost. A cycle on each stage was executed producing a prototype. This process was repeated until a version that fulfilled the requirements was produced. In these iterations the output from one cycle was considered the input for the next one.

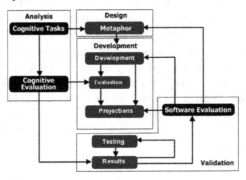

Fig. 5. Model of educational software for blind children

Analysis: In this stage we defined the set of tasks to be accomplished by the student which lead to define software requirements (such as navigating, using orientation resources, solving certain problems, and others). According to these requirements different content was shown to the user, using a treasure hunt metaphor, where learners explored and interacted with the virtual world. **Design:** In this stage the navigated virtual environment that users navigate was defined. The game rules were settled, defining how the different metaphors (scripts) utilized connected with each other. The world was designed as a set of scenarios grouped in different zones with common characteristics (cities, forests, islands and others). **Development:** This cycle consisted in the computer implementation of the models that represented the fictional world and the user. We used an incremental model which allowed the user to navigate some zones created in a coherent and simple fashion when the first cycle ended. This way, on each cycle new zones, characters, and functionalities were added to the game. The projections for different models were designed and new information inputs and outputs flowed from and to the user, mainly using 3D sounds. **Validation:** A usability evaluation was implemented to obtain information about the user's acceptance of the software, and the match between his or her mental model and the representation included in the software. Four instruments were considered for usability evaluation: end-users questionnaire, heuristic questionnaire, direct observation sheets and the facilitator evaluation questionnaire. Below we discuss the main results obtained in the usability evaluation of the software. The data obtained was analyzed and studied to figure out how the metaphors, models, and projections could be improved.

4 Usability Evaluation

Formally, the ISO organization proposed some usability definitions, depending on the terms considered when specifying or evaluating usability [0], "The capability of a software product to be understood, learned, used, and attractive to the user, when used in a specified Context-Of-Use" (ISO/IEC 9126) and "The extent to which a product can be used by specified users to achieve specified goals with effectiveness, efficiency, and satisfaction in a specified Context-Of-Use" (ISO 9241). The main importance of usability in software development is that it is a critical factor for the system to reach its objective [0]. Users should have a real feeling that the system will help them to achieve their tasks, avoiding becoming reluctant to their use.

In spite of the known value of usability, there is still a trend in software engineering to disregard the end-user, leaving to developers the self-testing of the interfaces [0], making changes based on their own experience, mental model and preferences. The problem with this is that developers cannot simulate the behavior of blind end-users because their cognition and mental models are not alike. They cannot assume their feelings and tastes when interacting with digital devices.

A usability evaluation was implemented in this study to ensure that the software proposed was usable for blind children. End-user and heuristic evaluations were implemented; concluding that the final software product developed can be utilized by blind users independently. It was also verified that *AudioLink* is appealing, encouraging and challenging software that stimulates interaction.

5 Scenario and Sample

Software evaluations were carried out at the school for the blind "Santa Lucía", located in Santiago, Chile. Two special education teachers expert in vision disorders also participated in the evaluations. The sample consisted of 20 students divided into two groups: a group of eight children with ages between 8 and 12 years old, half of them had low vision; and a second group conformed by 12 children, with ages between 9 and 16 years old, where 9 of them had low vision.

All users were legally blind, which according to Chilean laws means that *"an eye is blind when its corrected visual accuracy is 1/10, or when the sight field is reduced to 20 degrees"*. This means that a legally blind person is able to see at one meter (3.2 feet) what a sighted one can see at 10 meters (32 feet). They were all familiar with interacting with a computer through a keyboard. All of them also had expressive and comprehensive language skills and could utilize reading and writing systems (Braille or Macro-type), and had an IQ higher than 70. Some users had some previous experience with game-oriented software; therefore they were more critical when evaluating this type of software.

6 Instruments

Four instruments were used for the usability evaluation: 1. End-users evaluation, 2. Heuristic evaluation, 3. Facilitator evaluation, and 4. Direct observation. *End-user evaluation* consisted in blind users answering a short usability questionnaire elaborated by Sánchez [0] to evaluate the system usability considering interaction attributes such as learning, efficiency, memory, errors and satisfaction. End-user evaluations focused on opinions such as how users liked the software, what was pleasant to them, what was not, and how useful the software was to them. The *heuristic evaluation* [0, 0] is a methodology to find usability issues in the design of interfaces, and involved expert evaluators that judged the interface considering a series of validated usability principles –the heuristics– that are general rules that describe usable interfaces (Table 1). Heuristic evaluation was implemented through an extended questionnaire with a likert-type scale elaborated by Sánchez [0]. *Direct observation* was applied to get to understand the fluidity of particular situations in a fast and direct way. The *facilitator evaluation* was designed considering facilitators as end-users when facilitating the interaction of children with the software. Apart from their own interaction with AudioLink, facilitators were present during the interaction of children with the software, acquiring knowledge and unique points of view that shaped them when evaluating this software usability.

Table 1. Usability Heuristics.

Number	Heuristic
1	Visibility of system status
2	Match between the system and real world
3	User control and freedom
4	Consistency and standards
5	Error prevention
6	Recognition rather than recall
7	Flexibility and efficiency of use
8	Aesthetic and minimalist design

9	Recognize, diagnose, and recover from errors
10	Help and documentation
11	Content design
12	Velocity and media

7 Procedure

End-users evaluation considered the interaction of blind children with a series of incremental prototypes. Users interacted with the interfaces independently and could ask facilitators for assistance. When the interaction session was over, a usability questionnaire was applied. Questions were read and explained to children by the facilitators who also wrote down their answers. Six evaluations with end-users were implemented, from September to November (2005), each of them of approximately one hour of duration.

Three evaluators –experts in usability with experience in working with software for visually impaired people– participated in the heuristic evaluation. During the evaluation session, each expert inspected the interface independently, judging each component against the heuristics. This procedure provided a list of usability issues, classified by heuristic (visibility, flexibility, and so on). Then, we conducted dialogue rounds in order to understand the problems faced by the experts and to discuss possible redesigns. The heuristic evaluation was taken in one session of 40 minutes for each usability evaluator.

The facilitator evaluation was taken by two special education teachers, expert in vision disorders. They had not interacted with the software before the evaluation session –only observed the children's interactions. The facilitators interacted with the software and then evaluated it by answering the facilitator questionnaire independently. The evaluation was taken in one session of 30 minutes.

In all of these evaluations an observer was present without interacting with the participants, but recording the usability problems detected, and taking a photographic register of the evaluation sessions. This information that was later analyzed and considered for interface redesign.

8 Results

The first significant result of the usability study was that in all evaluations a very high rate of acceptance was obtained. End-users evaluation showed that the navigation model and the proposed interaction were appropriate and highly accepted by users, who were able to carry out all interaction features embedded in the software. Fig. 6 shows the end-user evaluation of the first prototype (first test) and the final product (last test) for children with low vision (left) and totally blind children (right).

Users liked the software during all implementation stages and always found it entertaining. The final product was more challenging, simple to use, and highly encouraging. End-users always stated that they would play again the software, reflecting that the interaction was attractive and pleasant to them. The importance of usability evaluations is reflected in the affirmation about the software being easier to use in its final version rather than in the first prototype. This happened not only because the level of appropriation of users was higher, but also because the software was adjusted after each evaluation session, reflecting more accurately the needs and interests of end-users through incremental prototypes.

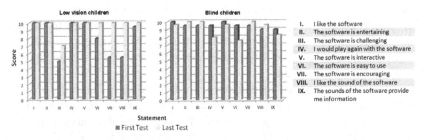

Fig. 6. Results of usability evaluations by children with residual vision.

Software audio cues and sounds were also modified in order to achieve a higher quality and making them more representative of the audio stimuli and more attractive for children. This influenced users by assuming a significantly higher score in the affirmation about how they liked the sounds of the software, when comparing prototype and final product evaluations. Thus, according to the evaluation taken to end-users with low vision, we can conclude that the interface is highly interactive, attractive, and appropriate to them.

Even though during the blind children's evaluation it was possible to observe a small decrease in the final score of some statements –when comparing the first and last evaluation– in average a favorable score still remains. The main score decrease was in the statement *"the software is easy to use"* because a virtual environment of higher extension and more a complex storyboard was obtained in the final product, so users had to interact with a higher number of elements and a greater number of characters. This imposed greater cognitive load to users, because it was designed with the purpose of obtaining a more challenging and encouraging game. Another collateral effect of increasing the complexity of the game was observed in the decrease of the score for the statement *"I would play again with the software"*. This seems to be somewhat contradictory when considering the increase to a perfect score in statements that evaluate this software as entertaining, challenging and encouraging. It can be explained because by making the virtual environment more complex, which implies a higher audio memory capacity of users, leading to a higher cognitive loading, and thus decreasing the scores about whether they would play again the software. Also, they did not use the game saving functionality, so each evaluation began from the same starting point, thus losing interest in the game. In spite of these slight decreases we can conclude that considering the high scores obtained, the proposed interfaces are appropriate and were highly accepted by these users.

The tutorial embedded in the software showed to be useful and provided an added value to the game by teaching users to learn the basic interactions independently at their own pace. Evaluations showed the appropriateness of using quadraphonic sound for the mental construction of the space by blind users (the first prototype had only stereo sound). The appropriate and correct design of the interfaces favored visually impaired users to play and achieve goals effectively and efficiently, gaining satisfaction during interaction. These characteristics allowed adding a greater complexity to the virtual environment by adding more missions, characters, and elements. Users also showed acceptance and encouragement to interact with the mini-games presented. Although each prototype evaluated had a greater complexity than the previous one, they also demonstrated in each interaction session a greater degree of software appropriation.

The heuristic evaluation also provided positive results for software improvement. Some software errors were detected thanks to this evaluation and fixed for the final version. This evaluation also led us to find some problems with icons and navigational issues, and even to suggest new functionalities for the software. The facilitator evaluation also indicated that this software presents and integrates science contents clearly. This makes AudioLink an appropriate tool for children to learn curriculum contents and to develop and exercise problem-solving skills. Facilitators also mentioned that this software had a very usable interface for low vision users, encouraging blind users to use it.

8.1 Cognitive Evaluation

As part of this study, a preliminary cognitive evaluation was implemented to measure the impact of using AudioLink on the development of scientific thinking skills. Two instruments were used: 1. Logging the actions taken by users during playing –which were recorded automatically by the computer– and 2. An open question questionnaire. We first analyzed the actions that are implicit part of the development of scientific thinking skills, such as observing, identifying problems, looking for solutions and evaluating. We considered variables such as interaction time, rate of visited zones, and number of items that were found and used. We concluded that users were able to perform most interactions, they highly motivated themselves, and they developed scientific thinking skills. Likewise, the ways hypermedia stories are presented encouraged users to interact with the software in the long run, since there are several alternative endings depending on the user decisions in the game.

Additionally, an open question questionnaire –with a problem-solving orientation– was applied. Users were asked to indicate what problems they faced in the game, how they knew when something was a problem, and how they solved it. Finally, they were asked to make an evaluation of their own interaction. Results showed that users identified problems, when mentioning, for instance, that *"we must do things that are not said"*; meaning that there were things not explicitly stated in the game that they had to infer. Users also understood that information was distributed in different zones and to gather it they had to navigate the virtual environment. They also recognized that they enjoyed and solved different problem situations after planning and executing diverse strategies.

Last year, we implemented an in-depth study to evaluate the impact of working with AudioLink and cognitive tasks on science learning by blind children, in a six-month field study [0]. This study showed us that blind children were able to learn and practice scientific method processes and enjoyed learning new topics by widening and enhancing their theoretical conceptualizations and acoustic perception. There was a manifest physics learning gain and analytical cognitive skills were enhanced. In some participants these gains meant significant achievement. Children were also able to map, use and understand a game with a complex dynamic and interaction, and solved complicated science problems. We concluded that the use of AudioLink, combined with cognitive activities, promoted scientific content learning and also enhanced problem-solving skills during experimentation conveyed through the application of the scientific enquiry method.

9 Conclusions and Future Work

In this study we have designed, developed, and evaluated the usability of Audio-Link, interactive audio-based multimedia software for visually impaired children for the learning of science. A usable product was developed for the user's independent utilization. We verified that the software was appealing, encouraging, engaging, and challenging. In addition, users rated the usability of AudioLink highly, demonstrating that user-centered design favors the final interaction of end-users with the software product.

This software has an enormous potential by incorporating new scenes and adventures from an external file. This makes it possible to think that in the near future the teachers of blind children, their parents and even themselves, could be able to create their own games and extend existing ones. Modifying the game by means of an external file (for instance, using the game editor currently being developed), can partly help to overcome the lack of educational software for people with visual impairments.

We validated that users developed abilities and strategies to identify a problem, solve it, and know when it is solved. We also observed that users spontaneously contrasted information they cooperatively exchanged to help each other. Children were able to play and understand a game with increasing complexity. They were able to solve problems of high difficulty and to explore a world of a higher magnitude than anything they may had experienced previously.

When creating a generic RPG engine for blind users, this software can be applied for learning concepts of any given subject. This game genre has shown to be very appropriate, useful and appealing for most children that played it. It was also very important to experiment with a widely used game model developed for sighted users and successfully implemented in commercial console games. This demonstrated that perhaps it is not necessary to redesign the whole model to make this type of software available for visually impaired users. Rather, it is possible to consider some adjustments, oriented to support users in their own particular needs.

Finally, the role that AudioLink can play is in the same direction of those tools that help to provide opportunities to children with visual impairments to be more integrated and included in the society.

References

1. Bevan, N. (2001). International standards for HCI and usability. In: International Journal of Human-Computer Studies, Vol.55, No. 4, Oct 2001, pp. 533-552.
2. de Freitas, S., Oliver, M. (2006). How can exploratory learning with games and simulations within the curriculum be most effectively evaluated? Computers and Education 46 (3), pp. 249-264.
3. Eriksson, Y., & Gärdenfors, D. (2004). Computer games for children with visual impairments. Proceedings of The 5th International Conference on Disability, Virtual Reality and Associated Technologies, 20-22 September 2004, New College, Oxford, UK, pp. 79-86.
4. Fowler, M. (1998). Mocks objects aren't stubs, Testing Methods: The Ugly Duckling, Keeping Software Soft. Retrieved January 4, 2007 from http://www.martinfowler.com/distributedComputing/duckling.pdf
5. Kish, D., Bleier H., Moser S. (1998). Facilitating Movement and Navigation in Blind PreSchoolers: A Positive, Practical Approach. Online report. Retrieved Jan. 13, 2007 from http://www.waftb.org/Facilitating%20Movement.pdf.
6. Kurniawan, S. H., Sporka A., Nemec, V. and Slavik, P. (2004). Design and user evaluation of a spatial audio system for blind users. Proceedings of The 5th ICDVRAT, 20-22 September, 2004, New College, Oxford, UK, pp. 175-182.
7. Mastropieri, M., Scruggs, T. (1992). Science for students with disabilities. Review of Educational Research, Vol. 62, No. 4 (Winter, 1992), pp. 377-411.
8. Molich, R., Nielsen, J. (1990). Improving a human-computer dialogue, Communications of the ACM 33, 3 (March), pp. 338-348.
9. Nielsen, J. (1993). Usability Engineering. Academic Press Professional, Boston, MA.
10. Nielsen, J. (1994). Heuristic evaluation. In Nielsen, J., and Mack, R.L. (Eds.), Usability Inspection Methods. John Wiley & Sons, New York
11. Panchanathan, S., Black Jr, J. A., Tripathi, P., and Kahol, K. (2003). "Cognitive Multimedia Computing". Proceedings of IEEE International Symposium on Information Science and Electrical Engineering (ISEE 2003), November, Fukuoka, Japan, pp. 13-15.
12. Sánchez, J. (2001). Visible Learning, Invisible Technology. Santiago: Dolmen Editions.

13. Sánchez, J., Baloian, N. (2006). Modeling 3D interactive environments for learners with visual disabilities. In K. Miesenberger et al. (Eds.): ICCHP 2006, LNCS 4061, pp. 1326 – 1333, 2006. Springer-Verlag Berlin Heidelberg 2006.

14. Sánchez, J., Elías, M. (2007). Science Learning by Blind Children through Audio-Based Interactive Software. Annual Review of CyberTherapy and Telemedicine (in press).

15. Sánchez, J., Flores, H. (2004). Memory enhancement through audio. Proceedings of ASSETS 2004, Atlanta, Giorgia, USA, October 18-20, pp. 24-31.

16. Sánchez, J., Flores, H. (2006). AudioMedia: Multimedia for blind people. 11th Annual CyberTherapy 2006 Conference: Virtual Healing: Designing Reality. June 13 - 15, 2006. Gatineau, Canada, pp. 65

17. Sánchez, J., Sáenz, M. (2005). Developing Mathematics Skills through Audio Inter-faces. Proceedings of HCI 2005. Las Vegas, Nevada, USA, July 22-27, 2005.

18. Sánchez, J., Sáenz, M. (2006). 3D sound interactive environments for blind children problem solving skills. Behaviour & Information Technology, Vol. 25, No. 4, July - August 2006, pp. 367 – 378

19. Shaftel, J., Pass, L., Schnabel, S. (2005). Math Games for Adolescents. TEACHING Exceptional Children, 37(3), pp. 25-30

20. Strangman, N., Hall, T. (2003). Virtual reality/simulations. Wakefield, MA: National Center on Accessing the General Curriculum. Retrieved 4/3/2007 from http://www.cast.org/publications/ncac/ncac_vr.html.

Towards the Introduction of Accessibility Resources in Public Telecentres

Cesar Mauri, Agusti Solanas, Toni Granollers

GRIHO Research Group. Dept. of Computer Science and Industrial Engineering. Lleida University. C/ de Jaume II, 69, Campus Cappont, 25001 Lleida, Spain.
cesar.mauri@urv.cat, tonig@diei.UdL.es

CRISES Research Group. UNESCO Chair in Data Privacy. Dept. of Computer Engineering and Mathematics. Rovira i Virgili University. Av. Països Catalans, 26, 43007 Tarragona, Spain.
agusti.solanas@urv.cat, asolanas@ieee.org

Abstract In this chapter we tackle the problem of studying the Digital Divide (DD) and we pay a special attention to its relation with disabled people. We emphasise on the importance of the fight against the DD and we report a number of projects that aim to reduce it in Catalonia (Spain). The main contribution of this work is the study of the DD from the point of view of the relation between Information and Communication Technologies (ICTs) and disabled people. We analyse the problems that disabled people have to face in order to use ICTs. Therefore, we have defined a number of measures to determine the degree of accessibility that a given user has and we have carried out some experiments to evaluate the proposed measures. Our work is deeply related with the Òmnia Project and the telecentres network impelled by the Catalan Government. Thus, we must understand our work in the context of these innovative initiatives. In this chapter we concentrate on the Human-Computer Interaction (HCI) issues related to the DD in order to explain our experience in this field. At the time of writing this text, the experimental part is still in progress, however some previous results are given. Moreover the current work and experiences are also reported.

M. Redondo et al. (eds.), *Engineering the User Interface*,
DOI: 10.1007/978-1-84800-136-7_8, © Springer-Verlag London Limited 2009

1 Introduction

Digital Divide (DD) is a term that defines the division between people, communities, states, countries, etc. with respect to the access to the new Information and Communication Technologies (ICTs). Nowadays, it is essential to have technological skills to work in a variety of jobs (*i.e.* administration, education, etc.). Moreover, ICTs have become ubiquitous and they affect almost every aspect of our daily life.

The way in which people face the task of using ICTs varies depending on a plethora of variables. The most analysed ones are the technological literacy and the educational level. These are two very important factors that strongly affect the success of the individuals in accessing ICTs. Unfortunately, these are not the only variables to consider. Some people suffer from mental and physical disabilities that are real impediments to access ICTs, and they must be studied in detail. How can we help disabled people to access ICTs? Can public telecentres deal with this task? Can the ICTs be used to improve the accessibility of disabled people? Which projects aim to reduce the digital divide? Are they addressed to disabled people? These are some of the questions that we will try to answer, at least partially, in this chapter.

We believe that governments must invest to avert the DD, but they are not the only actors involved in this scenario. ICTs themselves should be used to improve the integration of some sections of the population which have trouble accessing them. Universities and research centres must help in the development of new techniques to make the normal and proper access to the ICTs to disabled people possible.

1.1 Contribution and Plan of the Chapter

The main contribution of this chapter is the study of the DD that the disabled people suffer. We introduce a number of measures with the aim to improve the techniques for assessing the accessibility to ICTs and we test these measures with real disabled people who frequently visit public telecentres.

The rest of the chapter is organised as follows. In Section 2, we introduce the Òmnia Project and its relation with the Telecentres Network and the NODAT Project. Section 3 gives an overview of the Accessible Computer Project and a set of measures that are specially interesting for being tested on disabled people are proposed. Section 4 is devoted to the explanation of our experience with disabled people in public telecentres. Finally, the chapter concludes in Section 5 with some final comments and future research lines.

2 The Telecentres Network and the Òmnia Project

In this section we elaborate on the main features of the Òmnia Project and we link it with the telecentres network and the NODAT Project. These Catalan projects have been designed to reduce the DD from a general point of view (*i.e.* they are not only intended for disabled people but for a wider range of sections of the society that have trouble accessing the ICTs).

2.1 The Òmnia Project

Technology already affects us nearly every minute of the day, and as we evolve towards a technological society, the need for well-trained people who are technologically literate will exponentially grow. Moreover, technological illiterates will have trouble finding a job or even buying a train ticket. The Òmnia Project (OP) [1] started in 1999 with the aim of overcoming these limitations by providing people with the possibility of integrating them in the new technological age. OP is mainly funded by the Catalan Government and some local organisations.

Òmnia is a Latin noun that means everybody, and in this project it is used as a metaphor for the main goal of OP *i.e.* to guarantee everybody the access to the ICTs and to fight against technological illiteracy. The idea is not new, but it represents a real milestone to minimise the DD in our country.

OP is specially focused on persons and groups with a difficult social situation (*i.e.* ethnic minorities, elderly, etc.). However, a wide variety of people have the risk of becoming technological illiterates.

With a view to getting going on this praiseworthy task, OP defined a network structure, which was made up of Òmnia Access Points (OAP). In 1999 the first 43 OAPs were created, in 2001 68 new OAPs were added to the network and currently there are 112 OAPs working to reduce the DD. OAPs are the building blocks of the OP and they can be defined in terms of physical space, technological equipment and technical support.

- **Physical space**: An OAP is located in a building provided by any of the organisations that take part in the project or by the Catalan Government.
- **Technical equipment**: A basic OAP consists of 9 personal computers with a wide band Internet connection, one scanner, one web-cam, two printers, one CD writer and common software such as a word processor, an e-mail manager, an Internet browser, etc. Some OAPs have increased their technical equipment due to the great welcome given to the project by the citizenship.
- **Technical support**: There is a person in each OAP who is responsible for invigorating the group by exploiting his/her pedagogical capacities; he/she is called "*invigorator*". The invigorator provides the group with technical support and promotes the socialisation and social integration of the group.

In order to work as a real network, the invigorator has to communicate with other invigorators and share his/her experiences in the OAP. The union of all the OAP forms a network that fights against technological illiteracy by following three main common action lines:

- **Community interaction**: This action line represents the philosophy that founds the project and can be divided in two principles:
    o   The access to the OAPs must be free to everybody namely individuals, organisations, groups and associations.
    o   Each OAP must be a place for social cohesion, and it must help in promoting the interaction between people and regions.
- **Labour and social insertion**: An OAP provides people with enough knowledge to address some basic tasks such as writing a Curriculum Vitae or sending an e-mail.
- **Education**: This line aims to guarantee a proper technological education to everybody. This education may let the users access to the information society and avoid their exclusion.

If we take a look at statistics in Catalonia in 2004, some results can be emphasised:

- The access to the OAP is perfectly balanced according to the gender. Specifically 49% of the OAP users were women.
- Regarding the age of the participants, 7% were elderly, 24% were children, 30% were young and 39% were adults. The complete distribution of participants is shown in Fig. 1.

There is no official information on people with disabilities using the telecentres resources but, to the best of our knowledge[3], few disabled people go to public telecentres. This behaviour is due to the lack of information that the disabled people receive from the public telecentres. In fact, they believe that they will not be properly helped in these environments.

It is clear, that it is necessary to increase the amount of information given to the disabled people in order to make them visit the OAPs.

---

[3] From conversations with several invigorators.

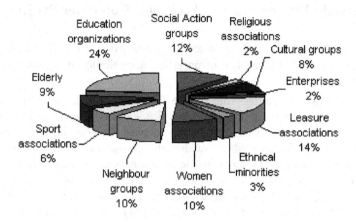

Fig. 1: Distribution of the participants in the Òmnia Project

2.2 Telecentres Network and the NODAT Project

Due to the great success of the OP and the existence of other projects promoting the access to the Internet, such as public Internet access points in libraries, tele-working centres, and Internet public centres amongst others, in 2001 the Catalan government decided to impel a larger project. To do so it merged all these projects. As a result of this merge, the NODAT Project started out with the creation of the telecentres network. The NODAT Project is founded over the next main principles:

- The telecentres must be distributed over the whole country (Catalonia).
- A tele-working community should be created.
- Technological education must be provided and new useful contents should be created.
- The whole network must be audited in order to evaluate the evolution of the information access of the citizenship.

As a result of the NODAT Project, the OAPs were transformed into telecentres and a global and larger telecentres network was created. Currently, the telecentres network is working properly to satisfy the objectives of the project.

3 Accessible Telecentres: the Accessible Computer Project

In this section we describe the foundations of our work and we show the way in which we deal with the problem of providing accessibility to disabled people in public telecentres.

Our study began as a toy-project in the *Ribera d'Ebre* telecentre[4] in Catalonia. A woman with severe mobility problems –lets call her Mary– used to visit the telecentre. Initially, her husband helped her in tasks like checking the e-mails and typing the answers because Mary was not able to use the standard mouse or the keyboard. We have been talking with the invigorators of the telecentre and we decided to test an alternative input system that could be useful to Mary. So we bought an inexpensive joystick and we installed an open-source joystick-to-mouse emulator and an on-screen keyboard. Since then Mary is able to check her e-mails and answer them without the assistance of her husband.

This experience let us think that it was possible to provide accessibility resources in a cheap and simple manner, so we proposed the idea to the Catalan government. Our proposal was accepted and, after a year, 23 Catalan telecentres were equipped with different assistive technology resources and their invigorators were trained with some basic accessibility courses.

The rest of this section includes a brief review of the state of the art in Spain. Next, our philosophy and desiderata are presented while some ideas about accessibility are proposed. Then, some assistive technology devices are commented. Finally, we present some performance measures, their aim being to help the invigorators in the evaluation of the accessibility.

3.1 Some Previous Work in Spain

Introducing accessibility resources and assistive technology devices in public telecentres is not new. The Internet Society, in a paper submitted to the UNESCO in 2000, said *"Self Sustaining Internet Training Centres should include some standard assistive technology as part of their access efforts"* [2]. There is a trend to include support for people with disabilities in public telecentres [3, 4]. In Spain the ONCE (Spanish organisation of blind and visually impaired persons[5]) has founded two telecentres in Sevilla and Valladolid equipped with assistive technology resources [5]. There is little information about these projects and we have not found the description of the methodology and resources used. Thus, we believe

---

[4] http://www.riberaebre.org/telecentre
[5] http://www.once.es/vocacion/webenglish/default.htm

that a relevant contribution of this chapter is to describe a possible approach to deploy accessibility resources in public telecentres.

3.2 Our Philosophy

Traditionally, accessibility and its related technical support were directly associated to complicated and very specialised devices. Moreover, these devices used to be very expensive. Our main idea is to break this trend (following the UNESCO recommendation) by using common hardware[6] controlled by specific software that, in some cases, is open source. The main advantages of using off-the-shelf hardware are: a lower price, higher availability and good quality. Although it is necessary to provide disabled users with some technical support, they are generally able to quickly understand and use the devices.

By following the ideas of the Òmnia Project and the telecentres network, our main goal is to provide a wide variety of disabled users with accessibility at a reasonable price but, we always consider specific problems and/or limitations (in some cases detailed attention and specific devices are necessary). Thus, the introduction of quantitative interaction performance measures [6] will be crucial to meet our objectives. These measures can help users and invigorators during the assessment process.

3.3 Assistive Technology Used

Next we describe some of the assistive technology that is commonly used.

- **Keyboard/Mouse extension lead.** It is useful to place keyboards, mice and trackballs where the users can better use them (*e.g.* on the wheelchair's table). Obviously using wireless mice and keyboards is the best approach; but an extension lead is a cheap option to reuse hardware.
- **Operating system technical aids.** Computers are equipped with Linux and Windows operating systems. Both have configuration options for various special needs such as hearing, sight and motion disabilities. For example, it is possible to configure the desktop theme with high contrast colours, large icons and large text fonts.
- **Joystick.** It is a well-known computer peripheral mainly used for gaming, in our scenario it is used for controlling the mouse pointer.

---

[6] We understand by "common hardware" the devices that we can find in commercial stores at affordable and standard prices.

- **Virtual keyboard.** This is an on-screen representation of a standard keyboard. As long as a person can control a mouse, a trackball or another pointing device, he/she can send keystrokes to any application.
- **Web-cam based head pointer.** This system consists of a web-cam and an application (in our case we use *Ratón Facial* [7, 8, 9, 10]) that let the user control the mouse pointer with slight movements of the head.
- **Screen magnifier.** A screen magnifier is a piece of software that shows enlarged screen content. It is suitable for visually impaired people with some functional vision.
- **Text-to-Speech Synthesis (TTS).** TTS systems are able to artificially produce human speech from an ASCII text. In our context this system is used to make the readings (*e.g.* from a web page) easier to visually impaired people with some functional vision.

3.4 HCI Measures

The use of HCI performance measures during the accessibility assessment process is not a new idea [6], but usually the assessment process is only based on qualitative criteria, that is, the invigorator observes the way in which the user interacts and decides which device better fits him/her. Although the qualitative assessment could be useful in some cases, we believe that it is necessary to introduce quantitative criteria (*i.e.* a set of measurements) for determining the quality of the interaction. This is interesting because it establishes an objective and common criterion between professionals. Moreover, some users could use the measures periodically in an autonomous manner, so they can monitor their improvements, and they can decide to test other devices or set-ups.

Although a variety of interaction technologies (*e.g.* switch-based) could be used, we have centred our efforts on the pointer-based interaction. We have developed a tool that implements an interactive task with the aim to analyse the user interaction when using pointing devices. The user should complete the task as fast and as accurate as possible. Performance data are collected in real-time (*i.e.* pointer movements, clicks). When the task is accomplished a summary is presented to the user.

3.4.1 Pointer control performance analysis

The most common assessment measurements for pointer devices are speed and accuracy. The ISO 9241-9 standard defines a single measure *i.e.* the performance measurement. Performance units are bytes per second and it is computed by considering the speed and precision of users. Performance is a good measure, but does not take into account the path followed to finish the task. So we decided to introduce some additional measurements [11, 12] that give us some more information.

The procedure is based on the ISO 9241-9 multidirectional "point and click" task with optional sound reinforcement. A set of targets (*e.g.* circles) arranged in a circle is presented to the user (*cf.* Figure 2). Users should click the highlighted target (*e.g.* a red coloured circle). Once the target has been clicked the next target is highlighted. The process finishes when users have clicked all targets.

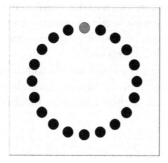

Fig. 2: Screen shot of the application used to collect data. The user should click on the coloured circle.

4 Our Experience

The invigorator has a key role in training and improving users' accessibility. He/she is at the user's disposal and must guide them through the assessment process bearing in mind their disability profiles. To that end, the invigorator must receive a practical instruction at the time of installing the accessibility hardware devices. This instruction is oriented towards the practical needs of the invigorator in terms of the accessibility components utilisation. Moreover, the instruction is inspired in a basic accessibility guide that is also given to the invigorator in order to aid him/her. Furthermore, we are introducing the HCI performance tool that complements the qualitative assessment process described in the guide. Different kind of resources are also available on-line, namely bibliography, forums for discussion and debate, FAQs, etc. Due to the great variability that exists on the disability degrees, the invigorator can be helped by a consultancy consisting of engineers, speech therapists and physiotherapists.

As we have mentioned, one of the main goals of the project is to provide disabled users with accessibility. However, it is also important to teach the users the basic knowledge that lets them properly use a computer outside the telecentres (*e.g.* at home). In addition, most of the required hardware is standard and the software is open-source, thus, the user can easily obtain them at reasonable prices. It is planned to receive feedback from the invigorators and users in order to guarantee the improvement of the proposed solution.

4.1 Disability Profiles

Two main disability profiles are taken into account in this project: impaired vision and motor problems. People with hearing problems are also taken into account by means of the operating system accessibility options; fortunately hearing problems are not serious barriers to use a computer.

A recommended assistive technology testing path is provided for each profile, going from the most common tools to the most specialised ones. In all cases users, assisted by the invigorator, must choose the most suitable combination of assistive technology.

4.1.1 Impaired Vision

We focus on people with impaired vision with moderate sight problems; so the users are able to vaguely see the computer screen. Note that each person is unique and his/her disability varies.

In these cases the testing path includes: using the largest available screen, lowering screen resolution progressively; increasing fonts, mouse pointer and icon sizes; using a high contrast desktop theme, using the screen magnifier and using the text to speech synthesis.

For blind people more specialised resources are needed such as Braille output devices or software for screen reading. We are now working in evaluating an affordable screen reader system for such cases.

4.1.2 Motor Problems

We are mainly interested in mobility problems related to upper limbs or hands that disturb the normal keyboard and mouse usage. It is clear that, people with disabilities in their legs and wheelchair users must be able to reach the computer and, to that end; all the architectural barriers must be suppressed. Although this is a very interesting subject, it falls out of the scope of this chapter.

We provide different approaches for keyboard and mouse access.

- **Keyboard.** Common keyboard access problems include lack of precision to hit the appropriate key, repetitive hits and the impossibility to hit two or more keys simultaneously [13]. All these problems are addressed though the operating system keyboard accessibility options. When this is not enough, an on-the-screen keyboard may be used if the users are able to control the pointing device or, in the worst case, hit some key (*i.e.* using the scanning mode).

- **Mouse.** The mouse requires better motor skills than the keyboard. First, users must be able to drag and stop the cursor accurately. Second, they must be able to push a button one or two times (double click) without moving the device. In this case the testing path includes: adjusting the mouse speed and acceleration settings, disabling OS desktop double click option, using the trackball, using the joystick and using the cursor keys emulation. If this is not enough a webcam-based head pointer (e.g. *Ratón Facial*) can be used in conjunction with the on-screen keyboard to provide a total replacement of the keyboard and mouse devices.

4.2 Preliminary Experimental Results

In order to test the proposed performance measures with disabled people, we have used the software explained in Section 3 and we have carried out a number of experiments with people suffering from cerebral palsy (*cf.* Table **Error! Reference source not found.**). Depending on the abilities of users we can adjust the difficulty of the task (*i.e.* changing the target size and the distance between targets). During the task execution the software collects the reaction time, the execution time, the performance, the trajectory data and the errors.

We have selected a reduced number of users suffering from various degrees of cerebral palsy[7]. Note that it is difficult to work with people suffering from cerebral palsy because they have a serious lack of concentration and attention. Thus, it is difficult to carry out experiments to assess their ability to use a given device. The results that we present here are preliminary results and, they are intended for an illustrative purpose only. They do not pretend to be considered statistically significant but they only give an idea of the first results that we have obtained from our study. The tests were carried out with the most appropriate devices (*i.e.* mouse and cursor keys) for each user. It is clear that controlling the screen cursor is much faster by using a mouse than by using cursor keys, so we selected the first device when possible.

---

[7] In general, cerebral palsy cannot be classified in different degrees. This is due to the fact, that cerebral palsy is not a simple problem but a complex merger of problems. When we speak about different degrees of cerebral palsy we want to express the fact that each individual suffering from this disease has different mental and physical capabilities to work with a computer.

Table 1: Average and standard deviation of the analysed measures

User & device	Reaction Time (ms)	Path Time (ms)	Errors %	Throughput
Cerebral Palsy & Mouse	275.83 ± 253.12	3568.77 ±3054.52	0.24±0.6%	1.44±0.77
Cerebral Palsy & Cursor keys	2406.43 ± 1025.16	18338.85 ± 8088.32	0	0.23±0.1
Normal & Mouse	71.27 ± 32.94	673.96±162	0.02±0.12%	5.33±1

During our experiments we have collected the next data (*cf.* Table 1):

- **Reaction Time**: It is the time that users need to start moving the pointing device after seeing a new coloured circle.
- **Path Time**: It is the time that users need to move the pointing device from its current location to the new coloured circle.
- **Errors**: An error is considered to occur when users click out of a coloured circle.
- **Throughput**: It combines speed and precision in a single unit whose units are bits per second.

After taking a look at the results in Table **Error! Reference source not found.**, we can reach the following conclusions:

- The reaction time of users suffering from cerebral palsy is clearly larger than the one of a non-disabled user. This result is not surprising, but it confirms that these disabled users require special attention. Specifically, it will be necessary to develop adapted graphical interfaces in order to make disabled people able to interact easily. The same conclusion can be reached regarding the path time.
- The path time is enormously shortened when a disabled user utilises a mouse instead of cursor keys. This result is due to two main reasons:

  1. Disabled users, who are able to deal with a mouse, have better movement capabilities[8] than the ones that can only work with cursor keys.
  2. The movement of the pointer is slower when using cursor keys than when using a mouse.

- The error rate obtained by the disabled users utilising cursor keys is 0 (or almost 0) and can be compared to the results of a non-disabled user. This result is really surprising and opens the door to the creation of cursor keys based interfaces[9].

---

[8] Note that the fact that a disabled user is able to properly manage a mouse does not mean that he/she is free of other mental problems, which make his/her interaction difficult.

[9] All graphical interfaces can be access by using cursor keys. However, most of them are designed to be used with a mouse. Thus, the design of new graphical interfaces oriented to the cursor keys could be a goal.

- The throughput obtained by a non-disabled user is far from the ones obtained by users suffering from cerebral palsy. Moreover, due to the fact that the throughput mainly depends on the utilised time, the use of a mouse increases the throughput.

5 Conclusions

This chapter reports an innovative experience in the framework of the Òmnia Project started up by the Catalan government. This project can be considered as an important step beyond the minimisation of the so-called Digital Divide with disabled people.

Our work highlights the importance of the quantitative assessment and all the related assistive technology that lets disabled people keep in touch with technology. We have focused the chapter on explaining our experience and how our quantitative measures can be used.

We have experimented on disabled people suffering from cerebral palsy, with the aim to provide experimental quantitative data extracted from the most used control interaction devices (pointer control and text input). At the moment of writing this chapter our results are still preliminary. It means that we have not enough feedback to be able to enumerate the advantages and disadvantages of the proposed experiments, but we can obtain some insightful ideas.

Currently we are studying some other disabilities in several Òmnia centres. One of these studies is related to the mouse and trackball interaction with motor disabled people. Another study tests the screen magnifier features on users with only 25% of vision. Globally, we are experimenting on fifteen different people.

We believe that sometimes disabled people cannot achieve higher personal autonomy levels because of the high cost of assistive technologies and, we think that the low cost systems that we have presented here can minimise this problem.

Disclaimer and Acknowledgments   The authors are solely responsible for the views expressed in this chapter, which do not necessarily reflect the position of UNESCO nor commit that organisation. Agusti Solanas is partly supported by the Spanish Ministry of Education through projects TSI2007-65406-C03-01 "E-AEGIS'' and CONSOLIDER CSD2007-00004 "ARES'', and by the Government of Catalonia under grant 2005 SGR 00446.

References

1. Government of Catalonia. The Òmnia Project. Retrieved on July 2, 2007 from http://xarxa-omnia.org

2. Maxwell, C., Global trends that will impact universal access to information resources. The Internet Society. Retrieved on July 2, 2007 from http://webworld.unesco.org/infoethics2000/documents/study_maxwell.rtf

3. Salamieh telecentre in Syria. Retrieved on July 2, 2007 from http://community.telecentre.org/en-tc/node/24519

4. UNESCO. Unesco supported telecentre for the blind opened in Uruguay. Retrieved on July 2, 2007 from http://portal.unesco.org/ci/en/ev.php-URL_ID=22399&URL_DO=DO_TOPIC&URL_SECTION=201.html.

5. ONCE Foundation (2006) Telecentros discapnet. Retrieved on July 2, 2007 from http://www.discapnet.es/Discapnet/Castellano/Telecentros/.

6. Mauri C, Solanas A, Granollers T., On the assessment of the interaction quality of users with cerebral palsy. In: ARES 2007 The International Conference on Availability, Reliability and Security. IEEE Computer Society, Los Alamitos, USA, pp 799–805

7. García M, Mauri C. (2005) Parálisis cerebral y nuevas tecnologías: Ayudas técnicas basadas en visión artificial. [Cerebral palsy and new technologies: Assistive technology based on computer vision]. In: IV Jornadas Onubenses sobre Parálisis Cerebral, Huelva, Spain..

8. García M, Mauri C., Experiencia de interacción persona-ordenador a través de webcam con usuarios con discapacidad motriz grave y moderadamente afectados. [HCI experience using webcam with serious and moderately affected motor disabled users]. In: Tecnología, Educación y Diversidad. Retos y realidades de la inclusión digital TECNONEET 2004, Murcia, Spain, pp 259–264

9. Mauri C., Interacción persona-ordenador mediante cámaras webcam. [HCI using web cameras]. In: Proceedings of Interacción 2004: V Human-Computer Interaction Congress. J. Lorés and R. Navarro (Eds.). Lleida, Spain, pp 366–367

10. Mauri C., Granollers T., Lores J, García M. (2004) Computer vision interaction for people with severe movement restrictions. In: Human Technology: An Interdisciplinary Journal on Humans in ICT Environments, 2nd issue. Agora Center, University of Jyväskylä, Finland, pp 38–54..

11. Mackenzie S, Kauppinen T, Silfverberg M. (2001) Accuracy measures for evaluating computer pointing devices. In: CHI '01: Proceedings of the SIGCHI conference on Human factors in computing systems. ACM Press, New York, USA, pp 9–16.

12. Keates S, Hwang F, Langdon P, Clarkson P, Robinson P. (2002) Cursor measures for motion-impaired computer users. In: Assets '02: Proceedings of the fifth international ACM conference on Assistive technologies. ACM Press, New York, USA, pp 135–142..

13. Trewin S. (1996) A study of input device manipulation difficulties. In: Assets '96: Proceedings of the second annual ACM conference on Assistive technologies. ACM Press, New York, USA, pp 15–22.

Access Control Model for Collaborative Business Processes

M. Sánchez, B. Jiménez, F. L. Gutiérrez, P. Paderewski, J. L. Isla

Department of Computer Languages and Systems - University of Granada
{miguesr, beajv, fgutierr, patricia}@ugr.es,

Department of Computer Languages and Systems - University of Cadiz
joseluis.isla@uca.es

Abstract One of the most important characteristics of current enterprise systems is the existence of collaborative processes where different users/subsystems communicate and cooperate in order to carry out common activities. In these processes, shared resources are often used and there are complex relationships between activities and users, so the definition and administration of different security levels (tasks, users, resources, etc.) is necessary. In this article, we shall focus on an important dimension related to the security aspect of collaborative systems: access control. We shall use an organization model that considers the necessary elements to represent authorization and access control aspects in enterprise systems. This model is used in a service-oriented architecture (SOA) in order to facilitate the implementation of a service which is responsible for these important functions.

Keywords: Collaborative System, Software Architecture, Role-based Access Control.

1 Introduction

Nowadays organizations need to operate in a flexible and efficient mode in order to solve the problems related with the complex business changes which will appear in the system. Modern systems evolve along the time to take the changes inside their organizations into account. A continuous adaptation of the system is necessary in order to obtain more effective business processes adapted to current requirements.

M. Redondo et al. (eds.), *Engineering the User Interface*,
DOI: 10.1007/978-1-84800-136-7_9, © Springer-Verlag London Limited 2009

Moreover, inside organizations there are special business processes for which communication, coordination and cooperation among different users are necessary in order to carry out common activities.

In this context, Internet and the Web have enabled us to change the way in which business and services are offered to global society. Furthermore, they have provided an extra support to allow organization interoperability.

Recently, web services technology has reached high levels. It has allowed IT departments to establish their business processes inside systems that incorporate architectures based on services. This is a logical consequence of the so many advantages achieved by Web Services, namely, standard-based middleware technology; business service high reusability level; easy business legacy system leverage; and integration among heterogeneous systems. In this global society, the security aspect is a crucial element in the business process performance. Information about security is related to the need of protecting information from non authorized access and modifications.

The main aims of information security are [5, 6]:

- Confidentiality: to ensure that information is not accessed by unauthorized users.
- Integrity: to protect information from unauthorized modifications.
- Availability: to ensure that information is accessible when it is necessary and inaccessible to malicious activities.
- Accountability: to ensure that the parts to interaction with the application or component cannot later reject the interactions.
- Assurance: the confidence level in the security system relative to the objectives of the prediction.

To achieve the security information aims of the business process inside an organization it is required to outline a set of protection mechanisms in the design stage of the business process. The main protection mechanisms are:

- Authentication: to provide mechanisms of users' identification.
- Access control: to provide mechanisms of access control and information workflow control.
- Data coding: to provide confidentiality.
- Summary function: to ensure data integration.
- Digital signature: to ensure responsibility.
- Auditing registry: to provide auditing measures.

Traditionally, these aspects have not been taken into account until the last phase of the software development. But we think it is essential to consider them from the initial phases if we want to develop reliable and usable systems. Consequently, security requirements must be integrated into all the development phases of the business systems [2, 3, 6].

In this paper, we will pay special attention to availability. We think that organization information is a key element in business processes because it must be shared and accessible by a great number of users. The access control mechanism is especially indicated to achieve the aim of availability.

Moreover, access control is an important complement to the characterization of users and/or systems interaction, because of its double function of protection and customization, as well as because of the fact of taking into account the characteristics of each organizational environment.

The rest of this paper is organized as follows: In Section 2 we will present and analyse some related work. In Section 3 we will illustrate the model we use to describe a collaborative system and how it includes the necessary elements for modelling access control policies. In Section 4 we propose the design of an access control mechanism as a set of Web Services in a service-oriented architecture. Additionally, we will present an application for collaborative learning called SisACo (Sistema de Aprendizaje Colaborativo) that is used to learn modelling use case of the UML (Unified Modelling Language). SisACo has been developed in order to validate our architecture. Finally, in section 5 we will draw our conclusions and expose future research tracks.

2 Related Works

Different models have been proposed to manage control access requirement for distributed applications. Traditionally, control access models have been characterised using discretionary access control (DAC) and mandatory access control (MAC). Soon after that, models as role-based access control (RBAC) or task-based access control (TBAC) have been proposed to manage the security requirement of a wide range of applications. We will now portray the characteristics and main differences among these models.

2.1 DAC - Discretionary Access Control Model

Discretionary Access Control, also called limited security model, is not oriented to control the information flow. All subjects and objects in the system are listed and there are specified authorization access rules for each subject and object. Subjects can be users, groups or processes.

DAC models are based on the idea that the owner of an object, its author, has the control over the object permissions. The author is authorized to allow or withdraw permissions for this object to other users.

DAC allows authorized users to copy data from one object to another. One user could allow the access to copy data to another unauthorized user. This risk could be extended to the whole system, thus violating a set of security objects.

The main advantage of DAC is that users benefit from great flexibility.

However, it is difficult for DAC to guarantee the integrity rules such as 'least privilege' and 'separation of duty', which are necessary for the enterprise environment. DAC is appropriate for environments where the shared information is more important than the protected one.

There are different representations of the DAC model, the most important being the HRU (Harrison, Ruzzo and Ullman) access control matrix (ACM) model. [8]

In ACM the access permissions are stored in an access matrix A. Subjects are represented by rows and objects are represented by columns. A[s, o] defines the access permissions that a subject, s, has over an object, o. If we split matrix into columns, for each object we have all the access modes for each subject. In this case, we have a model based on "authority". If we split by rows, the subjects know what they can do with each object; in this case we have a model based on "capacities".

There are different models based on ACM. Their main contribution is the inclusion of security types in the ACM model, for example: Schematic Protection Model (SPM) [12], Typed Access Matrix (TAM) model [13] and Dynamically Typed Access Control (DTAC) model [17].

2.2 MAC - Mandatory Access Control Model

MAC model is a multilevel security model. This model can be implemented using a multilevel security mechanism that uses "no read-up" and "no write-down" rules, also known as Bell-LaPadula restrictions [1]. These rules are designed to ensure that information does not flow from a higher sensitivity level to a lower sensitivity level. In this case, the goal is not to allow the flow of low integrity information to high integrity objects.

In a MAC model all subjects and objects are classified based on predefined sensitivity levels that are used in the access decision process.

An important goal of a MAC model is to control information flow in order to ensure its confidentiality and integrity, which is not addressed by DAC models.

Unlike DAC, MAC models provide more solid data protection mechanisms, and deal with more specific security requirements, such as the derived requirements of information flow control policy. However, the enforcement of MAC policies is often a difficult task, and in particular for Web-based applications. They do not provide feasible solutions because they lack sufficient flexibility [14].

2.3 RBAC - Role Based Access Control

The main goal of the RBAC model is to prevent users from having free access to the company's information [15]. To achieve it, the model introduces the role concept and associates users to roles. The access rights are associated with roles. The role is a typical concept used in enterprises in order to organize activities. RBAC admits to model security from an enterprise perspective since we can connect the security requirement with the roles and the responsibilities in the company.

The RBAC model is based on the definition of elements and the relationships among them (Fig. 1). This model describes a user group that can play a set of roles and carry out operations. In each operation, users need to use objects as resources. Within the organization, a role can be defined as a job function that describes the authority and responsibility conferred to a user assigned to the role.

The following relationships appear among these four elements:

- Relationships between users and roles: this relationship models the different roles that a user can play.
- Operation set that can be performed on each object: the elements of this relationship are called permissions.
- Relationships between permissions and roles: these relations describe each user's permissions to use specific objects when they are playing a certain role.

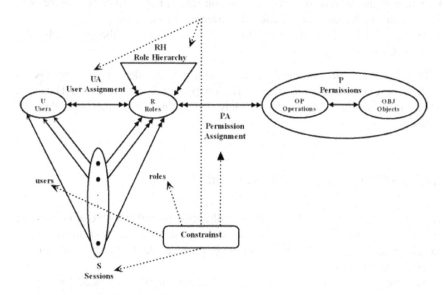

Fig. 1. RBAC model

The RBAC model includes a set of sessions. Each session is a mapping between a user and any possible roles. When users establish a session, they can activate the roles they have assigned. Each session is associated with a single user, although each user can be involved in one or more sessions.

The permissions available to the user are those assigned to the roles that are activated for all the user's sessions, independently from the sessions established by other system users.

It is also possible to include a role hierarchy so that generalisations and specialisations in access controls can be modelled. This enables us to define two types of role hierarchies: general role hierarchies and limited role hierarchies.

General role hierarchies provide support for an arbitrary partial order role. This type can be used to include the concept of multiple inheritance permissions and user membership among roles. Limited role hierarchies impose a restriction set, resulting in a simpler tree structure (i.e. a role may have one or more ascendants, but it is restricted to a single descendant). It should be noted that an inverted tree is also possible.

Another important aspect in the RBAC model is the possibility of specifying constraints on the users/roles relation and on the activation of role sets for users. These constraints are a strong mechanism to establish high level organizational policies. These restrictions can be of two types: static or dynamic. Static constraints enable us to solve interest conflicts and role cardinality rules from a policy perspective. The user association with a role can be subject to the following constraints:

- A user is authorized for a role only if the role is not mutually exclusive with any user's authorized role (Static Separation of Duty).
- The number of users authorized for a role cannot exceed the role cardinality (Role Cardinality).

Dynamic constraints define rules to avoid a pair of roles being designated as mutually exclusive regarding role activation (Dynamic Separation of Duty). In other words, a user may be active in only one of the two distinct roles thus designed.

2.4 TBAC - Task Based Access Control

Task Based Access Control rises to control access in collaborative environments represented by workflows. The TBAC model extends the traditional subject/object based access control models by including domains containing task-based contextual information [16].

This model makes a difference between assigning user's permissions or activating these permissions. A user will have a set of access permissions related to a task assigned; the user could only use these permissions in the activation of the related task.

In this model, access control is granted in steps related to the progress of the tasks. Each step is associated with a protection state containing a set of permissions. The contents of this set change depending on the evolution of the task. Hence, the model is an active one that admits dynamic management of permissions. Each step has a disjoint protection state as shown in Fig. 2. TBAC, unlike RBAC, supports type-, instance-, and usage-based access. Additionally, authorizations have a strict runtime usage, validity, and expiration characteristics.

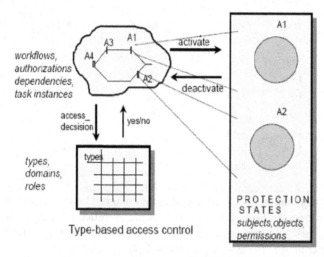

workflows,
authorizations
dependencies,
task instances

access_
decision

yes/no

types,
domains,
roles

Type-based access control

Instance and usage based access control

Fig. 2. TBAC model

3 Organization Model

In the previous section we have reviewed work related to access control models. Although each model has its own advantages, not all of them meet the necessary requirements for access control in enterprise environment where there are collaborative processes.

Table 1 shows a comparison about the characteristics of the control access model for collaborative systems. [7]

We can observe that the RBAC and the TBAC models are good to implement access control in collaborative systems in Table 1. However, these models do not support important characteristics as controlling the current context or performing a fine-grained control in collaborative systems.

In this section we present an extended model that includes additional elements to those that incorporate the RBAC and TBAC models to solve their problems.

In order to define the access authorization model, we use an organization model of the system actors (users, agents, subsystems, etc.) considering static and dynamic aspects. While static issues are related to the organization structure, dynamic aspects are related to modelling temporal changes in responsibilities, organization laws, capabilities, etc.

Table 1. Comparison between models

	DAC	MAC	RBAC	TBAC
Complexity	No	No	Low	Low
UnderStandability	Yes	Yes	Yes	Yes
Ease of Use	Low	Low	Yes	Yes
Applicability	Low	Low	Yes	Yes
Group of users	Low	Low	Yes	Yes
Policy Specification	Low	Low	Yes	Yes
Policy Enforcement	Low	Low	Yes	Low
Fine grained Control	No	No	Low	Low
To be Dynamic	No	No	No	Yes

Fig. 3 shows a conceptual model (using a UML class diagram) which allows us to describe the social organization of a system. This model reflects the most important elements appearing in any organization, such as those which have traditionally been used in collaborative system modelling [18].

This conceptual model defines an organization (for example a company, a department, a group of users who temporarily take part in common tasks, etc.) as a set of roles and functional dependencies between them. Consequently, we can model associations of a different nature, e.g. the possibility of a user passing from one role to another.

From a structural point of view (structural dependencies), an organization can be included in other organizations (for example, a department can be part of a company).

The actor concept includes both individuals (a user, a software agent, a robot, etc.) and organizations. An individual actor is at least part of an organization, and at any time, an actor (organization or individual) plays at least one role in an organization. Playing a role implies that the actor is responsible for performing activities associated with such role. We can implicitly assume that an actor must have the required capability and permission to carry out the corresponding activities and to use its associated resources.

Unlike the RBAC model, functional dependencies in this model enable us to specify and control the role changes that an actor can undergo in a system. For this reason, we can say that this model allows dynamic role-based access control. In addition, our model allows the assignment of permissions to groups of users working on a common activity, since an organization can play a role.

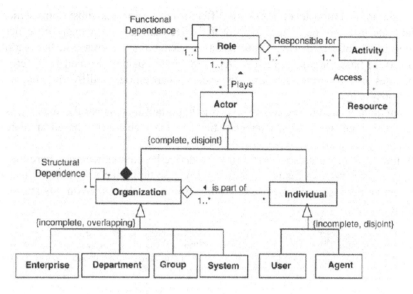

Fig. 3. Organization Model

In the following section, we will show an architecture based on the MDA paradigm (Model Driven Architecture). In it, the access control service is driven by a system organization model which contains all the information that the authorization service needs in order to carry out its operations. One of the advantages of this approach is that the changes in the model can be carried out dynamically and the general functionality of the system can be modified at runtime.

We implement two levels of changes:

- System evolutionary changes: changes in the model that are dynamically recalculated in the system. For example, we can change the permission assignment policies for a certain resource by adding a new role within the organization and distributing functions between the new role and pre-existing ones.
- Model adaptive changes: changes in the organizational structure that are predetermined in the model. For example, we can describe the policy of delegating existing authorizations in a bank for the granting of a loan: i.e. an assistant bank manager is authorized to play a bank manager's role in his/her absence.

4 An Architectural Proposal to Manage the Access Control

The Internet and Web evolution enable us to change the mode in which business and services are offered to global society. This progress makes information systems connect through the infrastructure supply by Internet and the Web.

On an architectural level, there are different interconnected subsystems which collaborate in many cases to carry out activities that have previously been performed in a centralized way. There has also been a sharp increase in the use of web service based architectures (WSA) to integrate business located in different companies or to describe collaborative processes carried out by different company users/subsystems.

From an architectural point of view, it is important to separate the security aspects from other application characteristics and the web service based architectures are a good platform to perform this separation.

In this section, we present part of a web service based architecture where there are a specific service to manage access control. We think that it is better to use a web service because it can be used by other systems without knowing its internal process.

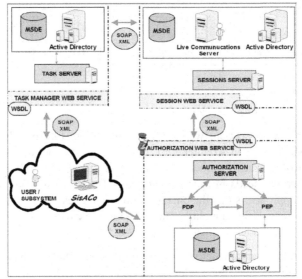

Fig. 4 . Architecture

One of the goals of our architecture is to allow the system to adapt to the current state of the company organization (the organizations are usually dynamic). Accordingly, it is necessary to know the business process definition and the organizational work flow as well as the execution context of these business processes (users/active roles, tasks or activities in execution, etc.). In order to achieve this goal, we include two new web services: one for process management and another to know and manage the execution context of the business process.

In previous works we have defined an architecture for collaborative systems where we have presented the necessity to use three web services related with the access control in collaborative systems: Web Service Authorization, Web Service Task Manager, and Web Service Session [10, 11, 4, 7].

In order to validate our architecture, we have developed an application for collaborative learning called SisACo (Sistema de Apendizaje Colaborativo). This application allows the development, in a collaborative mode, of a use case by a group of students as part of a task proposed by the teacher in the classroom. In Fig. 4 we partially show the architecture components which are necessary for access control into the SisACo application.

Web Services have been implemented using .NET technology and C# as program language over Windows Server 2003 operating system.

In the following sections, we will describe each of these services in more detail, including the main operations that they make available to the rest of the system.

4.1 Web Service Authorization

Web Service Authorization stores and manages information about system authorization policies. Other subsystems and applications in the enterprise will use this service to know if they have access to resources according to activities currently executed and to the users and their roles. Due to the dynamic characteristics of enterprise system processes and their adaptation to the current context (lack of personal, organizational structural changes, etc.), a wide range of information (roles, tasks in execution, moment when the access is requested, etc.) is necessary to determine access to the tasks and resources by means of the Web Service.

Two types of access are used to facilitate service management: "user mode access" used by applications to control access to shared resources, and "administrator mode access" with which modifications in the authorization models can be performed.

To implement this Web Service, SisACo has taken into account the next components: Authorization Server module, PDP (Policy Decision Point), PEP (Policy Enforcement Point), MSDE (Microsoft Server Desktop Engineer) database and AD (Active Directory).

The Authorization Server manages queries (request and response) from other subsystem into the organization about whether a user or subsystem has access permission to a specific resource or task. It is necessary for it to make XML/SOAP Parser functions in order to control communication. In order to do that, this module will need to communicate with Session Web Service to know the current context in the system.

The PDP (Policy Decision Point) module is in charge of deciding about access control using the policies defined in the organizational system.

The PDE (Policy Enforcement Point) module is in charge of carrying out access control according to the decision received by PDP.

The MSDE (Microsoft Server Desktop Engineer) database is used to store access control policies. In order to do that, we use the organization model we have described in section 3.

AD is used to manage the organizational structure in our system (role changes, users' connection, relation between roles and users, …).

Fig. . 5. Operations of Web Service Authorization

In Fig. 5 we show the main operations defined in WSDL (Web Service Description Language) that this service offers to the rest of the system.

4.2 Web Service Task Manager

We think that it is important to control the logic of communication and coordination in business processes. Therefore, it is necessary for the Web Service Task Manager to coordinate the tasks (activities and aims that are defined by business processes) and to store a task model with information about tasks, activities and subactivities. These tasks are performed by the elements within the system (either individually or collaboratively).

When we develop an application, we can derive part of the control flow from the tasks to the service task management. The application development and adaptation to the business model changes is facilitated with the introduction of this service.

In SisACo, the Web Service Task Manager implementation is composed by the next components: the MSDE database, AD and the Task Server module.

```
........
<operation name="LinkResourcesTask">
   <input message="y:linkResourcesTaskResquest"/>
   <output message="y:linkResourcesTaskResponse"/>
</operation>
<operation name="RegisterInitialStateActivity">
   <input message="y:registerInitialStateActivityRequest"/>
   <output message="y:registerInitialStateActivityResponse"/>
</operation>
<operation name="RegisterFinalStateActivity">
   <input message="y:registerFinalStateActivityRequest"/>
   <output message="y:registerFinalStateActivityResponse"/>
</operation>
<operation name="RegisterAim">
   <input message="y:registerAimRequest"/>
   <output message="y:registerAimResponse"/>
</operation>
<operation name="RegisterAimTask">
   <input message="y:registerAimTaskRequest"/>
   <output message="y:registerAimTaskResponse"/>
</operation>
<operation name="RegisterTransationRule">
   <input message="y:registerTransationRuleRequest"/>
   <output message="y:registerTransationRuleResponse"/>
</operation>
<operation name="GetInitialStateActivity">
   <input message="y:getInitialStateActivityRequest"/>
   <output message="y:getInitialStateActivityResponse"/>
........
```

Fig.6. Operations of Web Service Task Manager

The necessary information for tasks flow management in an organization is stored in the MSDE database. This information is necessary to represent the organizational structure, the task representation, the association between tasks and roles and resources used by tasks. All this information is obtained by applying the method presented in [7]. This method represents task models for a collaborative system using hypermedia networks.

In our system, AD is used to store the information into the organizational structure (roles-users), which is necessary for our task management.

The Task Server module is used to manage the task flow in our system. It indicates to users and subsystems which are the business processes they have to carry out in each moment.

In Fig. 6 we show the main operations defined in WSDL (Web Service Description Language) that this service offers to the rest of the system.

One of the most important requirements of these operations will be to have the system permanently in a consistent state. The changes performed in the context of the system can quickly be applied to the model and indirectly to the task services. This allows the system to rapidly adapt to the new changes.

4.3 Web Service Session

The knowledge of the current enterprise system context (roles, active users, tasks or activities in execution, etc.) is necessary to manage user and task access control.

In our architecture, we include a Web Service Session in order to prevent this functionality. The Web Service Session maintains a representation of the dynamic use of the system (current context and record of the finalization of the process). Its main goals are to register finished and active tasks performed by each user playing a specific role in the system. The service registers a set of elements related to the context in which the activities are carried out (used resources, reached goals, performed collaborations ...). Therefore, we can control the state of each user/subsystem using the information stored during a session.

In the case of SisACo we use: MSDE database, LCS (Live Communication Server 2005) and a Sessions Server module.

MSDE stores necessary information to describe the context in organizational system.

LCS allows us to modify current information about users and the subsystem.

AD stores organizational structure information necessary to control the current context. AD will give support to the LCS functions.

Finally, the Session Server module is responsible for managing the contextual information.

In Fig.7 we show the main operations defined in WSDL (Web Service Description Language) that this service offers to the rest of the system.

Fig. 7. Operations of Web Service Session

5 Conclusions and Future Work

In this work we have presented the necessity to bear in mind security requirements in all development phases, if we want to get reliable and usable systems. We pay special attention to access control requirements. They are basic elements in order to obtain a high availability grade of the information and the resources in an organizational system.

We have carried out a study about more important access control models (DAC, MAC, RBAC, and TBAC). We have presented the more relevant characteristics for each one, such as their lacks to define access control in collaborative systems. As a result of this study, we have observed that the RBAC and TBAC models are a good base for modelling access control in collaborative systems. Yet, these models do not support characteristics as important as the representing of the context in real time or the fine-grained control in collaborative systems.

We have presented an organizational model which is used to represent all information which is necessary for modelling access control in enterprise systems where there are collaborative processes.

We have proposed an approach that uses a Web Services based architecture to manage access control in collaborative systems. In order to evaluate this architecture we have developed an application for collaborative learning called SisAco.

Currently we are working in the proposal of a complete architecture for collaborative systems where we can include the Web Services presented in this work.

We think that modelling access control is very important to use conceptual patterns. This minimizes the shaped efforts and enables us to generate more optimized design solutions. Hence, we are finding specific patterns which allow us to model common security policies.

The organization model presented is being extended to include new elements in order to enable us to achieve the rest of the security requirements: confidentiality, integrity, accountability and assurance, as well as to improve the availability.

Acknowledgments   This research has been funded by the Comisión Interministerial para la Ciencia y la Tecnología (CICYT) (Spain), project AMENITIES, grant number TIN2004-08000- C03-02.

References

1. Bell DE, LaPadula LJ (1974) Secure Computer Systems: Mathematical Foundations and Models. Mitre Report M74-244, Mitre Corporation, Bedford, Massachusetts
2.. Firesmith DG (2003) Engineering Security Requirements. J Object Technology 2: 53-68
3. Firesmith DG (2004) Specifying Reusable Security Requirements. J Object Technology 3: 61-75
4. Garrido JL, Paderewski P, Rodríguez ML, Hornos M, Noguera M (2005) A software architecture intended to design high quality groupware applications. In: Proceedings of the ICSE Research and Practice, pp 59-65

5. Gerber M, von Solms R, Overbeek P (2001) Formalizing information security requirements. J Information Management & Computer Security 9: 32-37
6. Gutiérrez C, Fernández-Medina E, Piattini M (2004) A Survey of Web Services Security. Computational Science and Its Applications ICCSA 2004 vol 3043/2004 pp 968-977
7. Gutiérrez FL, Isla JL, Paderewski P, Sánchez M, Jiménez B (2007) An architecture for access control management in collaborative enterprise systems based on organization models. J Sci Comput Program 66: 44-59
8. Harrison MH, Ruzzo WL, and Ullman JD (1976) Protection in operating systems. Commun ACM 19: 461-471
9. Joshi JB, Aref WG, Ghafoor A, Spafford E H (2001) Security models for web-based applications. Commun ACM 44: 38-44
10. Paderewski P, Rodríguez MJ, Parets J (2003) An Architecture for Dynamic and Evolving Cooperative Software Agents. In: Computer Standards & Interfaces, vol 25, Elsevier Science, pp 261-269
11. Paderewski P, Torres JJ, Rodríguez MJ, Medina N, Molina F, A software system evolutionary and adaptive framework: Application to agent-based systems. Journal of Systems Architecture 50: 407-416
12. Sandhu RS (1988) The schematic protection model: its definition and analysis for acyclic attenuating schemes. J ACM 35: 404-432
13. Sandhu RS (1992) The typed access matrix model. In: Proceedings of the 1992 IEEE Symposium on Security and Privacy . IEEE Computer Society, Washington, DC, pp 122-136
14. Sandhu RS (1993) Lattice-based access control models. IEEE Computer 26:9-19
15. Sandhu RS, Coyne EJ, Feinstein HL, Youman CE (2006) Role-based access control models. IEEE Computer 29: 38-47
16. Thomas RK, Sandhu RS (1997) Task-based Authorization Controls(TBAC): A Family of Models for Active and Enterpriseoriented Authorization Management. Proceedings of the IFIP TC11 WG11.3 Eleventh International Conference on Database Securty XI: Status and Prospects, pp 166-181
17. Tidswell J, Potter J (1998) A Dynamically Typed Access Control Model. In: Proceedings of the Third Australasian Conference on information Security and Privacy C. Boyd and E. Dawson (eds), Lecture Notes In Computer Science, vol 1438, Springer-Verlag, London, pp 308-319
18. Van Welie M, Van der Veer GC (1998) An ontology for task world models. In: Design, Specification and Verification of Interactive System'98, Springer Computer Science

An Ontology to Model Collaborative Organizational Structures in CSCW Systems

Victor M. R. Penichet, Maria D. Lozano, Jose A. Gallud

I3A-UCLM, Av. España s/n, 02007 Albacete, Spain
{Victor.Penichet, Jose.Gallud, Maria.Lozano}@uclm.es

Abstract This paper presents a conceptual model to represent the organizational structure of the users in a CSCW system and their cooperative interactions, that is, interactions between them through the system. We define this conceptual model and its associated ontology with the aim of defining in a precise way the main concepts and their relationships used in the development of CSCW systems. This vocabulary description eases the representation, specification, analysis, and design of this kind of environments. Such common concepts are absolutely necessary because all the artefacts needed to model a collaborative system will be built starting from them. Therefore they should be used in a coherent and non-ambiguous way. This ontology will be the base for the further definition of the models involved in the development of collaborative systems.

1 Introduction

The evolution of the working style of human beings and the improvements of computer technologies, in terms of communication and interaction mechanisms, have deeply altered the classical concept of Human-Computer Interaction (HCI) towards a new Human-Computer-Human Interaction and the necessity of working in collaboration with other people. These changes have produced what is known as CSCW (Computer-Supported Cooperative Work).

In order to achieve an appropriate representation of the domain problem, the specification of such systems must include how users are distributed, organized, and how they communicate, coordinate, and collaborate among them.

Software Engineering, HCI, CSCW, Sociology, Psychology, and so forth are important areas which have been traditionally involved in the study of the user and his/her interaction with computer systems. A problem arises due to this variety of research fields: the same term could be used to express different ideas in different areas of knowledge; and different terms from different areas may refer to the same

M. Redondo et al. (eds.), *Engineering the User Interface*,
DOI: 10.1007/978-1-84800-136-7_10, © Springer-Verlag London Limited 2009

concept. All in all, there is not an agreement among the different authors about the set of concepts and their subjacent abstractions.

Defining an ontology to specify concepts related with the "collaborative environment" knowledge domain provides us with a common and well-defined vocabulary, a list of terms and meanings, which describes objects and relationships among them in a formal way.

Terms such as group, actor, role or cooperative task have been previously defined in related works showing the need to formalize these abstractions. They will be briefly discussed in the related work section. The meaning of every term is not always exactly the same from one definition to another.

In this paper, we propose a solution to the lack of a common vocabulary for CSCW systems, by means of the formalization of a list of terms, defining a list of concepts around the collaborative environments knowledge domain to provide us a complete and coherent specification of the collaborative organizational structures of users in these environments.

This ontology is proposed in order to have a firm base to specify the organizational structure of the users of a collaborative system, as well as the relationships that take place among them. In this way, designers are provided with a common language to avoid ambiguities when they use such terms in the organizational structure and collaboration modelling.

The ontology presented in this work is used as a base in some diagrams we have defined to represent collaborative environments. Such diagrams support a user-centred modelling technique, which takes into account the user as a member of an interacting organization. Therefore, the user is not an isolated person, but a component of an organization. The user has some characteristics, belongs to one or more groups, plays roles, and performs cooperative tasks in order to achieve some objectives which would be unreachable in an individual way. This ontology defines the vocabulary which is used to specify this organizational structure and the relationships among the different users.

The rest of the paper remains as follows. Related work is briefly discussed in the following section. A discussion about why we have chosen ontologies rather than other techniques is presented in section 3. The concepts gathered in the ontology are defined in section 4 as a conceptual model to describe organizational structures and the human-computer-human interactions within them. Section 5 briefly describes the ontology metamodel that relates the concepts. Lastly, some conclusions about the work are presented in section 6.

2 Related Works

Actor, role, group or similar concepts are commonly used in the analysis and design of complex systems in which many and different types of users must interact with each other. For instance, these concepts are addressed in [18] who models the tasks of a workflow participant according to the four dimensions to describe work introduced in [6]. With our proposal, the study of such participants is achieved by identifying their position within the organizational structure, which helps designers to have better, clearer and more structured information about the final users of the system.

Role modeling is used as a mechanism for the separation of concerns to increase the understandability and reusability of business process models [2]. In some modeling techniques for developing groupware systems [13, 15, 19], role or actor concepts are also considered when modeling the existing collaboration among the users of a system. We propose a notation, which provides designers with a more flexible way to represent social structures and interactions. It is a view of the system that eases the design and the analysis of the users' collaborations and provides a way of classifying, organizing, and representing the roles and the groups to which the final users will belong.

When talking about agents, roles are very important in order to achieve a more expressive model. Odell argues that without considering organizational issues, designers will not be able to leverage benefits, such as emergence and scalability [10]. Thus, a superstructure specification is proposed whereby agents are classified by using these concepts.

An agent diagram is proposed in [8] to show the organization of the system according to the roles, their tasks and their relationships. These and other concepts are used in [21] to describe organizational structures -based on UML [11]- in the analysis, specification, and design of multi-agent systems.

Other works such as FOAF (Friend-Of-A-Friend) vocabulary [1] are used to express information about people and their relationships. This RDFS/OWL ontology is centred on describing people and their basic properties such as name, e-mail address, etc., rather than describing the organizational structure of the users within an organization and the cooperative tasks they perform.

Some methodological environments for designing cooperative systems, such as AMENITIES [3] or CIAM [9], take into account and define several important concepts for collaborative systems. The first one is based on tasks models and it considers dynamic issues about how users may move from playing a role to play another different role by means of a set of laws and capacities. The second one proposes four views to design the user interface in a groupware system, and defines several concepts around this kind of applications.

Such methods use these concepts to make the comprehension of the system easier, and to allow designers to know who is doing what, or what kind of features or functions a particular user performs. Our proposal makes it possible to represent the components structure of the system organization to be built. After modelling the organizational structure of the users, we suggest a graphical notation to represent the person-computer-person interactions, which provides an easy-to-grasp view of the collaborations among such users.

3 The Ontology: Why and How

Getting a common well-defined vocabulary is very important when people from different fields work together as in the case of CSCW. There are several approaches to classify and/or specify concepts related to a specific domain. In this section we describe the different methods used to formalize these concepts and we explain the solution we have adopted.

Taxonomies have been used from the beginning, probably from the classification of species in Biology. In Computer Science, this concept has been considered too simple and too fixed. Some authors defend the use of folksonomies instead of using taxonomies: *"Yes, folksonomies are interesting in contrast to taxonomies. Taxonomies limit the dimensions along which one can make distinctions, and local choices at the leaves are constrained by global categorizations in the branches. It is therefore inherently difficult to put things in their hierarchical places, and the categories are often forced"* [4].

Folksonomy [20] is a new concept associated to Web 2.0. The following definition from O'Reilly [12] shows, in a very clear way, what a folksonomy is: *"a style of collaborative categorization of sites using freely chosen keywords, often referred to as tags. Tagging allows for the kind of multiple, overlapping associations that the brain itself uses, rather than rigid categories"*.

Microformats are another new way to define and classify information [17]. Microformats are a way of thinking about data. The official definition for microformats says they are *"designed for humans first and machines second, microformats are a set of simple, open data formats built upon existing and widely adopted standards. Instead of throwing away what works today, microformats intend to solve simpler problems first by adapting to current behaviours and usage patterns"*.

Lastly, we have ontologies. This term comes from two Greek terms: *ontos* (to be), and *logos* (science, study, theory). As a branch of Philosophy, it studies the nature of being, the reality and the substance in its fundamental forms. In [7], a study about the different uses of this concept in the various research fields is pointed out, but in Computer Science it could be seen as a data model that represents a set of concepts within a domain and the relationships between those concepts. Probably, the most widely accepted definition is the following: *"An ontology is an explicit specification of a conceptualization"* [4]. The same work introduced a larger and clearer explanation about ontologies: *to support the sharing and reuse of formally represented knowledge among AI systems, it is useful to define the common vocabulary in which shared knowledge is represented. A specification of a representational vocabulary for a shared domain of discourse - definitions of classes, relations, functions, and other objects- is called an ontology.*

The definition of an ontology for some specific subjects can be very complicated, as complicated as you need. The W3C even provides a language, OWL Web Ontology Language, which is designed to be used by applications that need to process the content of information instead of just presenting information to humans [22].

In this paper, we propose a solution to the lack of a common vocabulary, by means of the formalization of a list of terms which are well defined and related between them, a list of concepts around the knowledge domain of collaborative environments to provide us a complete and coherent specification of the collaborative organizational structures of users in CSCW systems.

For this reason, the method we use to represent, define and put into relation the concepts we consider fundamental when modelling the organizational structure of the users of a CSCW system is an ontology. It is necessary to specify and associate related concepts in order to have a common vocabulary; therefore it is not essential to develop a complex ontology with such concepts. On the contrary, it is necessary, at least, to define and put into relation these concepts. Thus, the ontology to model collaborative organizational structures in CSCW systems presented in this work is considered as a set of specifications regarding essential concepts.

4 An Ontology to Describe Organizational Structures and Interactions among Collaborators within a CSCW Environment

Nowadays, software applications are more and more complex and the number of users is constantly rising. Users may be geographically distributed, running the application in a synchronous way, and collaborating to achieve common objectives. In the specification of cooperative systems, the social structure and the users' collaborations need to be taken into consideration so that the cooperative analysis can be done in depth.

In such specifications, we use some terms whose meaning could differ in different fields. Therefore, we are going to briefly explain the meaning of these terms considered in our approach.

The study of a collaborative system starts with the structure of the users that will use it. Hence, the first concept we are going to define is the *organizational structure* of the final users of the system.

Most software applications are used by different users, but not all these users have the same rights, or can use software applications in the same way. A complex application usually needs also a complex variety of final users. However, there are several types of users: users with similar features or users related between them because they share a common goal, etc. This logical structure of final users, classified by means of groups and roles, is what we mean by ***organizational structure***.

The *organizational structure* of the users is defined according to some other concepts we call *organizational items* (*group*, *role*, and *actor*) and some *organizational relationships* among them (*play*, *aggregation*, and *cooperative interaction relationships*). Items and relationships will be defined in the following subsections. Some other concepts are also taken into account, but they are not the objective of this work.

4.1 Organizational Items: Collaborators

Regarding organization, we use three concepts that we call **organizational items**: *group*, *role*, and *actor*. These items compose the *organizational structure* of the users of an organization, that is, they compose the logical structure of the users that will use a collaborative application. The organizational items are defined in such a way that they can classify, describe, and characterize such users.

In general, the concept ***collaborator*** refers to a *group*, a *role*, or an *actor*, because interactions in a collaborative application happen among them. The human-computer-human interaction takes place among *collaborators* interacting with each other to perform a cooperative task, in order to achieve a common goal.

The first *organizational item* we identify is the ***group***. A *group* is a set of individual or collective *actors* that play *roles*. It is a set of *actors* that need to work together and to collaborate in order to reach a common *group objective*. Common *group objectives* would not be reachable without such collaboration. *Groups* could also become part of other *groups*, thus, the whole organization could appear as the largest *group*.

A ***role*** is defined by the set of tasks that an actor performs. Therefore, a role can be seen as a set of actors that share the same characteristics and perform the same tasks.

An ***actor*** is one or several persons or another external system that interacts with the system. Actors directly interact within the collaborative system to accomplish individual tasks, but they can also interact with each other, through the system, to perform cooperative tasks.

A ***user*** is a person who interacts with the system, but we understand that some other elements could also interact with the system, and these elements could not be people. All the *users* are *actors*, but not all the *actors* are *users*.

It is important to note that we have defined this ontology as a base to model collaborative environments. Our modeling technique is centred on the role that users (*actors* in general) play in a system and in the collaborations among them. Therefore, isolated users do not make sense here.

An *actor* is what it is, due to the *roles* it plays. That is, an *actor* does not make sense in the system if it does not play at least a *role*. Consequently, the *task* concept is linked to the *role* concept. An *actor* does not have any *task* directly associated, but *tasks* are associated to *roles*. Thus, *actors* can perform *tasks* depending on the *roles* they play.

Table 1. Organizational Items. Example

Organizational Item	Example
Group	Researchers
Role	Research staff, Graduate fellow, Visiting fellow, Doctoral Student
Actor	Victor M. R. Penichet, Maria D. Lozano, J. Gallud

In the same way that an *actor* does not have any *task* directly associated, *actors* cannot directly belong to a *group*. Thus, *actors* belong to *groups* depending on the *roles* they play, because groups are organized with the roles needed to form that group.

Table 1 shows a simple example where there is a *group* called "researchers", four *roles*: "Research Staff", "Graduate Fellow", "Visiting Fellow", "Doctoral Student"; and some *actors* with concrete names. There are no connections among these organizational items because they are only examples about *group*, *role*, and *actor* respectively.

4.2 Organizational Relationships

Three types of organizational relationships have been defined to connect the *organizational items* (*group*, *role*, and *actor*) described in the previous sub-section. This way, the *organizational structure* of the *collaborators* in a system is composed of the organizational items and the different **organizational relationships** that we can establish among them: *play*, *aggregation*, and *cooperative interaction*. We distinguish two kinds of relationships among the *organizational items*: *structural* and *collaborative*.

On the one hand, a **structural relationship** describes dependency relationships among items, that is to say, how the items of the *organizational structure* are related to each other. We identify two *structural relationships* in our ontology: *play* and *aggregation* relationships.

Between a *role* and an *actor* playing such a *role* there is a **play relationship**. In other words, it is possible to know what the *actor* is (features) and what the *actor* can perform (*tasks*) according to the *role* it plays. An *actor* is a general *organizational item*, an entity linked to the *role* concept by means of this *play relationship*.

An **aggregation relationship** is an association between the whole and its parts. It is the traditional definition of aggregation in UML [11]. This relationship shows the elements composing every *group*. Aggregation makes sense among *groups* and their *roles*, but also with other *groups*. Since *actors* belong to *groups* by the *roles* they play, there are not *aggregation relationships* between *groups* and *actors*.

On the other hand, we identify the *cooperative interaction* as a **collaborative relationship**. A *Cooperative interaction* is a relationship that can take place between any of the *organizational items* and expresses an interaction among them.

Every kind of *organizational item* can be related with another one through a *cooperative interaction*. A *cooperative interaction* means the performance of a cooperative *task* among several *actors*, *roles*, or *groups* in order to reach a common *objective*.

In short, *play* and *aggregation relationships* define the organizational structure of the users of a system, while *cooperative interaction* specifies the collaborations within such an organizational structure.

4.3 Objectives

When large problems need to be solved, usually the "divide-and-conquer" technique is used to obtain smaller sub-problems from the first one. Such sub-problems are easier to solve. The technique we use to specify collaborative systems is based on this idea and divides the collaborative problem into three granularity levels: *organization objective*, *group objective* and *task objective*, from a bigger to a smaller level respectively.

The **organization objective** represents the largest granularity level. The *organization objective* refers to the problem to solve, that is, to the largest and the most general of the problems for which the application has been developed. The *organizational structure* of the users of the system is organized to achieve such *organization objective*.

As it was defined previously, a group is considered as a set of *actors* that need to interact together and to collaborate in order to reach a common **group objective**. Common *group objectives* would not be reachable without such collaboration among the members of the group. *Group objective* is a new concept, the following granularity level in the decomposition of problems. A *group* achieves a *group objective*, which is part of the system *organization objective*. A *group objective* is a sub-problem in which the main problem has been divided. Thus, a *group* (actually, the *actors* playing *roles* which belong to such *group*) performs the necessary *tasks* to achieve a *group objective*.

In the same way, every *group objective* is decomposed into **task objectives**, whose granularity level is the smallest one. A *task objective* is a little sub-problem which is solved by a *task*. It might be also possible to talk about atomic problems as simple as to press a button.

Therefore, an *actor* could achieve different *task objectives* performing different *tasks*. Such *tasks* could only be performed by *actors* which are playing particular *roles*. Collaboration among grouped *actors* eases the achievement of *group objectives*. When all the *group objectives* have been achieved, the general *organization objective* is also considered to be achieved.

An *actor* could participate in the achievement of several *group objectives* because it could play different *roles* within different *groups*.

4.4 Tasks

The concept of Task has been defined many times along the computer science history, thus we are not going to discuss all the possible variants. We include our concept of task in the ontology as the modelling technique we propose uses it. Another important thing to remark is that collaboration and cooperation are not exactly the same; however, we talk about cooperation and collaboration as the same in this work because of their similarity.

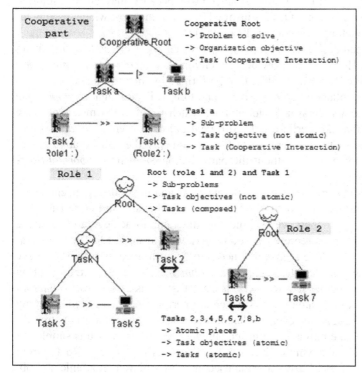

Fig. 1. *Objectives*, and *tasks* correspondence in CTT

Problem to solve	Application	Organization Objective	Tasks	Composed
Sub-problems	Sub-systems	Group and Task Objectives	and	
Atomic pieces		Task Objectives	Cooperative Interactions	Atomic

Fig. 2. Correspondences among objectives and tasks.

In the ontology proposed for collaborative environments, the concept of task is a very wide concept. A task is a piece of work required to achieve an objective. The term is so generic that we could say that there is a task, the most general and complex task from which the other tasks are daughters, whose performance solves the organization objective, that is, the main problem.

All the pieces of work are considered tasks, neither actions nor activities as in other works, only tasks. Some tasks are divided into other more specific tasks, and these into other more specific ones, and so forth. Finally, there are atomic tasks which cannot be divided into other smaller tasks because they are the solution themselves. This definition of task is inspired in one of the most widely used notations for task modelling: ConcurTaskTrees [13].

Tasks have been defined as a piece of work which is performed by *actors* in an individual way. However, as previously mentioned, the *cooperative interaction* could be considered as a cooperative task performed by different *collaborators* to reach a common collaborative *objective*. Therefore, it is clear that a *cooperative interaction* is like a general task, not atomic, which is solved by means of some other sub-tasks that are performed by different *actors* (different *collaborators*). The performance of the cooperative task (consequently the collaborative objective) would be unreachable without the participation of such *collaborators* performing the atomic *tasks*.

Fig. 1 and 2 show an example of different *tasks* and their correspondence with the *objective* concepts. The notation selected to show the tasks in Figure 1 is CTT. Figure 1 shows the cooperative and the role diagrams to achieve a cooperative work. That is the way to represent a cooperative work using CTT. The "cooperative root" is the most general *task* that needs to be performed in order to achieve the main problem, that is, the *organization objective*. Since this *task* is not an atomic one, it is decomposed in several *tasks*. "Task a" is a *cooperative interaction* decomposed in two atomic *tasks* which are performed by two *actors* playing different *roles*. "Task a" achieves a collaborative *task objective* that is not atomic.

CTT does not take into account group and actor concepts, thus this simple example does not show anything about *group objectives* or *groups*. "Root" (from role 1 and 2) and "Task 1" are also composed tasks to achieve non-atomic task objectives that solve sub-problems. The other tasks are atomic tasks performed by actors to achieve atomic task objectives that solve atomic actions just like "push a button". The "Task 1" granularity level is bigger than the "Task 3" granularity level, but smaller than the "Cooperative root" one. Therefore, "Task 1" solves a more abstract problem than "Task 3", but not so abstract and general as the "Cooperative root" one.

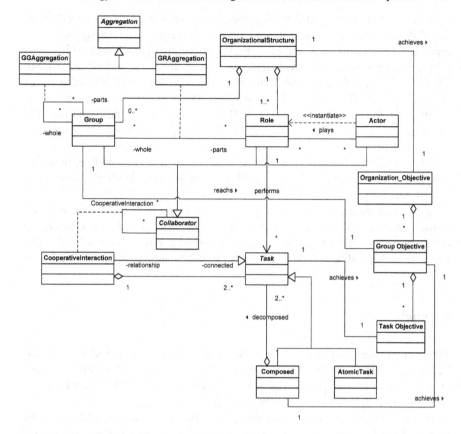

Fig. 3. Metamodel for the Organizational Structure of Collaborative Systems

5 Organizational Structures Metamodel

Once we have presented the ontology to describe organizational structures and interactions among the users of a CSCW environment, it is important to define a conceptual model where all the previously described terms fit together to constitute a metamodel from which specific models to represent real collaborative scenarios can be instantiated.

With this idea, the metamodel depicted in Fig. 3 represents the concepts, and relationships, related to the proposed ontology to describe the organizational structure of collaborative environments. The metamodel is not described in depth as the main aim of the paper is to present the ontology but not the associated metamodel. Nevertheless, we have considered including it, at least to show the next step we follow to model these environments.

Although the ontology defines the vocabulary we will use in the specification of collaborative systems, the metamodel shows the relationship among these concepts in a semi-formal way. In this way, the conceptual model from which other concrete models to represent real situations will be derived is defined using UML 2.0 [11]. We have defined several diagrams to model the organizational structure of the system (OSD, Organizational Structure Diagram), the interactions among the users of the collaborative system (CD, Collaborative Diagram) and the individual tasks users have to perform (TD, Task Diagram) among other artefacts [14].

It is important to remark that the proposed metamodel is extensible, in such a way that new concepts could be included as for instance to characterize *tasks*, *groups*, *roles*, etc.

In a collaborative system, collaborations are established to achieve concrete goals. Therefore, goals are an important issue to take into account when modelling collaborative systems. In this sense, in our metamodel, goals are considered at different levels depending on which term it is associated, as depicted in Figure 3.

6 Conclusions

This work presents an ontology and its associated conceptual model that is the base of a common and well defined vocabulary to model collaborative environments, concretely, to represent the organizational structure of the users of a system, and the collaborations established among them.

In this paper, we propose a solution to the lack of a common vocabulary by means of the formalization of a list of terms which are well defined and related among them, a list of concepts around the collaborative environments knowledge domain to provide us a complete and coherent specification of the collaborative organizational structures of users in CSCW systems.

Concepts such as group, role, actor, cooperative interaction, aggregation, play relationship, organizational structure, and so on, are key terms in the representation of this kind of environments. Due to the different definitions of these and other terms between different areas, we present this set of expressions to make the representation of the user, role, and group interactions easier. That is, the ontology defines a set of terms around the human-computer-human interactions instead of only around the human-computer interactions.

Thereby, cooperative tasks in a system can be identifying, analyzing, designing, even, if necessary, re-designing in an intuitive and explicit way.

References

1. Brickley, D., Miller, L. (2005) *FOAF Vocabulary Specification.* http://xmlns.com/foaf/0.1/,
2. Caetano, A., Silva, A. R., and Tribolet, J. (2005) *Using roles and business objects to model and understand business processes.* In Proceedings of the 2005 ACM Symposium on Applied Computing.L. M. Liebrock, Ed. SAC '05. ACM Press, New York, NY, 1308-1313
3. Garrido Bullejos, José Luis (2003) *AMENITIES: Una metodología para el desarrollo de sistemas cooperativos basada en modelos de comportamiento y tareas.* Tesis Doctoral. Granada
4. Gruber, T.R. (1993) *A translation approach to portable ontologies.* Knowledge Acquisition, 5(2):199-220.
5. Gruber, Th. (2005) *Ontology of Folksonomy: A Mash-up of Apples and Oranges.* Invited paper/keynote to the First on-Line conference on Metadata and Semantics Research (MTSR'05), November 2005
6. Marshak, R.T. (1997) *Workflow: Applying Automation to Group Processes.* In: Coleman, D. (ed.): Groupware - Collaborative Strategies for Corporate LANs and Intranets. Prentice Hall PTR, 143-181
7. McGuinness, Deborah L. (2002) *Ontologies Come of Age.* In Dieter Fensel, J im Hendler, Henry Lieberman, and Wolfgang Wahlster, editors. Spinning the Semantic Web: Bringing the World Wide Web to Its Full Potential. MIT Press,
8. Mellouli, S., Mineau, G. W., and Pascot, D. (2002) *The integrated modeling of multi-agent systems and their environment.* First international Joint Conference on Autonomous Agents and Multiagent Systems: Part 1. AAMAS '02. ACM Press, New York, , 507-508
9. Molina, A. I. (2006) *Una Propuesta Metodológica para el Desarrollo de la Interfaz de Usuario en Sistemas Groupware.* Tesis Doctoral. Universidad de Castilla-La Mancha.
10. Odell, J., Nodine, M., and Levy, R. (2005) *A Metamodel for Agents, Roles, and Groups.* Agent-Oriented Software Engineering (AOSE) V, James Odell, P. Giorgini, Jörg Müller, eds., Lecture Notes on Computer Science volume, Springer, Berlin,
11. OMG, Object Management Group. (2005) *UML Superstructure Specification,* v2.0;
12. O'Reilly, T. (2005) *What Is Web 2.0. Design Patterns and Business Models for the Next Generation of Software.* Published on O'Reilly (http://www.oreilly.com/). http://www.oreillynet.com/pub/a/oreilly/tim/news/2005/09/30/what-is-web-20.html.
13. Paterno', F. (1999) *Model-based Design and Evaluation of Interactive Applications.* F. Paternò, Springer Verlag, November 1999, ISBN 1-85233-155-0
14. Penichet, Victor M. R.; Paternò, Fabio; Gallud, J. A.; Lozano, M. (2006) *Collaborative Social Structures and Task Modelling Integration.* Proceedings DSV-IS 2006. Lecture Notes in Computer Science, Springer Verlag; I.S.B.N.: 978-3-540-69553-0. Dublin, Ireland. 27 Jul 2006
15. Pinelle, D., Gutwin, C., Greenberg, S. (2003) *Task analysis for groupware usability evaluation: Modeling shared-workspace tasks with the mechanics of collaboration.* ACM Transactions on Computer-Human Interaction (TOCHI) Volume 10 , Issue 4, Pages: 281 - 311. ISSN:1073-0516
16. Rumbaugh, J.; Jacobson, I.; Booch, G. (1999) *The Unified Modeling Language. Reference Manual.* Addison-Wesley.
17. Tantek, Ç. (2005) *Microformats.* http://tanket.com http://microformats.org.
18. Traetteberg, H. Modeling work: Workflow and Task Modeling. CADUI'99. 275-280

19. Van der Veer, G. C.; Van Welie, M. (2000) *Task based groupware design: Putting theory into practice*. In Proceedings of the 2000 Symposium on Designing Interactive Systems. New York, ACM Press, 326–337.
20. Vander Wal, Th. (2004) *Off the Top: Folksonomy.* http://www.vanderwal.net/random/category.php?cat=153.
21. Van Dyke Parunak, H. and Odell, J. (2001) *Representing social structures in UML*. In Proceedings of the Fifth international Conference on Autonomous Agents. AGENTS '01. ACM Press, New York, NY, 100-101
22. W3C. (2004) *OWL Web Ontology Language* http://www.w3.org/TR/2004/REC-owl-features-20040210/

Semantic Web Query Authoring for End-Users

Diego Moya, José A. Macías

Escuela Politécnica Superior, Universidad Autónoma de Madrid.
Ctra. de Colmenar Km. 15. 28049 Madrid.
{diego.moya, j.macias}@uam.es

1 Introduction

Generally speaking, the search for information on the web is mostly based on the documents' popularity and similarity. This significantly enhances the way to estimate the information relevance and produce successful outcome [3]. The Semantic Web can greatly help improve the search for information, mostly due to the semantic relationships that can be explicitly defined and exploited.

The Semantic Web is an evolving extension of the World Wide Web by which web content can be expressed not only in natural language, but also in a form that can be read and used by software agents, thus permitting them to find, share and integrate information more easily. It derives from the W3C director Sir Tim Berners-Lee's vision of the Web as a universal medium for data, information, and knowledge exchange. The Semantic Web features ontologies to describe the relationships between elements, which helps determine the relevance of data based on the context of use [1, 5].

In both computer and information sciences, an ontology is a data model that represents a set of concepts within a domain and the relationships between those concepts. It is used to reason about the objects within that domain. Although ontologies can be considered as a flexible and expressive notation to enhance knowledge creation and retrieval, ontology management can turn out to be a problem when a web user deals with such data representation. This is due to the fact that ontologies usually comprise high level of abstraction that users cannot afford when carrying out common information-management tasks such as creation, classification and query.

As an example, the project [9] automatically translates data structures defined in the standard MPEG7 into RDF, with the aim of annotating multimedia information. The resulting RDF graph defines an ontology that facilitates automatic reasoning. However, this vocabulary, mostly defined by experts, is inadequate for end-users in order to deal with the desired information.

The solution adopted by the software industry is focused on the use of web ontologies to build user interfaces exploiting vocabularies and tasks adapted to the user's concrete necessities. Unfortunately, this limits the user's ability to access

M. Redondo et al. (eds.), *Engineering the User Interface*,
DOI: 10.1007/978-1-84800-136-7_11, © Springer-Verlag London Limited 2009

the semantic annotation of contents, requiring the intervention of an expert programmer to define new tasks and objects.

When the user explicitly manifests the need to change the software behaviour, the expert proceeds to analyze the problem and the context of use where it appeared, with the aim of capturing complete specifications for the solution. These specifications are in turn taken up by the development team in order to build the final software which overcomes the problem reported.

End-User Development (EUD) paradigm [8] empowers users to make their own changes to software tools, significantly reducing the dependency on experts. This idea is very useful in order to present to the user a further high-level view of the system's (domain) ontology. In doing so, user actions, captured while interacting, are recorded and transformed into commands performing on the ontology. This way, automatic inference takes place on changes from concrete actions. In order to assist the user as much as possible, results are shown as feedback to the user so that s/he can interactively control the changes in an iterative process.

This book chapter describes an interface for searching and classifying ontology data included in the S5T project, which involves the creation of a search engine for a sample corpus of multimedia archives annotated with metadata [18]. The goal of this interface is for end-users to easily design relatively complex queries for the mentioned corpus by accessing its semantic model and avoiding the users to have any technical knowledge about ontologies or programming. The system incorporates EUD tools so that the user can easily handle ontological concepts and create new categories to classify content. The developing of new categories allows users to implicitly construct vocabulary to describe information. In this task, the end-user is assisted by inference algorithms which derive data types from user actions. So, in addition to a query interface, the tool supports knowledge acquisition techniques to allow for developing ontologies on demand and maintaining an acceptable trade-off between expressivity and ease of use.

The rest of the book chapter is structured as follows. Section 2 describes related work, highlighting the aspects that are mostly related to our research. Section 3 presents the visual language used by our query system, the elements composing it and the kind of both interaction and inference that it supports. Section 4 shows the system's software architecture, which is put it into the context of the S5T's search engine. Finally, Section 5 discusses conclusions and future work.

2 Related Work

Interaction design is a multidisciplinary field. Our research is inspired by previous works on *information visualization and recovery, end-user development and cognitive psychology*, among others.

2.1 Information Retrieval

Information retrieval embodies a great deal of techniques and methods intended to efficiently extract information from data sources. It is worth mentioning two end-user related techniques for information retrieval, which are *directed search* and *visual query*. Those are related to our work and will be discussed in this section.

Directed Search. Research on information retrieval has been traditionally based on keyword-based queries. Teevan [21] shows, by means of qualitative research, that personal information retrieval (particularly in non-structured information spaces) can be split up and achieved by smaller context-guided search steps, rather than by direct queries. These results agree with the work of Pirolli [17], who establishes a theoretical frame to describe information-searching strategies. The visual language of our system follows the principles proposed by Teevan for the design of search tools, as it facilitates the feature of context-based information retrieval.

Visual Queries. Visual languages are frequently used to facilitate the construction of queries by users. The goal is to facilitate the use of predefined domain concepts, as visual representations may reduce the abstraction level. Detwiler [7] proposes an interface to build queries in Protégé, an application for authoring ontologies. The concepts extracted from the ontology are combined to make up phrases in a subject-verb-object format used by RDF. Baeza-Yates [2] proposes a visual representation of queries by achieving pattern-matching on the hierarchical structure of an XML document, visually represented by nested boxes. Both interfaces are intended to navigate through the whole ontology using a tree-like visualization. Our proposal does not assume any predefined structure for the navigation. Each concept is represented with a label that can be freely positioned on the screen, and it shows only parts of the ontology that are meant to be relevant within the current context.

2.2 Knowledge Building

As indicated in the related bibliography, knowledge construction can be successfully applied to user-interface modelling in order to carry out a real end-user approach. Sometimes, this implies to reduce the implicit expressiveness of the resulting application to increase the final ease of use. In this section, we discuss such issues and relate them to our work.

Modelling. Recent research used uniform representations to model personal information in PIM (*Personal Information Management*) applications with the aim of managing information by means of a reduced set of homogenous tools [20]. These environments combine structured information together with free-format one (without structure). Although this representation is difficult to be automatically processed, it is easier to be exported to different applications as well as stored and manipulated by generic tools. Translating data into a uniform representation makes it easier to automate.

Völkel [22] proposes an annotated *Wiki* environment that offers a smooth transition between the syntactic, structural and semantic levels of the information models. Jones [10] utilizes labels to represent documents and store them as concepts; the labels allow for connecting documents and storing them in a hierarchical structure. Our work uses the same label metaphor, but originates from a different idea. In our system, labels are bidirectional connections that also allow browsing the reverse path from concrete instances of objects to the semantic information stored in the hierarchy.

The existing low-level granularity is probably the major shortcoming of these previous works, as they allow metadata annotation only for complete documents. By contrast, our labels can annotate specific elements within a document and hence leverage these premises.

End-User Development. End-User Development (EUD) is a set of techniques or activities that support the creation and modification of software artefacts by people with little or no knowledge in programming [6], [8]. This paradigm is based on user-centred techniques to make the use and understanding of the system easy, as well as on machine learning techniques such as Programming by Example (PBE), which supports the creation of software from examples that end-users provide to the system, thus avoiding the user to deal with programming and specification languages [11]. EUD systems analyze user actions, generalize the acquired knowledge and apply it automatically to similar tasks, avoiding achieving repetitive patterns. In our system, a similar method is used for the knowledge creation: the system extrapolates the attributes which define a collection from a set of elements provided by the user.

Burnett [4] shows that including semantic-level affirmations in EUD systems radically increases the correctness and efficiency when developing software artefacts. In our interface, each association of semantic label implies an "is-a" relation, which is an explicit assertion of the user about the data.

Miller [15] discusses an inference algorithm that learns the syntactic structure of a text and predicts multiple selections of text fragments to perform simultaneous "edit" actions. Our interface carries out inference on data types from collections of elements, although it would benefit from a model of interaction based on a similar algorithm for multiple selections and editions as well.

Model-Based User Interfaces (MBUI) paradigm enables the specification of the different conceptual levels by which a user interface can be represented [16]. When defining a user interface in a declarative way, Puerta [19] identifies the *mapping problem* between different levels of abstraction. Macías [12] presents a mechanism of reverse engineering that builds a semantic model representing the changes on the interface, taking into account the user's actions and the domain information.

Initially, the MBUI paradigm was based on concrete ad-hoc specification languages. Later on, these languages converged with the technology of the Semantic Web to obtain further expressiveness in the representation of domain data and the specification of services and applications, as well as a better integration among such issues.

3 A Visual Language for Querying and Authoring Ontologies

The visual language is one of the most important points when designing a direct-manipulation interactive system. In our work, we have carried out a trade-off between expressiveness and ease of use by means of designing a visual language which enhances interaction with users and provides suitable mechanisms to carry out inference and data integrity.

3.1 Elements of the Visual Language

Fig. 1 shows a schema of the interface used for manipulating visual elements in our system. The main aim is to represent elements intended to build queries and classify data using direct manipulation. Semantic Labels are exploited to represent metadata, and query bars show the definition of an ontology concept keeping a low abstraction level. More precisely, a RSS feed based on news from The New York Times is annotated with semantic labels that show some metadata of the items in the feed. Labels allow the user to explore the semantic structure of the content and extract collections of similar elements, all without having to read the underlying XML description of the news. Each label has a query bar that presents the metadata of the labelled object and shows a collection of all related objects.

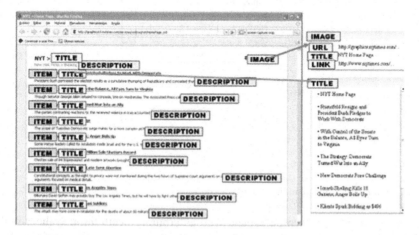

Fig. 3. The user interface used for manipulating visual elements in our system

Semantic Labels. The user can freely label any individual or grouping of objects contained in our system. The left part of Fig. 1 shows the labels "Title", "Description", "Item" and "Image" in different entries of an RSS feed. The names and positions of these semantic labels are extracted from the tags of the XML-feed description, which can be polled by applications, affiliate websites or systems using other languages, such as C++, Perl, .NET, etc., to display the information in XML readable format.

Each semantic label represents a concept of the ontology, and is used as an access point to the metadata of any labelled object. An information column called Query Bar can arise from any visible label. This shows the definition of the concept associated to the list of the data that belong to the same class.

Attaching a label to an object has a deliberately ambiguous meaning: it symbolizes either that the object belongs to the class defined by the label or that the concept represented by the label is an attribute of the object. This ambiguity facilitates the labelling process to the user, as s/he does not need to be aware of the precise and formal semantic aspects of the tool. The disambiguation task is accomplished by inference algorithms and is based on the context of use.

Query Bar. Query bars contain forms with search parameters and object lists with the search results. Since each query bar is equated with a concept, the search form can be meant as the definition of the class represented by the related semantic label, and the object list as the instances of the class. Also, the query bar acts as both a search interface and an ontology browser. Attributes defining the class are automatically inferred by an appropriate data-based inference algorithm when the label is assigned to one or several objects. The object list gives access to the object's inferred attributes and the attribute values, thus enabling users to explore the metadata definitions of objects related in the domain.

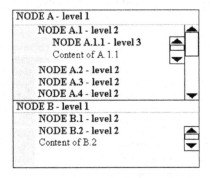

Fig. 4. Hierarchical structure of the ontology graph

The ontology graph can be expanded to an arbitrary depth through the visual object-list component, which offers functionality similar to a *treeview* widget. Its hierarchical structure is depicted in Fig. 2, where the lower part of a query bar is the Objects List, a visual component that enumerates all the instances of the class defined by the semantic label. It can be seen as the result of the query defined by the class attributes. The object list shows a hierarchy where each node contains a collection of related semantic labels. The headers containing node names can be collapsed or expanded to show the attributes associated to the object

As an example, Fig. 3 shows a Macromedia Flex [13] implementation with real data. In this example, a new class is defined by attaching the labels "Name", "Price" and "Image" to several parts of a product, and by creating a new label "Product" to group all parts. The type-based inference is focused on the labels that the user has previously provided in order to define the "Purchase" class. Any on-screen object assigned by metadata can be labelled. In the virtual store of the example, we have labelled the data "Image", "Name" and "Price" of the product at the left, and we have assigned the label "Purchase" to that list of labels. By opening the query bar associated to the label "Purchase", the search engine locates other objects having the same attributes. The query definition can be edited to build a new list containing objects that match the modified attributes (1). Individual data objects can be extracted from the result (2). Data-flow dependencies appear while navigating through the meta-data, so that the user can see and access the data definitions at any time

The first levels of nodes correspond to the database objects satisfying the current class definition. Each node contains the values of the metadata instances, and can be expanded to show the attributes of the object. The headers act themselves as semantic labels that can be expanded to show new query bars, representing the metadata in the ancestor nodes. When a node is expanded, the content is shown in a rectangular region in order to maximize the visual space. Nodes contain a sequence of attributes and values that are shown in the same interface. The object list offers larger clickable areas than a *treeview*, and nodes in level 1 are always present onscreen - whereas in a *treeview* the shallowest nodes are located out of the vision-area when the deepest nodes are expanded.

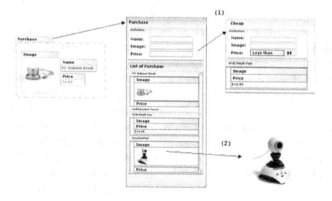

Fig. 3. Implementation with real data

3.2 Interaction

Navigation. Semantic labels act as bidirectional hyperlinks. This is a key point to ensure the ease of use while addressing the concepts in the ontology. From any visible label, the users have access to the object definition and the query bar by which labelled data can be retrieved. Objects found while navigating can be dragged to the work area. They can be expanded to directly work on them and their metadata. This mechanism associates abstract concepts to instances of a concept, therefore reducing the cognitive load of the ontology by also reducing the abstraction gap. The idea of "class" or "metadata" is mapped to a collection of concrete objects. Each semantic label can be used as a symbol that represents the associated data collection.

Knowledge Building. The simplest way to define new classes is to type the corresponding keywords in the search forms. As values are supplied to the class-definition attributes, the objects list is updated to reflect the items that agree with the query. Since a class corresponds to a collection, the updated list corresponds indeed to a different class of data.

Once created, a new label is attached to the class. This can be stored for later reuse, acting as a link to the new class. It is possible to assign the label to different objects, adding them to the objects collections that belong to the class. Also, when a query is generated, a label can represent the collection considered as input to an operator in an expression. This mechanism helps to manage knowledge, building it as well as possible in most common user tasks, instead of requiring a separate activity to generate knowledge. This way, writing queries provides a user-designed vocabulary adapted to the information domain.

Queries. As mentioned earlier, queries can be used to create new classes and retrieve content from the knowledge base. They are constructed by visually manipulating labels in the definition area of the class, in order to create a description of the desired data. User can write expressions in Attribute-Value, Attribute-Range and Subject-Relation-Object forms. Complex queries can be constructed by adding or removing attributes, typing an attribute name or dragging a semantic label to the definition area. Attributes and values can be user-defined classes or concepts taken from the ontology.

For example, Fig. 4 depicts a query used to search for the last openings of Jazz music. Defining a class is achieved by composing concepts from the ontology (represented by semantic labels) in the query construction process. The list of objects in the query bar is updated to show the objects corresponding to the new definition. In the definition area of the class [SONGS], an attribute [RELEASE DATE] is included. A restriction on its value is added by means of the labels [AFTER] and [LAST MONDAY], both extracted from the ontology. A second attribute is specified by labels [MUSIC GENRE] and [EQUAL TO] [JAZZ]. As long as conditions are added to the query, the list is updated to reflect the objects of type SONG that contain attributes [RELEASE DATE] and [MUSIC GENRE] with values satisfying the restrictions.

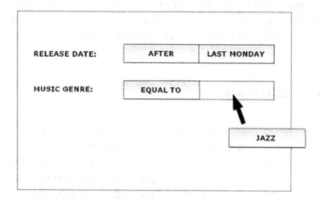

Fig. 4. A sample query to search for the last openings of Jazz music

When opening the query bar associated to a label, the search algorithm recovers all the objects manually associated with the label in addition to the objects with attributes matching the class description. This includes objects belonging to the class and also those where the label represents an attribute or relation corresponding to the labelled object. When this is done, all the related information will appear when navigating through the collections.

This kind of manipulation allows users to define queries based on examples. Instead of building a query from an empty form, the user can label an object similar to the one s/he wants, helping her/him find others that match the description. This also improves the information retrieval process, as objects labelled in previous sessions can be easily located by their corresponding semantic labels.

Inference Control. Inference is utilized to create definitions for new classes by generalizing common object properties that are associated to same-name labels. Whenever a new instance is associated to an existing class, the data-type inference algorithm is activated. This way the system shows the user the minimal changes to the definition that would be necessary to include in the new object as a member of the class. The user is given the option to accept those changes, thus altering the definition of the class. If s/he explicitly rejects the changes, the system infers that the new labelled object does not belong to the class. In this case, the semantic label is assigned to other possible meanings (i.e. the concept represented by the label is an attribute of the object). The user can also choose to ignore the suggestions, thus maintaining the ambiguity.

The advantage of this mechanism is such that when the user finds an error in the automatic class definition, s/he can either correct the inference by changing the explicit definition or attempt to improve the generalization by adding new examples to the class. This is quite a common practice in most PBE environments, where the user can add new knowledge to the system without explicit use of programming languages.

The proposed interaction mechanisms support several inference algorithms, where the input is the label and the metadata of the labelled object, and the output is the list of attributes and restrictions composing the definition of the class.

4 System Architecture

Fig. 5 shows the modular architecture of our system, where the user ontology along with semantic annotations are used to store, evolve and produce sophisticated knowledge to reason about. To this end, a user with no programming-in-query-language skills can freely manipulate high-level representations of knowledge obtained from previous queries or directly from scratch. The system analyses the user's actions on domain information, which is automatically updated and maintained by the system from one session to another. The user can carry out graphical queries by a simple visual language that the system automatically transforms into an XML query-like representation to be processed by the underlying ontological engine. The data obtained from the query execution is processed later on to obtain feedback and update the visual information in the environment, in order for the end-user to compose far more expressive queries visually. Such an evolutionary approach supplies feasible customization of user queries, helping to extract sophisticated media knowledge from our system with the minimum effort. We based on cutting-edge End-User Development techniques such as PBE, automatically generalizing programmatic output from examples that the user provides to the system. Our Programming by Example techniques allow for inferring the user's intent in real interaction with domain objects at the visual level, with the aim of both visualizing and extracting information easily.

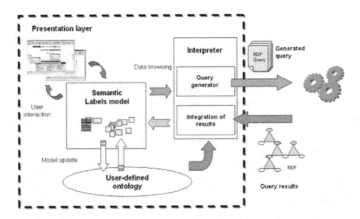

Fig. 5. Schema of our high-level tool.

The search engine provides a detailed ontology specifically created for the content. Users can easily describe the domain objects, and the interface visualizes the query results by using tokens from the user-defined ontology which is created from equivalent terms retrieved from the corpus.

In our work, it is first and foremost a concern to provide end-users with the ability to query and visualize the existing knowledge available in our ontological media repository. To this end, we propose a low-abstraction-level WYSIWYG authoring tool supporting end-user-intended inference and automatic customization of information retrieval. Such a tool lies on the basis of a far more complex environment (see Fig. 6), which comprises a complete audio annotation and management system to deal with multimedia information extracted from a Spanish news media group.

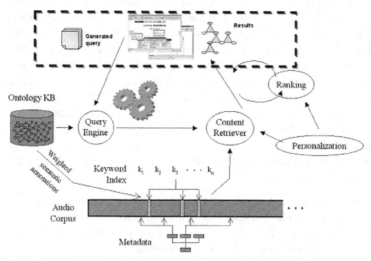

Fig. 6. The S5T Project, which includes the presented query authoring tool at the top

As shown in Fig. 6, our query tool is part of the S5T project, which addresses the problem of multimedia corpus annotation, management and retrieval by means of metadata. Our tool lies on the basis of an underlying ontology system, where the audio is extracted and automatically annotated. This information is used in turn to carry out a ranking of the information that will be finally queried by means of the tool we have presented. The source information comprises an audio core of media data extracted from a radio channel. This information is automatically processed and annotated and, in turn, an ontology is built in order to codify semantic information about the media pieces that will be stored in the ontology knowledge base. The ontology system deals with the ontology knowledge base and executes specialized algorithms for properly sorting and ranking the information. By means of the high-level query tool, end-users can query the information stored on the ontology knowledge base and so obtain the information from the audio core easily. As we mentioned earlier, the queries are the output of our tool whereas the query results, which are sent back from the underlying ontology system, are one of the inputs for our system. Nevertheless, the query tool is responsible for maintaining the domain model and the user ontology which are managed by the interface itself, also combining semantics from the query results to enrich the user interaction at the interface part and deploy meaningful information to improve the PBE inference algorithms.

5 Conclusions

This book chapter introduces a query system to help to meet knowledge management and end-user techniques, unifying search and classification through the use of metadata. The main contributions are the representation of metadata by *Semantic Labels*, and a visual language that allows the user to review and correct automatically inferred definitions. By exposing the user to data types, errors in the inference process can be corrected, providing the user with control over it.

Another novelty is the control of the ambiguity, enabling maintaining relationships partially defined. The semantic labels have an ambivalent relation with labelled objects. The user can decide either to solve this ambiguity or not. This increases flexibility in the use of labels in order to define concepts, and relaxes the restrictions when assigning a label through direct manipulation.

Our system's behaviour satisfies the design criteria of [21], which can be summarized as follows:

1. Search results are in the context defined by their associated labels and show the values of the attributes that define the class.
2. The results explicitly labelled in the past are considered as relevant at the present for evolving and improving inference.
3. The incremental refinement of the search is guaranteed.

Our design is aimed at simplifying the user's mental model by reducing the distance between the abstract concepts and the concrete examples.

The main goal of the inference mechanisms is the formulation of queries for data corpus, although combined with End User Development we have created an environment that provides support to activities such as directed navigation, knowledge classification and information recovery. The creation of simpler tools for the Semantic Web is a key point today. This will definitely allow people with no technical training to add knowledge, develop and create new functionality with the minimum effort.

Semantic labels provide the basis for the definition of information architectures for a Web site. Additionally, query bars can act as customizable search tools intended for end-user. All together, these mechanisms would allow users to address the management of contents and functionality, providing an essential support in the creation of end-user-oriented authoring tools for the Semantic Web.

As for future work, we are planning to carry out an empirical study of the tool usage with the aim of verifying its real utility and capability to capture the user's intent by analyzing the knowledge representation produced. Besides, it would be interesting to investigate the collaborative development of ontologies by end-users by means of label aggregation, as in *folksonomies* [14] (emergent vocabularies). We also intend to carry out an experiment with real users consisting in carrying out several query tasks and then evaluating the user's perception by means of a questionnaire. This will provide us with enough information to study the usability and ease of use of the proposed system and corroborate the theoretical explanations here presented.

Acknowledgments   The work reported in this book chapter has been partially supported by the Spanish Ministry of Science and Education in the National Program of Computer Science Technologies, project number TIN2005-06885.

References

1. Aleman-Meza B, Halaschek C, Arpinar I. B, Sheth A. (2003) Context-Aware Semantic Association Ranking. First International Workshop on Semantic Web and Databases, Berlin, Germany, 7-8 September 33-50
2. Baeza-Yates R, Barrera C, Herskovic V. (2005) Lenguaje de Consulta Visual para XML y Visualización de Resultados vía Fisheye Trees. Interacción
3. Brin S, Page L. (1998) The Anatomy of a Large-Scale Hypertextual Web Search Engine. In Proc. 7th International World Wide Web Conference
4. Burnett M, Cook C, Pendse O, Rothermel G, Summet J, Wallace C. (2003) End-user software engineering with assertions in the spreadsheet paradigm. In ICSE'03, Proceedings of the 25 International Conference on Software Engineering, Portland, OR, 3-10 May 93-103
5. Chirita P A, Ghita S, Nejdl W, Paiu R. (2005) Semantically Enhanced Searching and Ranking on the Desktop. L3S Research Center / University of Hanover Deutscher Pavillon, Expo Plaza 1 30539 Hanover, Germany
6. Cypher A, Kosbie D, Maulsby D. (1993) Characterizing PBD systems, in Watch What I Do: Programming by Demonstration, (A. Cypher, ed.), MIT Press, Cambridge, MA
7. Detwiler L T, Rosse C, Shapiro L G: An Intuitive Graphical Query Interface for Protégé Knowledge Bases. In Proceedings, 7th International Protégé Conference, Bethesda, MD (2004)
8. EUD-NET. Network of Excellence on End-User Development. http://giove.cnuce.cnr.it/EUD-NET
9. García R, Celma O. (2005) Semantic Integration and Retrieval of Multimedia Metadata. Presented at the 5th Knowledge Markup and Semantic Annotation Workshop, SemAnnot. Unpublished.
10. Jones W, Munat C F, Bruce H, Foxley A. (2005) The Universal Labeler: Plan the Project and Let Your Information Follow, paper accepted for inclusion at ASIST
11. Lieberman H: Your Wish is my Command. Programming By Example. Morgan Kaufmann Publishers. Academic Press, USA (2001).

12.Macías J A, Puerta Ángel R, Castells P. (2006) Model-Based User Interface Reengineering. HCI Related Papers of Interacción 2004. Jesús Lorés y Raquel Navarro (eds.). Springer-Verlag Volume 155-162

13.Macromedia Flex. http://www.adobe.com/go/gnavtray_prod_flex_home

14.Mathes A. (2004) Folksonomies – cooperative classification and communication through shared metadata. Computer Mediated Communication, Dec

15.Miller R C, Myers B C. (1999) Lightweight Structured Text Processing. In Proceedings of USENIX

16.Paternò F. (1999) Model-Based Design and Evaluation of Interactive Applications. Springer Verlag.

17.Pirolli P, Card S K. (1999) Information Foraging. Psychological Review, 106 (4). 643-675.

18.Proyecto S5T. (2005) Búsqueda Semántica Personalizada y Escalable de Contenidos de Texto y Habla en la Web Semántica. Financiado por el MEC en el Programa Nacional de Tecnologías Informáticas, TIN2005-06885

19 Puerta A, Eisenstein J. (1999) Towards a General Computational Framework for Model-Based Interface Development Systems. Proceedings of IUI 171-178

20 Quan D, Huynh D, Karger D R. (2003) Haystack: A Platform for Authoring End User Semantic Web Applications. In ISWC

21.Teevan J, Alvarado C, Ackerman M S, Karger D R. (2004) The perfect search engine is not enough: a study of orienteering behavior in directed search. In CHI '04: Proc. of the SIGCHI conf. on Human factors in computing systems. ACM 415-422

22.Völkel M, Oren E. (2005) Personal Knowledge Management with Semantic Wikis. Technical Report, AIFB Karlsruhe. December 2005.

A Methodological Approach for Building Multimodal Acted Affective Databases

Juan Miguel López, Idoia Cearreta, Nestor Garay-Vitoria, Karmele López de Ipiña, Andoni Beristain·

Laboratory of Human-Computer Interaction for Special Needs (LHCISN). University of the Basque Country.
{juanmi, idoia.cearreta, nestor.garay}@ehu.es

Computational Intelligence Group. University of the Basque Country.
isplopek@vc.ehu.es

Innovae Visión, L.C.
beristainandoni@yahoo.es

1 Introduction

Human beings are eminently emotional, as their social interaction is based on the ability to communicate their emotions and perceive the emotional states of others [1]. Affective computing is a discipline that develops devices for detecting and responding to users' emotions. Within affective computing, affective mediation uses computer-based technology which enables the communication between two or more people displaying their emotional states [2, 3]. In last years, the number of applications related to these two research areas is growing [4].

The main objective of affective computation is to capture and process affective information with the aim of enhancing the communication between the human and the computer. Within affective computing, affective mediation uses a computer-based system as an intermediary among the communication of certain people, reflecting the mood the interlocutors may have [3]. Affective mediation tries to minimize the filtering of affective information carried out by communication devices, due to the fact they are usually devoted to the transmission of verbal information and therefore, miss nonverbal information [5]. There are also other applications in this type of mediated communication, for example, textual telecommunication (affective electronic mail, affective chats, etc.).

It is remarkable that, in areas such as assistive technology, research is making it possible for people with special needs, mainly disabled people, to communicate, work, and perform daily activities that they were not able to perform efficiently and autonomously before the existence of these technological aids. Within assistive technology, Augmentative and Alternative Communication (AAC) research field is used to describe additional ways of helping people who find it hard to communicate by speech or writing. However, in the specific area of communica-

M. Redondo et al. (eds.), *Engineering the User Interface*,
DOI: 10.1007/978-1-84800-136-7_12, © Springer-Verlag London Limited 2009

tion, affective communication is an aspect that has received little attention from assistive technology researchers.

In the development of affective applications, affective resources, such as affective databases, are a good chance for training such applications, either for affective recognition or either for affective synthesis. Lang [6] proposed three systems involved in the expressions of emotions: Subjective or verbal information (reports on emotions perceived and described by users); Conductal expressions (facial and postural expressions and speech paralinguistic parameters, etc.); Psychophysiological responses (such as heart rate, galvanic skin response (GSR), etc.). Therefore, affective resources are often multimodal and they usually record images, sounds, texts, etc.

In this paper the procedure used to build an affective multimodal and bilingual database is described. It is multimodal because it stores several modalities that include conductal expressions (facial images and spoken utterances with different values of paralinguistic parameters) and verbal information (the semantics of the utterances is taken into account). It is bilingual because it stores sentences in Spanish and in Basque, the two official languages in the country the involved researchers are working. These researchers have found most of the affective resources in the literature are devoted to other languages (such as English) and they have found there is a need for developing this type of resources for Spanish and Basque –especially for Basque, due to the scope this particular language has. The resources have been obtained recording acted material, using both professional actors and amateurs.

On the following pages, a revision of the effort devoted to developing affective resources is presented. Next, RekEmozio database and its recording process are described. Finally, some remarks are mentioned and some future works that are taking place referred.

2 Related Work

Cowie and colleagues made a wide review on affective databases [7]. In this article it is mentioned that most technological research on emotion continues to be based on recordings of actors, skilled or unskilled. However, there are good reasons to move away from uncritical reliance on acted data, and that has been a major topic in recent database work. There have also been some references that naturalistic data seem an ideal alternative to acted sources, but the reality is not so straightforward. Problems of copyright and privacy are well recognized [8]. More fundamental, but less often noted, is the fact that key tools needed to deal with naturalistic data are still underdeveloped. They also note that between acting and pure naturalism lie various emotion induction techniques [7].

Cowie and colleagues also express that one of the key difficulties for database research is that induction remains an uncertain art, seriously complicated by ethical issues. Anyway, in the appendix of their article they give a list of affective databases and their characteristics [7].

Some of the applications to be developed starting from databases are enhancing human judgment of emotion in situations where objectivity and accuracy are required. These applications cover embedding affective systems in automatic tutoring applications, or game and entertainment industry [9], or even enhancing the quality of the messages composed by AAC systems. There are also studies about using artificial entities (such as animated avatars or autonomous robots) in order to validate affective models and systems trying to solve ethical problems [10].

Most references found in literature are related to English. Other languages have less resources developed, specially the ones with a relatively low number of speakers. This is the case of Basque. To the authors' knowledge, the first affective database in Basque is the one presented by [11]. These authors have developed a database of 130 stimuli of acted speech using neutral texts and texts semantically related with six basic emotions: Anger, Disgust, Fear, Joy, Sadness and Surprise. In Spanish, the work of [12] can be emphasized. They developed an initial corpus with 336 speeches in which 8 actors simulated seven basic emotions (Happiness, Desire, Anger, Fear, Surprise, Sadness and Disgust).

A non-exhaustive list of acted affective databases and their characteristics can be showed in Table 1. Following instructions provided by [8], three of the five main issues have been considered in this table:

- Scope: characteristics such as language, description given of emotions, and the number of subjects or actors have been defined.
- Naturalness: characteristics such as whether semantics of the speech is taken into account or not, the material used in the database, and whether the same text has been used expressed in different emotions or not.
- Context: modality of the resource has been defined.

In the next section we are presenting RekEmozio affective database: the procedure to obtain it and the characteristics and features it has.

3 RekEmozio Database

3.1 Database Description

RekEmozio database is created with the aim of serving as an information repository to perform research on user emotions. RekEmozio database lies on data acquired through user interaction, metadata used to describe and label each interaction, and provides access to the data stored and the faculty of performing transactions over them, so new information can be added to the database by analysing the data within. As most existing affective resources are composed only of data, our aim when building RekEmozio resource has been to add descriptive information about the performed recordings, so processes such as extracting speech parameters and video features may be done lately on them. Members of different work groups involved in research projects related to RekEmozio have access on it and have performed several speech and video feature extracting processes. This information has been lately added to the database.

Table 1. Several affective databases and their characteristics found in the literature.

	SCOPE			NATURALNESS			CONTEXT
Reference	Language	Description given of emotions	Number of subjects (male/female)	Semantically meaningful content	Material	Same text per emotion	Mode
[13]	Danish	neutral, surprise, happiness, sadness, anger	4	No	13 utterances	Yes	Audio
[11]	Standard Basque	anger, disgust, fear, joy, sadness and surprise + neutral	1	Combined	130 utterances	Yes	Audio
[14]	Japanese	anger, joy and sadness	2 (1/1)	Yes	73 texts	No	Audio
[12]	Spanish	desire, disgust, fury, fear, joy, surprise, sadness	8 (4/4)	No	336 utterances	Yes	Audio
[15]	English	happiness, sadness, anger and fear + normal	5	No	1250 utterances	Yes	Audio
[16]	Russian	surprise, happiness, anger, sadness and fear + neutral	61 (12/49)	No	3660 utterances	Yes	Audio
[17]	Chinese	anger, fear, joy, sadness	9 female	No	288 utterances	Yes	Audio
[18]	English	four classes: joy/pleasure, sorrow/ sadness/ grief, anger, normal/ neutral	6	No	4800 utterances	Yes	Audio

[19]	German	anger, fear, boredom, happiness, sadness, disgust, neutral	10 (5/5)	Nonsense texts and normal everyday sentences	about 800 utterances	Yes	Audio
[20]	English	anger, happiness, sadness and neutral	1 female	Combined	357 utterances	No	Audio
[21]	Finnish.	happiness/joy, sadness and anger + neutral	14 (8/6)	Combined	a text of 120 words in neutral and 56 monologues reflecting basic emotions	No	Audio
[22]	German	hot anger, cold anger, anxiety, boredom, contempt, disgust, elation, panic fear, happiness, interest, pride, sadness, shame, despair	12 (6/6)	Neutral	2 semantically neutral sentences (nonsense sentences composed of phonemes from Indo-European languages) 1,344 voice samples	Yes	Audio-Visual (visual info used to verify listener judgments of emotion)
[23]	Italian	happiness, surprise, fear, sadness, anger and disgust, + neutral	8 (4/4)	?	1,008 short video clips (utterance and non-utterance)	?	Audio-Visual
[24]	Spanish	sadness, happiness, anger + neutral	1	Neutral	3 passages (4 or 5 long sentences per passage), 15 short sentences and 30 isolated words.	Yes	Audio

[25]	Chinese	neutral, happy, sadness, fear, anger, surprise and disgust	42 (18/24)	Combined	Laboratory recordings (15 neutral sentences, 15 non-neutral sentences, 2 passages for each non-neutral emotion) and extracts from movies and broadcast programmes.	No	Audio-Visual

Following instructions provided by [8], a multimodal affective resource can be described considering five main issues: scope, naturalness, context, descriptors and accessibility. These issues are considered in this section.

3.1.1 Scope

For audio recordings, professional and amateur actors were asked to speak both semantically meaningful and non-meaningful sentences in a concrete given emotion. For video recording, actors were asked to perform transitions from a neutral emotion to a concrete emotion, and then back to a neutral emotion. All actors received financial support for their cooperation. The scope of RekEmozio database is summarized in Table 2. "(pr./am.)" indicates that data about professional actors are expressed before the slash character and amateur actors' data after that character.

A categorical classification of emotions was used. Seven emotions were used: the six basic emotions described by [26], that is, Sadness, Fear, Joy, Anger, Surprise and Disgust; and a Neutral emotion. This number of emotions has been chosen because in their work, [26] suggest these emotions are universal for all cultures, which is interesting considering the bilingualism of RekEmozio database.

Table 2. Summary of RekEmozio database scope for acted recordings

Language	Type	Number of Actors (pr./am.)	Gender (pr./am.)	Average age (pr./am.)	Standard deviation (pr./am.)	Emotions
Basque	Contextualized acting	7/2	4/2 male, 3/0 female	31.28/27.0	5.15/0	Sadness, Fear, Joy, Anger, Surprise, Disgust; and Neutral
Spanish		10/10	5/5 male, 5/5 female	30.7/27.25	4.08/1.25	
Overall		17/12	9/7 male, 8/5 female	30.94/27.12	4.40/0.62	

3.1.2 Naturalness

Way of collecting material
Acted voice and images.

Material

Professional actors

(a) Audio in both languages (Spanish and Basque):
   For each of the seven emotions described above they used:

- Five semantically meaningful words and five non-meaningful words related to the given emotion. As non-semantically meaningful words were repeated in all emotions, 40 different words were used, but actors performed 70 recordings over them.
- Three sentences semantically related to the given emotion and three non-meaningful sentences. As non-semantically meaningful sentences were repeated in all emotions, 24 different sentences were used, but actors performed 42 recordings over them.
- Three semantically meaningful paragraphs related to the given emotion and three non-meaningful paragraphs. As non-semantically meaningful paragraphs were repeated in all emotions, 24 different paragraphs were used, but actors performed 42 recordings over them.

   Therefore, there are 88 different speeches with 154 recordings over them for each actor.

   Used paragraphs and sentences were built by using a group of words extracted from an emotional dictionary in Spanish (1987 words dictionary with nouns, adjectives, verbs and interjections). This emotional dictionary is built over words contained in [27] database. This database stores 95383 words taken from the Royal Spanish Language Academy Dictionary [28]. Most frequent words were selected, and only the most frequent 2358 were taken into account. Within these words, nouns, adjectives, verbs and interjections have been chosen to obtain a 1987 words emotional dictionary. For creating sentences and paragraphs for Re-kEmozio database, words from the emotional dictionary were labelled with the seven different emotions used with the assistance of words from ANEW [29]. As each word in ANEW has an associated value according to valence, arousal and dominance dimensions, by knowing where the emotions used were located according to those three dimensions [30], their corresponding emotion category was identified. Semantically meaningful paragraphs and sentences were built from this group of words, as for the non-semantically meaningful ones using words with the "neutral" label. The 40 words used in the recordings were obtained from this group of labelled words. On the other hand, Spanish texts were translated in order to obtain Basque texts.

The actors were asked to speak each word, sentence and paragraph with a given emotion and the resulting audio files were recorded.

(b) Video:

Until a three dimensional recording would be desirable, taking into account the cost, complexity and massive data storage, a different approach was chosen. Videos were taken from front and left lateral views of the actor's face. This way, location and possible deformations, rotations and translations of all facial features relevant to emotional analysis were recovered.

There are two main ways for an actor to perform a given emotion [7]. The first one is based on applying stimuli on him/her, so that it makes the emotion appear naturally. This is the best way to obtain a real emotional recording, but ethical implications related to producing affective states such as Sadness or Fear made us discard this approach. That is why a second way has been chosen: imitation. In this approach, actors were asked to imitate a certain facial expression, or at least to take them as an inspiration or departure point to perform each recording.

The procedure used lied on indicating the actor what emotion to perform and showing a visual aid in form of images from [26] database and asking the actor to try to reproduce them by imitation. For each emotion the subject was asked to initially keep a neutral state (without any expression) for around five seconds. Then, the subject had to slowly perform six consecutive transitions from a neutral state to the one corresponding to the given emotion (and back to the neutral state) and remaining between one and two seconds in both neutral and emotion-related facial features.

Amateur actors

(a) Audio in both languages (Spanish and Basque):

Per emotion, the actors were asked to speak a set of three words, sentences and paragraphs from previously defined texts with a given emotion and the resulting audio files were recorded.

(b) Video:

Using the procedure described before, the subject were asked to slowly perform three consecutive transitions from the neutral state to the one corresponding to the given emotion (and back to the neutral state) while remaining between one and two seconds in both neutral and emotion-related facial features.

3.1.3 Context

- Semantic context: As it has been described in the "Material" subsection, seven possible emotional intonations were combined with the semantic content of the given words, sentences and paragraphs
- Structural context: Texts with different length (words, sentences and paragraphs).
- Intermodal context: Audio and video were recorded separately.
- Temporal context: Single words, sentences and paragraphs were used with the aim of later studying the influence of certain speech parameters (such as rhythm, volume, length, tone...) and the temporal pattern of emotional expression in the audio files were collected.

3.1.4 Descriptors

- Psychological encoding: Categorical approach has been used to code recordings by using the seven emotions described above.
- Demographic encoding: Demographic data about the participating actor with parameters that can be valuable when analyzing speech and facial features such as the age, smoker/non-smoker, native tongue and expressivity.

3.1.5 Accessibility

The Wav format was used for storing the audio recordings, as it is a format with no data compression or data loss. This decision was made because formats with data compression lose accuracy when analyzing audio signals from the audio recordings. The only challenge in using Wav format is that massive hard drives must be used with a growing number of recordings, as there is no data compression.

On the other hand, for video recordings it was acceptable to use compressed data as there is evidence that this fact does not measurably affect emotion recognition. In this case, the Avi format was used, compressed using DivX 5.0 codec (with 320*240 points resolution). This way, recordings require much less space to be stored. The final duration of the recordings are summarized in Table 3.

Table 3. Duration of the recordings

	Professional actors		Amateur actors	
Language	Audio duration	Video duration	Audio duration	Video duration
Basque	130'41''	53'52''	4'08''	2'11''
Spanish	166'17''	40'04''	19'44''	11'54''
Overall	296'58''	93'56''	23'52	14'05

3.2 Recording Procedure

3.2.1 Environment

A recording set was used to perform database recordings. In this recording set, a chair was placed for the actor to sit on and stay there while performing the recordings. In front of the actor and on his/her left-hand side two cameras were located for the video recordings. Those cameras recorded videos from both frontal and left-hand side perspective, so there was more material to work with. A microphone was placed in front of the actor to record the sound of the different speeches he/she had to perform.

A calibration process was performed before the beginning of the recordings to check that both audio and video were properly received. It was done by checking the distance from the microphone, adjusting cameras so the actor's head was centred in the image with a blank background and checking the microphone was not visible in video recordings. Each actor was asked to test some trial recordings to do so.

There was an operator with a computer guiding the actor's sessions. All the recording process was performed using applications for session guiding and video and audio recording which where executing in the operator's computer. Information with instructions for the session and the different blocks of emotions was provided to the actor by retro-projecting video output from the operator's computer's graphic card to a projector. All the words, sentences and paragraphs the actors had to interpret were provided to the actors in the same way. Special care was taken with all possible sources of sound distortion, so they did not affect the process of recording audio.

3.2.2 Tools

The recording session for each actor was performed using Eweb, a framework originally designed for designing and implementing controlled experiments in web environments [31]. This framework has been developed within the Laboratory of Human-Computer Interaction for Special Needs in the University of the Basque Country.

An XML-based specification file for the experimental design was created using the Session Design Module in order to define user sessions. All different variables used in this experiment were coded in this design. This specification file was later used by the Session Monitor and Guidance Module, which, based on its information, distributed the different tasks users had to perform.

In this case, the Session Monitor and Guidance Module communicated via sockets with two applications, one for performing audio recordings and another one for performing video recordings. Two different kinds of messages were sent, one for starting recording and another for stopping recording. Fig. 1 shows the applications used in performing recordings.

Both applications use DirectShow, which is part of Microsoft DirectX technology, as the way for capturing and rendering. Both have been created as independent modules that communicate with the process guiding application by means of sockets. In both cases a specific nomenclature was used to automate the process of storing multimedia files, so these files were organized in different directories by means of the actor, media type and the given emotion. In the case of audio recordings another additional distinction was made according to the source text type, length and semantics.

The audio recording application allows recording audio files with the features described above and hearing the recorded sound. This is very valuable for the operator to check the quality of the recordings made. The video recording application is able to record video from both frontal and left lateral views simultaneously.

All data were stored to a database, labelled according to actors, emotions and texts, as we are going to mention in the next subsection.

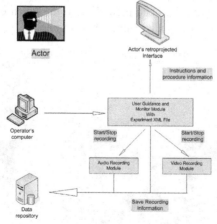

Fig. 1. Applications used in performing recordings

3.2.3 Procedure

Before the session started, each actor was provided with information about the session. After the actors were sat and ready, the recording session began for each of them. First of all, the actor had to provide the operator information to fill a demographic questionnaire launched in the beginning of the session. The recording procedure was the same for each language and it is described below.

The operator managed the recording process from the control interface created by Eweb. Moreover, interfaces from audio and video recording applications were always visible so that the operator could see and hear (using headphones) recordings without interfering the actor's recording session. Fig. 2 shows the operator's interface.

The actor saw the actor's interface retro-projected. There, the actor was provided with instructions for the session. The different blocks of emotions he was moving on were also visible for the actor in the interface every time. The actor was also warned about trial sessions. These sessions were performed for each block to ensure that the actor understood the process and had time to adjust his acting skills to the new emotion.

It must be highlighted that the order of the emotion blocks to be presented to the actor was randomly selected by Eweb, as the different recordings inside each emotion block. This was made to avoid that all actors could perform exactly the same session in the same order, which would enhance the effect of fatigue and learning over certain recordings. Being both emotion blocks and recordings to be performed randomized, the effect of fatigue and learning does not have relevance when comparing recordings from different actors.

Within video block, each actor was asked to perform, using exclusively facial features, six transitions from a neutral emotion to the given emotion and back to the neutral emotion. A frontal and a lateral shot were taken for each recording.

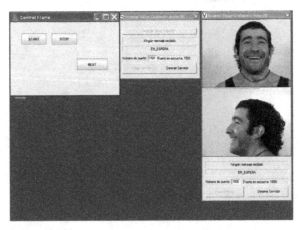

Fig. 2. Control (operator's) interface.

In the case of the audio block, given an emotion by the system, the actor was asked to express all the words, sentences and paragraphs the system offered to him/her.

In the case of audio recordings, before the actor had to perform a recording, the text to be acted for each concrete recording was shown to the actor in his/her interface. This way, the actor had time to memorize it. There was also an image with the shape of a white bulb on the interface, indicating that the recording had not begun yet. In order to perform a recording, the operator had to push the "Start" button in the control interface as he/she saw the actor was ready to perform the recording. Then, that command was sent to the proper recording application (audio or video, depending on the current recording) and the application began to record. At the same time, the image with the shape of a white bulb on the actor's interface turned to an image with the shape of a red bulb, indicating that the actor could begin to perform the recording. By pushing the "Stop" button, the operator was sending the order to stop, so the proper application stopped recording and the bulb in the actor's interface turned again to white. In the case that the recording was not considered as a valid recording by the operator, the recording could be repeated by pushing the "Start" button once again. In this case the previously stored file was overwritten with the new one. If the recording was considered valid by the operator, the "Next" button was pushed so that the session could move on.

When a recording was performed, it was stored in a concrete path, depending on the actor, the emotion, the type of recording and, if audio, if the recording belonged to a word, sentence or paragraph.

Another relevant issue is that Eweb labelled all recordings to record all videos and audios and store them in a database, so metadata about each recording, as the path where the recording was stored and the information about current recording (actor, emotion, word/sentence/paragraph, semantics) was labelled and stored in this database. Metadata stored in the database was used to obtain relevant information about each recording, by analyzing the characteristics each recording had and filling the database with such information.

The total session length for each professional actor was around two hours. Having in mind that the session was shorter for amateur actors, the total session length lasted around twenty minutes for each of them.

3.3 Outcome

After completing the recording process, the outcome is a database where there are data in files with their corresponding video and audio recordings in both languages. On the other hand, metadata or descriptive information about performed recordings is composed by demographic data about the actors that took part in recordings and information about each recording, such as the recording path, the actor, emotion and type of recording. For audio recordings, the type of speech and information about semantics significance are stored. In case of video recordings, whether the recording view was frontal or lateral was recorded.

Apart from recordings performed by professional actors, recordings performed by amateur actors are also considered. This decision was taken with the aim of providing affective material provided by people with limited acting skills in order to establish comparisons among recordings performed by both skilled and non-skilled actors.

4 An Application of RekEmozio Database for Automatic Emotion Recognition in Speech

The development of affective systems is a challenge that involves analysing different multimodal data sources. A large amount of data is needed in order to include a wide range of emotionally significant material. As previously mentioned, affective databases are a good chance for developing such applications, either for affective recognizers or either for affective synthesis.

RekEmozio database is currently being used as the basis for researching automatic emotion recognition in speech. One of the most important questions for this research is to determine which features from the voice signal are relevant in emotion expression in humans. Previous studies show it is difficult to find specific voice features that could be used as reliable indicators of the emotion present in the speech [32].

A wide range of speech parameters have been extracted from RekEmozio database recordings, in order to select the most relevant ones applying different Machine Learning (ML) techniques. [33] and [34] describe how results obtained by ML techniques applied to emotion classification can be improved automatically by selecting an appropriate subset of classifying variables by Feature Subset Selection (FSS) [35]. The FSS proposes additional methods to reduce the number of features so as to improve the performance of the supervised classification algorithm. In this particular case, Estimation of Distribution Algorithm (EDA) [36] has been used to select speech feature subsets that optimize noticeably the automatic emotion recognition success rate.

The obtained results [33, 34] have shown that automatic emotion recognition rates vary from 66 and 75%, depending on the actor. It shows that material recorded in RekEmozio database is useful for research in emotion recognition in the speech area.

5 Conclusions and Future Work

In this paper an application of Eweb tool [31] in the creation of RekEmozio affective database is presented. Eweb has proven to be useful in providing a methodology that can be used for the recording of the affective resources. Recordings have been carried out by experimentation with human subjects based on cognitive psychology theories. As a result, RekEmozio is a valid, consistent affective database. It is multimodal (speech utterances, both semantically meaningful and non-meaningful texts and dynamic facial expressions) and bilingual (Spanish and Standard Basque) and metadata is used to describe and label each interaction.

The approach used for recording RekEmozio database using Eweb can be used for any database. To perform this, an experimenter should create a proper XML file with the Session Design Module. Thus, recording sessions can be performed by creating the proper variables (in our case Language, Actor, Media, Text Length and Semantics), indicating the path of each recording to be stored in the data repository.

RekEmozio database is being currently used to train some automatic emotion recognition systems applied to the particular localization where authors make their research [33, 34]. Furthermore, a validation or normative study has been performed by experimental subjects in order to obtain affective values for each recording and see what the validity of recorded material and the affective values for each recording are [37]. Achieved results show that the material recorded in RekEmozio database is correctly identified by experimental subjects in most cases, with an accuracy of 78% for audio recordings and 90% for video recordings.

All the affective information in the database is being described in an ontology with multimodal elements associated. It is expected that using this ontology in combination with software engineering applications will help to develop affective systems [38].

Acknowledgments   The involved work has received financial support from the Department of Economy of the local government "Gipuzkoako Foru Aldundia" and from the University of the Basque Country (University-Industry projects modality). The authors would like to express their gratitude to the people that participated in the making of RekEmozio database.

References

1. Casacuberta D (2001) La mente humana: Diez Enigmas y 100 preguntas. Océano (Ed), Barcelona, Spain. ISBN: 84-7556-122-5
2. Garay N, Abascal J, Gardeazabal L (2002) Mediación emocional en sistemas de Comunicación Aumentativa y Alternativa. Revista Iberoamericana de Inteligencia Artificial 16: 65-70
3. Picard RW (1997) Affective Computing. MIT Press, Cambridge, MA

4. Tao J, Tan T (2005) Affective computing: A review. In: Tao J, Tan T, Picard RW (eds) Proceedings of The First International Conference on Affective Computing & Intelligent Interaction (ACII'05). LNCS 3784. Springer, pp 981-995.
5. Garay N, Cearreta I, López JM, Fajardo I (2006) Assistive technology and affective mediation. J Human technology, Special Issue on "Human Technologies for Special Needs" 2 (1): 55-83
6. Lang PJ (1979) A bio-informational theory of emotional imagery. J Psychophysiology 16: 495-512
7. Cowie R, Douglas-Cowie E, Cox C (2005) Beyond emotion archetypes: Databases for emotion modelling using neural networks. J Neural Networks 18: 371-388
8. Douglas-Cowie E, Campbell N, Cowie R, Roach P (2003) Emotional speech: Towards a new generation of databases. J Speech Communication 40: 33–60
9. Fragopanagos NF, Taylor JG (2005) Emotion recognition in human-computer interaction. J Neural Networks 18: 389-405
10. Canamero L (2005) Emotion understanding from the perspective of autonomous robots research. J Neural Networks 18: 445-455
11. Navas E, Hernáez I, Castelruiz A, Luengo I (2004) Obtaining and Evaluating an Emotional Database for Prosody Modelling in Standard Basque. In: Sojka P, Kopecek I, Pala K (esd) TSD'04. Brno, Czech Republic, pp 393-400
12. Rodríguez A, Lazaro P, Montoya N, Blanco JM, Bernadas D, Oliver JM, Longhi L (1999) Modelización acústica de la expresión emocional en el español. J Procesamiento del Lenguaje Natural 25: 159-166
13. Engberg IS, Hansen AV, Andersen O, Dalsgard P (1997) Design, recording and verification of a Danish Emotional Database. In: Kokkinakis G, Fakotakis N, Dermatas E (eds) Eurospeech'97. Rhodes, Greece, pp 1695-1698
14. Iida A, Higuchi F, Campbell N, Yasumura M (2002) A Corpus-based Speech Synthesis System with Emotion. J Speech Communication 40(1-2): 161-187
15. Dellaert F, Polzin F, Waibel A (1996) Recognizing emotion in speech. In: Proceedings of the ICSLP. Philadelphia, PA, USA
16. Makarova V, Petrushin VA (2002) RUSLANA: a database of Russian emotional utterances. In Proceedings of ICSLP'02. Denver, Colorado, USA, pp 2041-2044
17. Yuan J, Shen L, Chen F (2002) The Acoustic Realization of Anger, Fear, Joy and Sadness in Chinese. In: Proceedings of ICSLP'02. Denver, Colorado, USA, pp 2025-2028
18. Oudeyer P-Y (2003) The production and recognition of emotions in speech: features and algorithms. J International Journal of Human-Computer Studies 59(1-2): 157–183
19. Burkhardt F, Paeschke A, Rolfes M, Sendlmeier WF, Weiss B (2005) A database of german emotional speech. In: Proc. INTERSPEECH'05. Lissabon, Portugal, pp 1517-1520
20. Bulut M, Narayanan SS, Syrdal AK (2002) Expressive speech synthesis using a concatenative synthesizer. In: Proc. of ICSLP'02. Denver, Colorado, USA, pp 1265-1268
21. Seppanen T, Vayrynen E, Toivanen J (2003) Prosody-based classification of emotions in spoken finnish. In: EUROSPEECH'03. Geneva, Switzerland, pp 717-720
22. Banse R, Scherer KR (1996) Acoustic profiles in vocal emotion expression. J Journal of Personality and Social Psychology 70(3): 614-636
23. Battocchi A, Pianesi F, Goren-Bar D (2005) The Properties of DaFEx, a Database of Kinetic Facial Expressions. In: Tao J, Tan T, Picard RW (eds) Proceedings of The First International Conference on Affective Computing & Intelligent Interaction (ACII'05). LNCS 3784. Springer, pp 558-565
24. Montero JM, Gutiérrez-Ariola J, Palazuelos S, Enríquez E, Aguilera S, Pardo JM (1998) Emotional speech synthesis: from speech database to tts. In: Proceedings of the 5th International Conference of Spoken Language Processing. Sydney, Australia, pp. 923–926

25. You M, Chen C, Bu J (2005) Chad: a Chinese affective database. In: Tao J, Tan T, Picard RW (eds) Proceedings of The First International Conference on Affective Computing & Intelligent Interaction (ACII'05). LNCS 3784. Springer, pp 542-549

26. Ekman P, Friesen W (1976) Pictures of facial affect. Consulting Psychologist Press, Palo Alto, CA

27. Pérez MA, Alameda JR, Cuetos Vega F (2003) Frecuencia, longitud y vecindad ortográfica de las palabras de 3 a 16 letras del diccionario de la lengua española (RAE, 1992) 8(2): 1-20

28. Real Academia de la Lengua (1992) Diccionario de la Lengua Española (21ª edición). Espasa Calpe, Madrid

29. Bradley MM, Lang PJ (1999) International affective digitized sounds (IADS): Stimuli, instruction manual and affective ratings. (Tech. Rep. No. B-2 by The Center for Research in Psychophysiology, University of Florida, Gainesville, Florida)

30. Cowie R, Douglas-Cowie E, Savvidou S, McMahon E, Sawey M, Schröder M (2000) 'Feeltrace': An Instrument For Recording Perceived Emotion In Real Time. In: ISCA Workshop on Speech & Emotion. Northern Ireland, pp 19-24

31. Arrue, M, Fajardo I, López JM, Vigo M (2007) Interdependence between technical web accessibility and usability: its influence on web quality models. J International Journal of Web Engineering and Technology 3(3): 307-328. Inderscience

32. Laukka, P (2007) Vocal Expression of Emotion. Discrete-emotions and Dimensional Accounts. Acta Universitatis Upsaliensis. Comprehensive Summaries of Uppsala Dissertations from the Faculty of Social Sciences, 141, 80 pp. Uppsala University ISBN 91-554-6091-7

33. Álvarez A, Cearreta I, López JM, Arruti A, Lazkano E, Sierra B, Garay N (2006) Feature Subset Selection based on Evolutionary Algorithms for automatic emotion recognition in spoken Spanish and Standard Basque languages. In: Sojka P, Kopecek I, Pala K (eds) Text, Speech and Dialog. LNCS 4188 LNAI. Springer, pp 565-572

34. Álvarez, A, Cearreta, I, López, JM, Arruti, A, Lazkano, E, Sierra, B, Garay, N (2007). A comparison using different speech parameters in the automatic emotion recognition using Feature Subset Selection based on Evolutionary Algorithms. V. Matousek and P. Mautner (Eds.): TSD 2007, LNAI 4629, Springer, pp. 423–430

35. Liu, H, Motoda, H (1998) Feature Selection for Knowledge Discovery and Data Mining. Kluwer Academic Publishers

36. Pelikan, M, Goldberg, DE, Lobo, F (1999) A Survey of Optimization by Building and Using Probabilistic Models. Technical Report 99018, IlliGAL

37. López JM, Cearreta I, Fajardo I, Garay N (2007) Validating a multilingual and multimodal affective database. In: N. Aykin (ed) Usability and Internationalization Part II, HCII2007, LNCS 4560. Springer, pp 422-431

38. Obrenovic Z, Garay N, López JM, Fajardo I, Cearreta I (2005) An ontology for description of emotional cues. In: Tao J, Tan T, Picard RW (eds) Proceedings of The First International Conference on Affective Computing & Intelligent Interaction (ACII'05). LNCS 3784. Springer, pp 505-512

Audiovisual Analysis and Synthesis for Multimodal Human-Computer Interfaces

Xavier Sevillano, Javier Melenchón, Germán Cobo, Joan Claudi Socoró, Francesc Alías

GPMM – Grup de Recerca en Processament Multimodal ,Enginyeria i Arquitectura La Salle Universitat Ramon Llull, Quatre Camins 2 – 08022 Barcelona

{xavis, jmelen, gcobo, jclaudi, falias}@salle.url.edu

Abstract　Multimodal signal processing techniques are called to play a salient role in the implementation of natural computer-human interfaces. In particular, the development of efficient interface front ends that emulate interpersonal communication would benefit from the use of techniques capable of processing the visual and auditory modes jointly. This work introduces the application of audiovisual analysis and synthesis techniques based on Principal Component Analysis and Non-negative Matrix Factorization on facial audiovisual sequences. Furthermore, the applicability of the extracted audiovisual bases is analyzed throughout several experiments that evaluate the quality of audiovisual resynthesis using both objective and subjective criteria.

1 Introduction

Currently, the way human beings interact with computers is far from resembling the natural communication acts between people [4]. Thus, in order to access the growing volume of digital information available, users are required to be familiar with the information and communication technologies. However, it is well known that, for large segments of population, this fact implies a severe obstacle to become full-fledged members of the information society, giving rise to the so-called digital gap. For this reason, the human-computer interaction research community has focused intensively on the development of human-computer interfaces (HCI) capable of emulating the natural interaction between human beings [1, 22].

The construction of such interfaces requires that the design of every module in the HCI (e.g. dialog engines or user models) is oriented towards the development of a natural interaction [1, 4]. A common element in HCI architectures is the so-

M. Redondo et al. (eds.), *Engineering the User Interface*,
DOI: 10.1007/978-1-84800-136-7_13, © Springer-Verlag London Limited 2009

called *presentation module* [4], responsible for acquiring the users' messages and generating the appearance (or *front end*) of the HCI [4]. Regarding this latter issue, creating a presentation module capable of emulating all the modes encompassed in interpersonal communication would be a big step towards natural human computer interaction. However, developing natural looking-and-sounding audiovisual front ends is a very challenging task [1].

In this context, most previous works on audiovisual synthesis treat the auditory and visual modes separately [7, 19], which often results in a perceptible decrease in the naturalness of the synthesized message due to synchronization errors [8]. For this reason, this work is focused on the application of *joint audiovisual* techniques for the generation of HCI front ends based on *facial appearances with synthetic speech*. The rationale behind our proposal is to take advantage of the existing dependencies between the auditory and visual information in a facial audiovisual sequence [9, 11]. To do so, it is necessary to take a joint audiovisual signal processing approach.

This paper is organized as follows: section 2 describes several state-of-the-art approaches for the generation of audiovisual HCI front ends. In section 3, our proposal for conducting a joint audiovisual analysis of facial video sequences is described. Next, section 4 outlines the procedure for synthesizing audiovisual sequences upon the data extracted from the audiovisual analysis stage. Section 5 presents several objective and subjective experiments regarding audiovisual analysis and resynthesis, and, finally, the conclusions of this work are discussed in section 6.

2 Audiovisual HCI Front Ends

In the last years, audiovisual (AV) fusion has emerged as a promising research area in the signal processing field. Most proposals posed in this context are intended to analyze the dependencies between the auditory and visual modes of AV sequences so as to locate the regions of the video scene where the soundtrack is generated [9, 11]. The underlying concept of these approaches is the maximization of the mutual information between both modes, which has been tackled by means of several techniques such as AV covariance estimators [11], non-parametric density estimators [9], Canonical Correlation Analysis [25] or Markov chains [3]. Alternatively, data representation techniques based on statistical independence constraints have been applied to the detection of AV correlations operating on audiovisual feature spaces [26].

Whereas several research efforts have been conducted towards the development of joint AV analysis techniques, far fewer works have been carried out so as to build joint audiovisual synthesis systems. Rather contrarily, the most usual trend in AV synthesis is synthesizing both the auditory and visual modes separately and synchronizing them *a posteriori* [2, 19].

Alternatively, only one proposal –to our knowledge– has been put forward so as to conduct *joint* audiovisual synthesis [8], thus being able to avoid the decrease of the naturalness of the synthesized audiovisual message caused by errors in the AV synchronization process. The following paragraphs briefly describe previous approaches to AV synthesis.

2.1 *Audiovisual Synthesis*

The most common approach for developing AV synthesis systems consists of extending concatenative speech synthesis strategies to the audiovisual framework [6,8]. In short, the procedure is as follows: firstly, training AV sequences are analyzed and segmented into auditory and visual units, which are stored in an AV database (or corpus). Subsequently, when a synthetic AV message is to be generated, the most appropriate –according to some criteria– auditory and visual units from the corpus are selected and concatenated so as to synthesize the auditory and visual modes. Finally, both modes are synchronized, giving rise to the AV message.

Several examples of AV synthesis approaches can be found in the literature. One of the pioneering works in this area presents an audio-driven facial animation technique, in which the training audiovisual sequences are segmented according to the auditory mode in order to generate the AV corpus [2]. However, the synthesis process is speech-driven: given a natural speech fragment, synthetic video is generated by concatenating the most suitable visual units (i.e. a *partial* synthesis is conducted [2]). Despite this approach allows synthesizing high quality AV messages, the large size of the training AV corpus constitutes one of its main drawbacks.

Alternatively, previous works by our research group have been focused on the development of HCI front ends based on text or speech-driven photorealistic talking heads [19, 20, 21]. In comparison to [2], these proposals use an efficient training scheme that largely alleviates computational and storage requirements [21], and generate the facial appearance by frame interpolation (instead of concatenation) [19, 20]. Furthermore, they allow a *complete* corpus-based text-to-audiovisual synthesis by animating the facial appearance from an input text. Other relevant proposals in the field of synthetic photorealistic talking heads are [6, 7], which are based on unit selection and multidimensional morphable models, respectively.

2.2 *Joint Audiovisual Synthesis*

To our knowledge, the first and –for the moment– only joint concatenative photorealistic audiovisual synthesis system is the Joint Audio-Visual Unit Selection (JAVUS) speech synthesizer [8]. It is based on creating an AV corpus containing both visual (video frames) and auditory data (e.g. phonemes duration and pitch, among other parameters extracted from the training sequences). At synthesis time, unit selection is conducted using joint audiovisual criteria, concatenating video frames so that they are synchronous with the synthetic audio.

The main coincidence between JAVUS and our proposal is the joint use of audiovisual information extracted from AV sequences for creating synthetic AV messages. However, whereas JAVUS follows an analysis-by-segmentation strategy for building the AV corpus, we propose projecting the training sequences on a dimensionally reduced linear audiovisual feature space. As a result, a set of AV bases and information regarding their activity across time are obtained. Subsequently, AV synthesis can be conducted, in a rather straightforward manner, upon this extracted audiovisual data. That is, our proposal allows reducing both the AV corpus size and the computational cost of the synthesis process. The next section describes the extraction process of the AV bases.

3 Extracting Audiovisual Bases

In this work, the audiovisual sequences analysis process is treated algebraically. That is, an AV sequence is conceived as a multivariate set, and as such, it is represented in matrix shape (denoted as **X** henceforth).

As we are aiming for joint audiovisual synthesis, matrix **X** must encompass both auditory and visual information of the training video sequence (see Fig. 1) [26]. Formally, let us consider the analysis of a sequence of N frames. For each frame, a M-dimensional audiovisual vector is created by concatenating $i)$ the M_a–dimensional vector corresponding to the parameterization of the audio segment associated to that particular frame, and $ii)$ the M_v–dimensional vector resulting from reshaping the frame (of size $M_v = M_v^x \times M_v^y$ pixels) into a vector (i.e. $M = M_a + M_v$). The repetition of this process for the N frames of the sequence gives rise to an $M \times N$ matrix **X** representing the whole AV sequence.

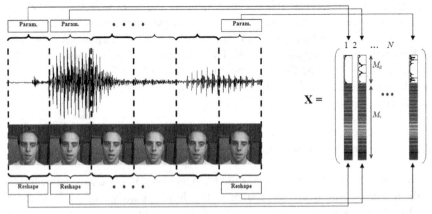

Fig. 1. Generation of matrix **X** from an audiovisual sequence

The next step in the extraction process of the AV bases consists of projecting the audiovisual data matrix $\mathbf{X}$ onto a more *meaningful* AV feature subspace (as compared to the original space). As aforementioned, a benefit of this projection is the obtaining of AV data representations in subspaces of reduced dimensionality, thus yielding a compression effect which can be advantageous in terms of data storage and processing. In this work, this process is conducted by means of two well-known feature extraction techniques, namely Principal Component Analysis (PCA) and Non-negative Matrix Factorization (NMF), extending previous works where these techniques were applied on visual [21] and musical data [27].

3.1 Extracting AV bases by PCA

Principal Component Analysis [14] is a feature extraction technique that projects the data under analysis onto the set of orthogonal directions in which its variance is greatest, besides yielding information regarding the relative significance of each projected component.

A usual method for conducting PCA is Singular Value Decomposition (SVD) [10], which is based on the factorization of the original $M \times N$ data matrix $\mathbf{X}$ (of rank K) according to the following product:

$$\mathbf{X}_{M \times N} = \mathbf{U}_{M \times K} \cdot \mathbf{\Sigma}_{K \times K} \cdot \left(\mathbf{V}_{N \times K}\right)^{T} + \mathbf{m}_{M \times 1} \cdot \mathbf{1}_{1 \times N} \tag{1}$$

where $\mathbf{U}$ and $\mathbf{V}$ are orthonormal matrices, $\mathbf{\Sigma}$ is a diagonal matrix, $\mathbf{m}$ is the mean column of $\mathbf{X}$ and $\mathbf{1}$ is a row vector containing N ones. Moreover, the columns of matrix $\mathbf{U}$ contain the principal components of $\mathbf{X}$, while the diagonal of $\mathbf{\Sigma}$ holds its singular values and, finally, the principal components of $\mathbf{X}^{T}$ are enclosed on the columns of matrix $\mathbf{V}$.

As aforementioned, SVD can also be applied so as to reduce data dimensionality [15], provided it yields the best approximation $\mathbf{\Lambda}$ of rank R (with $R<K$) of any matrix $\mathbf{X}$, in terms of the minimum mean square error [10]. Therefore, the rank R-SVD of the data matrix $\mathbf{X}$ can be used to represent its contents as a function of its first R principal components (see equation 2).

$$\mathbf{X}_{M \times N} \approx \mathbf{U}_{M \times R} \cdot \mathbf{\Sigma}_{R \times R} \cdot \left(\mathbf{V}_{N \times R}\right)^{T} + \mathbf{m}_{M \times 1} \cdot \mathbf{1}_{1 \times N} = \mathbf{\Lambda} \tag{2}$$

As a result of this dimensionally reduced factorization, we obtain R basis vectors (columns of matrix $\mathbf{U}$) and the projections of each column of $\mathbf{X}$ on this basis enclosed in matrix $\mathbf{C} = \mathbf{\Sigma V}^{T}$ (which represents, per rows, the activation levels of each column of $\mathbf{U}$, that is, of each basis vector). It is important to note that the basis vectors in $\mathbf{U}$ encompass two kinds of information: the first M_a dimensions of each column of $\mathbf{U}$ correspond to the auditory data, while the last M_v dimensions correspond to the visual component of the AV basis vector.

Nevertheless, the computational load of conducting PCA through SVD is not negligible when working on AV sequences (given the presumably large size of matrix $\mathbf{X}$). To tackle this problem, in previous works we defined a new method for improving the efficiency of the SVD computation process by updating the information yielded by SVD (matrices $\mathbf{U}$, $\mathbf{\Sigma}$, $\mathbf{V}$ and the mean vector $\mathbf{m}$) in an incremental fashion [21].

In a nutshell, the proposal is the following: the process starts from the initialization described in equation 3, which considers only the first S columns of the original data matrix $\mathbf{X}$; next, matrices $\mathbf{U}_{t+1}$, $\mathbf{\Sigma}_{t+1}$, $\mathbf{V}_{t+1}$ and the new mean column vector $\mathbf{m}_{t+1}$ are computed from the results of the preceding SVD (i.e. from $\mathbf{U}_t$, $\mathbf{\Sigma}_t$, $\mathbf{V}_t$ and $\mathbf{m}_t$, according to equation 4) when new S columns of $\mathbf{X}$, i.e., $\mathbf{x}_{tS+1}, \dots \mathbf{x}_{tS+S}$ are appended to $\mathbf{X}_t$ (equation 5).

$$\mathbf{X}_0 = [\mathbf{x}_1 \ \dots \ \mathbf{x}_S] = \mathbf{U}_0 \cdot \mathbf{\Sigma}_0 \cdot (\mathbf{V}_0)^T + \mathbf{m}_0 \cdot \mathbf{1} \tag{3}$$

$$\mathbf{X}_t = \mathbf{U}_t \cdot \mathbf{\Sigma}_t \cdot (\mathbf{V}_t)^T + \mathbf{m}_t \cdot \mathbf{1} \tag{4}$$

$$\mathbf{X}_{t+1} = [\mathbf{X}_t \quad \mathbf{x}_{tS+1} \ \dots \ \mathbf{x}_{tS+S}] = \mathbf{U}_{t+1} \cdot \mathbf{\Sigma}_{t+1} \cdot (\mathbf{V}_{t+1})^T + \mathbf{m}_{t+1} \cdot \mathbf{1} \tag{5}$$

Notice that, if the number of basis vectors computed at each iteration step is lower than the rank of matrix $\mathbf{X}$ (i.e. $R<K$), equations 3 to 5 will become approximations (i.e. the data will be projected onto a dimensionally reduced AV subspace).

3.2 Extracting AV bases by NMF

Non-Negative Matrix Factorization was introduced in [16] as a technique for decomposing a non-negative matrix $\mathbf{X}$ as the approximate product of two non-negative matrices $\mathbf{W}$ and $\mathbf{H}$:

$$\mathbf{X}_{M \times N} \approx \mathbf{W}_{M \times R} \cdot \mathbf{H}_{R \times N} = \mathbf{\Lambda}_{M \times N} \tag{6}$$

Just like Independent Component Analysis [13], NMF assumes a generative model, i.e. the multivariate dataset $\mathbf{X}$ is the result of the weighted sum of $R << \{M,N\}$ non-negative sources (or basis vectors). According to this generative model, the R non-negative basis vectors are contained in the columns of $\mathbf{W}$ and the weights associated to each base vector are contained in the rows of $\mathbf{H}$. In equation 6, matrix $\mathbf{\Lambda}$ is the approximation of $\mathbf{X}$.

As in the case of the AV basis derived through PCA, the contents of the approximating matrices **W** and **H** are audiovisual: the first M_a dimensions of each column of matrix **W** contain the auditory part of the corresponding AV base component, and the remaining M_v dimensions yield, after an appropriate reshaping, the visual mode of the associated AV source. On the other hand, each row of matrix **H** describes the level of activity of the corresponding AV source across the N frames of the audiovisual sequence.

From an algorithmic viewpoint, the NMF decomposition presented in equation 6 can be implemented through the optimization of a cost function which is proportional to the mean square reconstruction error (MSE) (equation 7) [17]. Such optimization process is conducted in an iterative manner by applying the following multiplicative update rules [17]:

$$D_{\mathrm{MSE}} = \left\| \mathbf{X} - \mathbf{\Lambda} \right\|^2 \tag{7}$$

$$\mathbf{H} = \mathbf{H} \otimes \frac{\mathbf{W}^T \cdot \mathbf{X}}{\mathbf{W}^T \cdot \mathbf{\Lambda}} \quad , \quad \mathbf{W} = \mathbf{W} \otimes \frac{\mathbf{X} \cdot \mathbf{H}^T}{\mathbf{\Lambda} \cdot \mathbf{H}^T} \tag{8}$$

where $\otimes$ denotes Hadamard product and divisions are computed entry-wise.

Finally, it is to note that, as aforementioned, the projection of the AV data onto dimensionally reduced spaces by means of PCA and NMF yields a data compression effect, as both techniques transform the original $M \times N$ data matrix **X** into a set of smaller matrices and vectors. Fig. 2 illustrates this compression effect, as it compares the size of the original data matrix **X** with the accumulated sizes of the PCA and NMF-derived AV representations for distinct values of R (the dimensionality of the audiovisual PCA or NMF feature space) across a range of usual values of the $M \times N$ product.

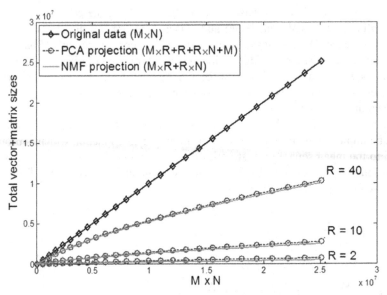

Fig. 2. Data compression effect achieved by PCA and NMF compared to the original data size $(M \times N)$ for distinct feature space dimensionalities (R=2, 10 and 40).

4 Audiovisual Synthesis upon the Extracted Bases

The bases extracted from the AV analysis process lend themselves to being employed for synthesis purposes. Moreover, the linear nature of the PCA and NMF decompositions suggests that synthesis can be conducted with a feasible computational cost.

However, synthesizing an AV sequence from a set of AV bases requires taking into account a few considerations. Firstly, the synthesis of the visual mode is straightforward, as it simply consists in reshaping the last M_v dimensions of the basis vectors (columns of **U** –PCA bases– or **W** –NMF bases–) into $M_v = M_v^x \times M_v^y$ matrices (i.e. frames). And secondly, synthesizing the audio mode implies using the auditory parameters contained in the M_a first dimensions of **U** or **W** columns with synthesis purposes. For this reason, the choice of the audio parameterization employed must take into account the subsequent audio synthesis process.

Keeping these considerations in mind, synthetic AV sequences can be created by linearly combining a selected set of base vectors. Moreover, as the rows of matrices ΣV^T (for PCA) and **H** (for NMF) describe the temporal activation of each AV base component, they can be used to segment the sequence according to the derived AV bases, thus allowing the creation of AV units. Subsequently, these audiovisual units can be linearly combined for generating synthetic AV sequences.

5 Experiments

The viability of our proposal has been evaluated in several experiments conducted on a video sequence of a speaker uttering the five Spanish vowels. Sampling frequencies are 24 frames/second for the video and 11025 Hz for the audio. In order to conduct the extraction process of the AV bases, a double implementation of PCA has been employed: the classic SVD factorization (henceforth denoted as classic PCA, or cPCA for short) and the incremental PCA (iPCA) computed by means of the SVD algorithm presented in [21]. As regards NMF, we have employed NMF algorithm available from NMFPACK that minimizes D_{MSE} as its cost function [12].

5.1 Audio Parameterization

As mentioned in section 4, the audio parameterization employed when generating the audiovisual matrix **X** must allow the creation of synthetic speech. In this work, two audio parameterizations are applied:

- Audio magnitude spectra: following [24, 26, 27], the auditory mode is represented by the magnitude of the M_a-points Fast Fourier Transform (FFT) of the audio segment associated to each frame. At synthesis time, thus, it is necessary to compute an inverse FFT (IFFT), which does not only require a magnitude spectrum (contained in the M_a first dimensions of the columns of **U** –for PCA– or **W** –for NMF), but also a phase response. In this work, this issue is tackled by using the phase of the original soundtrack for computing the IFFT [5].
- Partial correlation coefficients (PARCOR): this audio parameterization is based on the well-known linear predictive coding (LPC) [18], widely used for speech analysis and synthesis in compression applications. In this context, a basic requirement is the efficient coding of the LPC parameters of the vocal tract, which is usually modelled as an all-pole filter of order M_a. The partial correlation (PARCOR) coefficients set is defined to be equivalent to the so-called feedback parameters that define the inverse vocal tract filter [23]. With respect to the feedback parameters, the PARCOR coefficients present the advantage of guaranteeing the stability of the vocal tract filter if their magnitude is below 1 [23][10]. Moreover, these coefficients can be employed for synthesis purposes in a quite straightforward manner, as synthetic speech can be generated by filtering a suitable excitation signal by means of the inverse vocal tract filter defined upon the PARCOR coefficients. In this work, the residual error resulting from the analysis process is used as the excitation signal [18].

---

[10] As the application of NMF requires operating on strictly non-negative data, it is to note that the PARCOR coefficients values are made non-negative by adding a constant bias equal to 1 before applying NMF (which is subtracted afterwards).

5.2 Illustration of the Audiovisual Bases

The goal of this experiment is to provide the reader with an intuitive notion about the nature and contents of the AV bases. For this reason, Fig. 3 depicts the auditory and visual components, and the temporal activations of the bases obtained by applying cPCA and NMF with rank $R = 4$ on the training sequence, using FFT-based audio parameterization.

It can be observed that the visual components of the bases correspond to facial appearances uttering distinct parts of the sequence (Fig. 3a and 3d), as their temporal activations (depicted in Fig. 3b and 3e) indicate the time instants when they *take part* in the sequence. Last, as FFT magnitude has been used for parameterizing the audio, the auditory components of the bases (Fig. 3c and 3f) correspond to the spectra of the associated audio – see [24] for a more exhaustive interpretation of these AV bases.

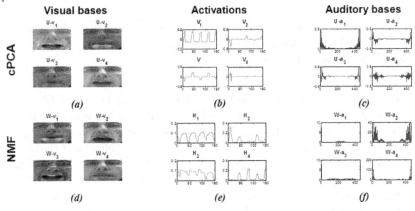

Fig. 3. Audiovisual bases and their corresponding temporal activations obtained by means of cPCA and NMF with rank R=4.

5.3 Objective Evaluation of Audiovisual Resynthesis

As a first step in the exploitation of the AV bases obtained from cPCA, iPCA and NMF with audiovisual synthesis purposes, the analyzed sequence $\mathbf{X}$ is *resynthesized*. That is, the approximated sequence Λ is generated according to equations 2, 5 and 6. Subsequently, both the resynthesized and the original sequences are compared objectively in terms of the normalized mean square error (NMSE) between the audio and video modes of both sequences. The influence of the AV feature space dimensionality (R) on the quality of the approximated sequence Λ is analyzed by conducting the resynthesis process with values of $R \in [2, 40]$.

Fig. 4a and 4b present the NMSE between the original and resynthesized auditory and visual modes when audio is parameterized by means of magnitude spectra. In this case, it can be observed that, as regards the visual mode, cPCA and NMF present a very similar behaviour, although cPCA achieves a slightly smaller error. In contrast, the iPCA decomposition introduces a much larger error when the data is projected onto low dimensional AV feature spaces, although it tends to approximate the NMSE achieved by cPCA and NMF as R increases. Note that, however, in the auditory mode, iPCA obtains the best results across the whole range of R. Again, as the value of R increases, cPCA and iPCA tend to converge, while NMF presents the worst behaviour. This is quite surprising provided that, although the magnitude of the audio spectra is used for parameterizing the audio, the auditory components of the cPCA and iPCA bases take both positive and negative values.

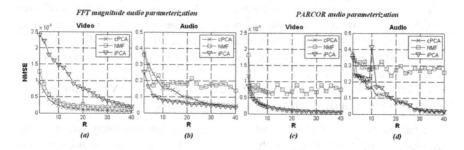

Fig. 4. Normalized mean square error (NMSE) between the original and resynthesized visual and auditory modes as a function of dimensionality R with *(a-b)* FFT magnitude, and *(c-d)* PARCOR audio parameterizations

The NMSE between the original and resynthesized auditory and visual modes in the PARCOR audio parameterization case are presented in Fig. 4c and 4d. It can be observed that cPCA and iPCA present a very similar performance in both the visual and auditory modes (apart from the outlier appearing at $R = 10$ in Fig. 4d). It is also to note that, although a decreasing trend is perceived in all the plots, the NMF error stabilizes at higher levels than in the case of cPCA and iPCA.

Last, but not least, it is interesting to highlight that using different audio parameterization schemes affects the NMSE of the visual mode, especially when the iPCA and NMF projections are employed (see Fig. 4a and 4c). Quite obviously, this cross-modal dependency is a consequence of using a joint audiovisual approach for deriving the AV bases.

5.4 Subjective Evaluation of Audiovisual Resynthesis

This experiment evaluates the quality of the resynthesized sequences from a subjective viewpoint. For this reason, 19 members of our faculty (males and females of ages between 21 and 45) are subjected to an individual preference test whose duration ranged from 8 to 10 minutes –including control points so as to detect in-

consistencies in the user's opinions. Each user is presented –in the same order–
with 24 pairs of audiovisual sequences combining the original and resynthesized
visual and auditory modes obtained by means of cPCA and NMF with rank R = 40
(as the NMSE tends to stabilize asymptotically, see Fig. 4), using the audio
parameterization schemes described in section 5.1. By doing so, we try to evaluate:

- the joint quality of the AV resynthesis, by making users compare fully synthetic sequences among them and also with the original sequences; this is what
  we call the *joint audiovisual preference test*, the results of which are presented
  in Fig. 5.
- the quality of the resynthesis of each mode separately, by making users compare sequences that combine synthetic video and original audio (and vice
  versa); this is what we call the *video-only* and the *audio-only preference tests*
  (note that pairs of AV sequences are compared in all cases, but differences between them are limited to one of the modes in these preference tests). Results
  are depicted in Fig. 6 and 7.
- the effect of using distinct audio parameterizations on the AV resynthesis process, which is evaluated across all the preference tests.

It can be observed that the most natural looking-and-sounding resynthesized
sequence is obtained when applying PCA audiovisual data projection plus
PARCOR audio parameterization (denoted by PCA_PRC), as it gets the highest
number of 'indistinguishable' votes (nearly 70%) when compared to the original
sequence for each one of the three evaluations (i.e. jointly audiovisual, video-only
and audio-only) – see Fig. 5, 6 and 7.

On the other hand, Fig. 5 reveals that PCA yields better AV resynthesis quality
than NMF regardless of the audio parameterization employed (however, when
FFT audio parameterization is used, the PCA preference margin is reduced with
respect to the PARCOR audio parameterization).

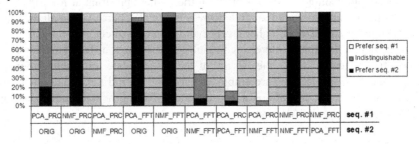

Fig. 5. Joint AV preference test between pairs of sequences. ORIG identifies the original sequence. PCA_PRC and NMF_PRC denote AV synthesis with PARCOR audio parameterization,
and PCA_FFT and NMF_FFT, with the magnitude of audio spectra. At each column, the white
portion of the bar denotes preference for the sequence labeled as #1, and the black portion, preference for sequence #2. The 'indistinguishable' option is drawn in grey

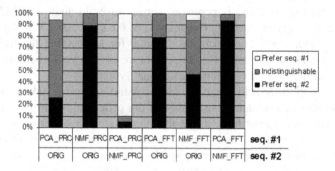

Fig. 6. Video-only preference test between pairs of sequences

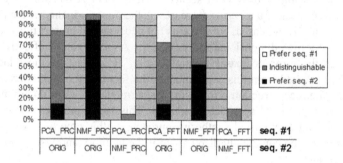

Fig. 7. Audio-only preference test between pairs of sequences

However, as regards PCA vs. NMF direct comparisons in the video-only evaluation (see Fig. 6), opposite preference trends are observed depending on the audio parameterization employed. In contrast, as regards the audio-only comparison (see Fig. 7), PCA-based resynthesis yields better results than NMF for both audio parameterization schemes.

The statistical significance of the subjective experiment results has been evaluated by means of the Wilcoxon signed rank test [28], revealing statistically significant differences ($p>0.95$) between the scoring distributions of PCA and NMF in all the preference tests.

6 Conclusions

In this work, Principal Component Analysis and Non-negative Matrix Factorization have been applied for joint audiovisual data projection in the context of AV analysis and synthesis of facial audiovisual sequences. Whereas most previous approaches to AV sequence analysis have been focused on detecting of audiovisual dependencies, and most works on audiovisual synthesis treat the auditory and visual modes separately, our proposal is oriented towards the use of the extracted joint AV bases with synthesis purposes, aiming to build audiovisual HCI front ends for natural user interaction. The analysis of the extracted AV bases suggests that their temporal activations can be valuable for segmenting the training sequences into audiovisual units. However, a lot of work is yet to be done so as to generate a corpus amenable for joint audiovisual synthesis.

As a first step towards this goal, we have conducted several audiovisual resynthesis experiments, evaluating the quality of the generated sequences using both objective and subjective criteria. In the objective evaluation experiments, we have compared the resynthesized and original sequences. As a result, it is observed that the lowest reconstruction error is achieved by PCA, either by its classic computation or by our incremental counterpart proposal. Thus, although the NMF algorithm employed also minimizes the mean square reconstruction error, the orthogonality constraint imposed by PCA seems to yield better AV bases. As expected, the normalized mean square error decreases as the dimensionality of the audiovisual feature space is increased, but it seems not necessary to project the training sequence on very high dimensional spaces (i.e. the AV data can be effectively compressed), as the error decreases asymptotically. However, the most interesting conclusion extracted from this experiment is the fact that the audio parameterization affects the reconstruction error of the visual mode, which is due to the intrinsically joint audiovisual approach employed. This fact reinforces our interest in following a joint audiovisual synthesis approach, as this type of cross-modal information would be completely disregarded if the auditory and visual modes were treated separately.

The subjective evaluation experiments corroborate the results of the objective analysis, as different preference trends are observed depending on the audio parameterization employed. Focusing on joint audiovisual evaluation, the most preferred configuration is PCA data projection plus PARCOR audio parameterization. However, given the level of dependence between the audio parameterization scheme and the perceived quality of the synthetic audiovisual sequence, more alternatives regarding both audio and video parameterizations must be explored in the future, as we conjecture that the cross-modal dependency detected is probably bidirectional. Thus, our next goal is to find a combined audio and video parameterization scheme that allows achieving high quality audiovisual synthesis results.

Acknowledgments   This work has been partially supported by the Ministerio of Educación y Ciencia of Spain (CICYT TEC2006-08043/TCM).

References

1. Allen J, Byron D, Dzikovska M, Ferguson G, Galescu L and Stent A (2001) Towards conversational human-computer interaction. AI Magazine 22(4):27–38

2. Bregler C, Covell M and Slaney M (1997) Video Rewrite: driving visual speech with audio. Proc. of the ACM Conference in Computer Graphics and Interactive Techniques, 353–360
3. Butz T and Thiran JP (2005) From error probability to information theoretic (multimodal) signal processing. Signal Processing, 85(5):875–902
4. Calle J, Martínez P and Valle D (2006) Hacia la realización de una interacción natural. Proc. of the VII International Conference on Human-Computer Interaction, 471–480 *(in Spanish)*
5. Casey MA and Westner A (2000) Separation of mixed audio sources by Independent Subspace Analysis. Proc. of the International Computer Music Conference, 154–161
6. Cosatto E and Graf HP (1998) Sample-based synthesis of photo-realistic talking heads. Computer Animation, 103–110
7. Ezzat T, Geiger G and Poggio T (2002) Trainable videorealistic speech animation. Proc. of the ACM Conference in Computer Graphics and Interactive Techniques, 225–228
8. Fagel S (2006) Joint Audio-Visual Unit Selection - The JAVUS speech synthesizer. Proc. of the International Conference on Speech and Computer
9. Fisher III JW, Darrell T, Freeman TW and Viola P (2000) Learning joint statistical models for audio-visual fusion and segregation. Advances in Neural Information Processing Systems, vol. 14
10. Golub G and Loan CV (1996) Matrix computations. The John Hopkins University Press
11. Hershey J and Movellan J (1999) Audio-vision: using audio-visual synchrony to locate sounds. Advances in Neural Information Processing Systems, vol. 12
12. Hoyer PO (2004) Non-negative matrix factorization with sparseness constraints. Journal of Machine Learning Research, 5:1457–1469
13. Hyvarinen A, Karhunen J and Oja E (2001) Independent Component Analysis. John Wiley and Sons
14. Jolliffe I (1986) Principal Component Analysis. Springler-Verlag
15. Kirby M (2001) Geometric data analysis: an empirical approach to dimensionality reduction and the study of patterns. John Wiley and Sons
16. Lee DD and Seung HS (1999) Learning the parts of objects by non-negative matrix factorization. Nature, 401, 788–791
17. Lee DD and Seung HS (2000) Algorithms for non-negative matrix factorization. Advances in Neural Information Processing Systems, vol. 13
18. Markel JE and Gray AH (1982) Linear prediction of speech. Springer-Verlag
19. Melenchón J, De la Torre F, Iriondo I, Alías F, Martínez E and Vicent Ll (2003) Text to visual synthesis with appearance models. Proc. of the IEEE International Conference on Image Processing, vol. 1, 237–240
20. Melenchón J, Iriondo I, Socoró JC and Martínez E (2003) Lip animation of a personalized facial model from auditory speech. Proc. IEEE International Symposium on Signal Processing and Information Technology, 187–190
21. Melenchón J, Meler L and Iriondo I (2004) On-the-fly training. Articulated Models and Deformable Objects, LNCS vol. 3179, pp. 146–153
22. Pantic M, Sebe N, Cohn JF and Huang T (2005) Affective multimodal human-computer interaction. Proc. of the 13th annual ACM International Conference on Multimedia, pp. 669–676
23. Papamichalis PE and Barnwell III TP (1983) Variable rate speech compression by encoding subsets of the PARCOR coefficients. IEEE Transactions on Acoustics, Speech and Signal Processing, 31(3):706–713
24. Sevillano X, Melenchón J and Socoró JC (2006) Análisis y síntesis audiovisual para interfaces multimodales ordenador-persona. Proc. of the VII International Conference on Human-Computer Interaction, 481–490 *(in Spanish)*

25. Slaney M and Covell M (2000) Facesync: a linear operator for measuring synchronization of video facial images and audio tracks. Advances in Neural Information Processing Systems, vol. 13

26. Smaragdis P and Casey M (2003) Audio/visual independent components. Proc. of the Fourth International Symposium on Independent Component Analysis and Blind Source Separation, 709–714

27. Smaragdis P and Brown JC (2003) Non-negative matrix factorization for polyphonic music transcription. Proc. of the IEEE Workshop on Applications of Signal Processing to Audio and Acoustics, 177–180

28. Wilcoxon F (1945) Individual comparisons by ranking methods. Biometrics, 1: 80–83

Creation and Evaluation of a Virtual and Collaborative Playground

Arturo S. García, Diego Martínez, José P. Molina, Pascual González

LoUISE Research Group. Instituto de Investigación en Informática de Albacete, Universidad de Castilla-La Mancha.
{arturo, diegomp1982, jpmolina, pgonzalez}@dsi.uclm.es

Abstract Focusing on the way users perform their tasks in Collaborative Virtual Environments (CVEs), there is still little research on understanding the impact of different platforms on the collaboration experience, as well as on which tasks a collaborative approach is worth using. Addressing both issues, this paper describes not only a CVE, being one that reproduces a block building game, but also an experiment aimed to evaluate the performance and the overall collaborative experience, as regards the impact that different input and output technologies employed by users and the tasks performed by them have on it. In addition, this paper also describes implementation details of the CVE that are rarely discussed in the literature, presenting an environment model that is based on the novel idea of *interaction views*.

1 Introduction

In the last years, computer networks have become a tool able to break the barrier of distance between people. This has caused a change in the software development process, since new theories, techniques and methods coming from anthropology, psychology, etc. need to be used to tackle the problems that computer mediated collaboration introduces [7, 11]. Thus, many research efforts move their attention from single user to multi-user systems where participants share data and collaborate, working together and simultaneously in the production of a result or to reach a common goal. An example of this is the design of a 3D model of a single piece or a whole environment, which is usually tackled by a single engineer or artist using their CAD/CAM or 3D authoring tool; however, it is now possible to work together with other people, collaborating in its realization, as in [1].

On the other hand, Virtual Reality (VR) seems to be suitable to simulate a virtual space where tasks take place and where people, even geographically distributed, collaborate to reach a common goal. This defines a Collaborative Virtual Environment (CVE) as a form of telecommunication technology that brings to-

M. Redondo et al. (eds.), *Engineering the User Interface*,
DOI: 10.1007/978-1-84800-136-7_14, © Springer-Verlag London Limited 2009

gether co-located or remote participants within a common spatial social and information context [17].

1.1 Related work

In the context of CVEs, this paper describes an educational and collaborative building game and its evaluation. Similar systems can be found in the bibliography [8, 10, 16], such as a two-handed 3D modeller [10], the building of a gazebo [18], or a puzzle similar to the Rubik's cube [8]. However, focusing our attention on the way users perform their task in these systems, there is still little research on understanding the impact of different platforms on the collaboration experience. From those cited before, only Heldal et al. [8] tackle this problem. Moreover, it is even more difficult to find studies which compare collaborative versus individual performance on the same task. Ruddle et al. [19] focused on cooperative manipulation, and Heldal et al. [9], continuing the work done in [8], may be the only published work on this regard. However, as these last studies are focused on only one task, it remains the question of how general the findings are.

1.2 Experiment goals

The evaluation described in this paper was planned as an experiment to get a better understanding on the previous issues, that is, to study collaboration when performing tasks in a CVE from different platforms, and to compare the results with the ones obtained from performing those tasks in the same platforms by an individual user. Furthermore, we wanted to compare those results with the physical – not computer-based– realization of the tasks. To do so, performance was measured in terms of task completion times.

For the first goal of the experiment, it was decided to compare performance using an immersive system –based on a VR helmet, trackers and data-gloves, which allows for a more natural interaction– with those using a desktop setup –based on a monitor, a keyboard and a mouse, which offers a less natural interaction–. For the second goal, the aim was to study whether collaboration actually improves performance, and how that improvement relates to the nature of the task, implying different tasks that could be carried out both individually and in collaboration. To account for the third goal, attention was driven to real-world tasks.

To accomplish all this goals, a block-based building game was chosen, named Prismaker. This game is three-dimensional in nature and can be played individually or in collaboration. Once Prismaker was chosen, the implementation of its virtual counterpart, as a CVE, started.

During the implementation of the CVE, the environment and the user interactions were given special attention. For them, a novel model currently under development by our research group was used. This model exploits the spatial, temporal and collaborative dimensions inherent to any entity in a CVE to guide the logic of the system. Given the spatial features required in this kind of games, the capabilities of the model were found interesting and worth mentioning.

Thus, this paper also describes the most relevant design concepts included in the CVE implemented to support our experiment. The most remarkable feature is that the elements that trigger the communication between the objects in the environment are given a spatial and collaborative context. Behaviours are not interconnected though completely logical routes, as in VRML [22], but are triggered taking into account the essential properties of every object in a Virtual Environment (VE).

1.3 Road map

This paper is organized as follows. Next section gives a brief introduction to the environment model used. Then, section 3 describes the CVE developed and explains how the model was applied to its development. Section 4 then presents the experiment carried out to evaluate the CVE developed and its main results. Finally, section 5 presents conclusions and the future directions of this research.

2 Environment Model

Some of the key elements of the model under development are explained in [12]. However, this section gives a brief introduction to them.

This environment model is based on the physical representation. Given the nature of VEs, whether collaborative or not, a spatial representation should be given for every object that allows interaction (even data and other "logical" elements). Even though this is an intrinsic characteristic of VEs, previous work on this field has not taken into account this kind of information when processing user actions. Object location and visual representation are usually stored in Scene Graphs, but the elements related to behaviours are in a logical context that does not exploit those spatial properties. This is the case of VRML [22] or InTML [2], where objects are modelled, behaviours are coded, and then static links connect them all. Besides, these systems do not even take into account the organizational context of the user in a CVE to guide the processing of their actions.

The model presented here, on the other hand, exploits the spatial context of the elements, even to manage behaviours, and so all these elements are given a spatial representation. The following section explains some basic elements needed to understand the rest of the environment model, especially those related to the communication processes and the representation of the environment.

2.1 Basic Elements

To help to understand the behaviour of the model proposed, some key concepts are explained:

- **Action**: Any user input: a gesture made with a data glove, a key press, etc. is considered as an *action*. *Actions* are no more than messages and, as such, they should be processed. The *interaction views* in the objects are the filters that process these messages, and they decide whether this *action* ends up changing the state of the world or not. The *action* by itself just contains information about the user who performed it, the message contained (gesture performed, tool used, etc.) and the associated geometry to process that gesture.
- **Interaction**: If a given *action* is performed on the appropriate object, the target object will produce an *interaction*. *Interactions* are responses of the system to a user *action* through a given object, which may change the state of the world. Given that every change in the world will be performed in response to an *interaction*, it is important that all the clients who have the target object in their Scene Graphs perform the same *interactions*. Also, given the distributed nature of a CVE, the execution of the *interactions* must be synchronized with the other clients granting exclusive access to the necessary objects. Therefore, a tight control over *interactions* becomes necessary to achieve consistency.

2.2 Users and Actions

As a part of the environment, every user needs a representation. This model assumes that each user is represented by means of two virtual hands and a virtual head, but the *actions* they can perform must be identified by the developer. For instance, in MASSIVE [5] a set of MEDIUMs are identified. They include text, voice and, in general, every possible channel of communication between two participants in the environment.

In the same way, the model presented here allows developers to identify the possible communications or interactions that any user can start, and associate them with a logical channel. Therefore, an object that allows a user to interact through a given channel will define an *interaction view* for that channel. This can include the set identified in MASSIVE to communicate with other users, and, more interesting, the particular messages the user can create (pick, drop, point, etc.) to interact with the objects of the VE.

In order to completely define an action, both the message contained by that action –identified in the logical channels above (user inputs, tools, MEDIUMs)– and the geometry defining its spatial constraints need to be taken into account. As a simple example, user *actions* may be modelled with a sphere in a virtual position, and then the message within will be the gesture performed by the user. This definition is enough to allow the user to interact with objects directly, but other behaviours may need more complex *actions*. For *interactions* in which the user must use a tool to operate on an object (to cut, join, etc.), it is not the user's hand but the handheld object the one which is interacting. This way, every object held by the user transforms the *actions* received, modifying both its geometry and its content according to its own rules.

Once the different types of messages available for the user have been identified, each of the local user systems has to adapt the user inputs into a homogeneous representation of the actions defined by this model. Thus, local systems match the available user inputs (tracker, joystick, keyboard, etc.) to this unique representation, and they can also adapt it, as we will see in the CVRPrismaker desktop system.

Also, this homogeneous representation of the *actions* allows the definition of agents in an easy way. These agents can be programmed to perform the appropriate *action* or they can be obtained by simply recording real users interacting in the system and replaying the recorded virtual actions when desired.

2.3 Object Views

The proposed model, as most VR applications, uses a kind of Scene Graph, but one of a completely different kind. As in any Scene Graph, it contains the definition of the position and status of every object in the VE, but the information available for each object is different, since they are defined as a set of different views. Some of the views define the appearance of the object, while others define the kind of *action* that will trigger an *interaction* over the object, and thus, change the state of objects of the world.

2.3.1 The Appearance view

Every object in the VE will have one, or more, appearance views. This view, or set of views, defines the "visual" aspect of the object and contains information usually complex and useless for its use in interaction decisions. The union of all the appearance views of the objects of the VE would correspond to the classical definition of a Scene Graph given in the literature. To manage this information, common Scene Graphs such as OpenSceneGraph [15] or more complex game engines such as Ogre3D [14] could be used.

The model proposed defines a restrictive interface to the actual "appearance Scene Graph" used, allowing it only to define the position of the objects, its appearance and the definition of one object position relative to another object. This restricted interface is one of the key concepts that allow the model to keep its independence from the actual Scene Graph used in the implementation. Only the appearance views will be Scene Graph-dependant.

2.3.2 The Interaction views

Apart from the appearance views available for every object, if it is an interactive object, it will contain, at least, one *interaction view*. These views determine the geometrical place where a user can perform their *actions* to trigger an *interaction* over the object. Besides, every *interaction view* contains the conditions the user *action* has to fulfil to trigger the *interaction*. These conditions may vary from one object to another and they are based on the geometries of both the *interaction view* and the user *action* itself, and on the status of the objects involved in the *interaction*.

The idea underneath is that users are not interested on the whole object, but only on those regions where they can interact. For this purpose, *interaction views* can be defined with a set of very simple geometries, for instance spheres, as in the implementation of CVRPrismaker.

Another interesting point is grouping these regions in different sets, each responsible for processing different user messages. Applying this model in this way, objects define one *interaction view* for each kind of user's message they can process.

3 Application of the Model to CVRPrismaker

Prismaker is a block-based game designed for children over three years old, consisting of several types of blocks with which different models can be built. This work follows previous single-user implementation of this game [13], but this time Prismaker is presented as a game where several people can collaborate to build a model.

Collaborative Virtual Reality Prismaker (CVRPrismaker) is a CVE developed as an experimental platform where collaboration in cyberspace can be studied and compared to collaboration in real places. For that reason, a shared virtual playground was created, where several users can pick new pieces, build models, save them or load the previously saved ones using their own hands (Fig. 1).

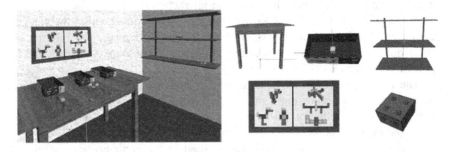

Fig. 1. The virtual environment.

Focus is then on communication and interaction between subjects, but also on how interaction was managed by each of the distributed systems to allow users to share a common perception of the environment. For these purposes the system was built taking into account the environment model presented in the previous section. For this purpose, three main tasks must be completed:

- first, the CVE and its desired functionality must be studied;

- then, as it was explained in section 2.2, the kinds of *actions* available for different users must be identified;
- finally, the *interaction views* that each object needs to process the identified user actions will be designed.

The following points explain, step by step, how these tasks have been solved in the implementation of CVRPrismaker.

3.1 Users and Actions

At this point, it is important to explain how the interaction was adapted for the desktop users, since testing interaction in low-cost platforms was another of the interests of the experiment. To achieve this, the interaction model establishes a unique rule: desktop users will generate their interactions in the same way than an immersive user, through their virtual hands and head and a set of discrete data associated with each virtual hand. This way, desktop systems will be responsible for translating the inputs generated (key presses and mouse movements, mainly) to the homogeneous representation of the users given in the system, but also, it allows the definition of adapted interaction features. Particularly, CVRPrismaker allows restricted rotations of 90 degrees for the desktop systems.

Regarding the *actions* that users will be able to produce, they will interact by means of two different gestures: "pick" and "drop". These gestures will be used for picking and dropping pieces from the boxes, and loading and saving models in the shelves. Also, the pick gesture can be used to separate a piece or a set of pieces from a given model.

However, to join a piece to a model or glue two models together, a new "join" *action* is needed. To do so, when a user is holding a figure, the "drop" *actions* generated by the user will be translated by the figure into "join" *actions*.

3.2 Object Views

In this implementation, more importance is given to the interaction views rather than to the appearance views, since they are the most innovative aspect of the model.

Thus, once the possible user *actions* are identified, each interactive object in the environment will define the required *interaction views* to respond to these *actions*. Thus, each object will define up to three views (one for each kind of message). However, most of the objects will not define views for all the actions, as they will not be able to respond to all these kinds of messages.

Figure 2 shows the *interaction views* defined for each action. Boxes and shelves only define views for the "pick" and "drop" messages and these views show the places where user will be able to perform "pick" or "drop" actions. Pieces also define a view for "join" actions. As it can be seen, this view defines a geometry which is placed outside the piece itself. This is because pieces define the places where other pieces can be added.

It is also remarkable the fact that pieces do not define a view for "drop" messages. This is logical as they will not respond to "drop" messages. Nothing can be dropped over a piece.

On the other hand, when a user wants to drop a piece or a figure in the environment (not over another piece or figure), the drop *action* generated by the user will be filtered by the hand-held piece, which will translate it into a "join" message. This message will be received by the Room object, which will process it allowing the piece to be removed from the user's hands. The priority associated to this interaction will be the lowest, so any other *interaction* triggered in the same cycle will be performed instead of this one. The *interaction view* for the Room object is not shown but it covers the whole environment.

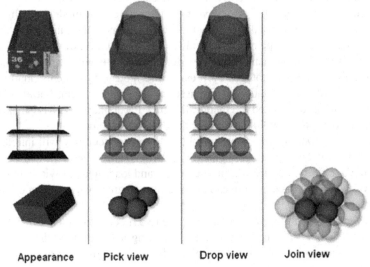

　　　Appearance　　　Pick view　　　Drop view　　　Join view

Fig. 2. Interaction views for each of the user's possible actions.

3.3 Architecture Overview

As regards the software platform chosen, the development of the system mostly relied on VRJuggler [21]. VRJuggler includes a layer for device abstraction that allows the developer face user inputs without worrying about how they were generated. This abstraction was useful for the definition of the logical *actions* used in our model, although some additional programming had to be done.

Besides, it is also independent of the graphics API used to render the scene. Regarding this, OpenGL was selected as it is a standard supported by many different platforms. The VRML/X3D file format was used to store the playground model, the user-built models and the users' avatars. The *interaction views* were defined in a dedicated file format.

To implement the communication with the rest of the CVE, a free and widely used library for networked games, Raknet [16], was selected for the transmission of data over the network.

4 Data-Sharing Mechanism

Communication in CVRPrismaker is based on the idea of a shared Scene Graph. As in other CVEs described in the literature [3], the clients communicate changes in a Scene Graph that they all share. However, CVRPrismaker clients do not broadcast every change, but just the *interactions*, which are then executed in every other client locally, producing the same changes in all of them.

To ensure consistency, and according to the classification of distributed data consistency by Greenhalgh et al. [6], the system described in this paper follows a total ordering approach. Thus, each client will wait for a server acknowledgement before performing any *interaction*. Performance is, however, improved, as it allows clients to move their hands without having to wait for a server acknowledgement. As it has already been said, they will only communicate with the server when an interaction occurs and thus, a change in the world may happen.

To prevent this situation from breaking the consistency of the system, each *interaction request* delivered to the server contains the local data (such as the positions of the objects in the client who generated the interaction) which caused the *interaction* to happen. The server broadcasts a *confirmed interaction* to each connected client, sending also these local data. This way, each change in the state of the world (*interaction*) happens in the same order and with the same data in all the clients.

This logical behaviour had a strict impact on the network architecture of the CVE. There are several options to consider when choosing the appropriate architecture for a CVE, from client-server, to peer-to-peer, or even more complex hybrid models [20]. However, given the tight ordering restrictions of the communication model desired, a client-server architecture was chosen for implementing CVRPrismaker. The server is used to order the user *interactions* and broadcast them to all the connected clients when appropriate. Given the behaviour of the server, it does not store a copy of the Scene Graph, it just acts as a moderator. This is not the case with the clients, each one keeping their own copy, but they are all modified applying changes in the same order and with the same operands, according to the update messages sent by the server.

4.1 Hardware Platforms Tested

For the development of this system, an immersive VR setup was used. It was composed of a HP Compaq XW6000/PL station (dual 2.4GHz Intel Xeon, 512

MB, 3Dlabs Wildcat III 6110), an Ascension Flock of Birds tracking system with three trackers, a pair of Fakespace Pinch Gloves and a ProView XL35 stereoscopic head mounted device (Fig. 3a and 3b).

For the desktop system, a HP Compaq XW4000 station (P4 2.4 GHz Intel, 512 MB, NVIDIA Quadro4 900 XGL) was used with a conventional mouse, desktop and keyboard (Fig. 3c). Some keys of the keyboard were labelled with symbols representing its associated function, to make it easier for the user to use (Fig. 3d).

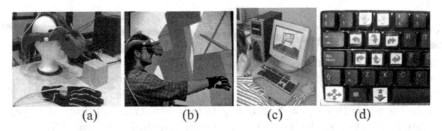

    (a)   (b)   (c)   (d)

Fig. 3. Hardware used in the immersive (a-b) and desktop configuration (c-d).

5 Evaluation

This section describes an experiment that was carried out to get insight into this kind of systems. As a first approach to them, our main concern is to evaluate the performance in different configurations. This way, it is not only our interest to test an immersive platform, but also to check if a desktop-based system is also useful as a platform for a CVE. The opinion of the users taking part in the evaluation was also taken into account.

5.1 Task Design

It was our hypothesis that collaborative work is more efficient than individual work. To verify or refute that hypothesis, several participants took part in an experiment that followed a within-groups design, that is, each participant had to repeat the same tasks under different conditions. As for the tasks, they had to build two different models: a duck and an airplane. They where chosen with collaboration in mind, thinking that the duck was difficult to divide but the airplane had easily distinguishable subparts.

As measuring the performance at different platforms was the objective of the experiment, participants had to fulfil the tasks using the virtual game in both desktop (D) and immersive (I) platforms, and also the real block system (R). In order to test the hypothesis, they used each platform once individually and once or twice collaborating with another participant. Obviously, when the real game is chosen, both participants carry out the tasks with the real blocks (R-R). And because only one immersive system was available for this experiment, no (I-I) test could be planned but, instead, participants had to alternate its usage –(D-I) and (I-D) trials–.

In any case, the dependent variables were the time to complete the task by the individual or the couple, and the subjective ease of use of the system as perceived by each participant.

5.2 Participants

Eighteen people took part in this experiment. There were 11 men and 7 women, with ages ranging from 19 to 31 years old. The different number of participants of each gender was thought not to have a significant influence on results, based on our experience on previous evaluations [4]. All of them were technically-literate, recruited from computer science courses and from teaching and research staff, but not related to our lab.

5.3 Experiment Procedure

For each trial, participants were first instructed on how to play with the blocks and were given some time to get used to them. To help participants in their tasks, different views of the models –shown in Fig. 1, as a picture inside the environment– served as graphical instructions.

Each participant completed 6 individual trials (3 platforms x 2 models) and 8 more in pairs (4 platform combinations x 2 models). The order of trials for each participant differed from the others so as to counterbalance any influence of learning on performance. Time taken to fulfil each task was annotated, and then each participant filled in a questionnaire that was designed to get insight into the problems faced when using each platform, and whether the participants preferred to work alone or collaborate in pairs. In that questionnaire there was also a blank space for them to express their thoughts regarding the platforms and collaboration.

5.4 Results and Analysis

The bar charts shown in Fig. 4 represent the average times and standard deviation for each task. It can be clearly stated that there is one platform that outstands from the others, as the time taken to complete the tasks with the real game (R, individually, and R-R, working in pairs) is much less than using any computer platform. This may mean that the implementation did not achieve the same degree of naturalness as the real one, mostly because block manipulation was limited by the input devices, forcing us to use a gross hand-block interaction instead of a fine finger-block one.

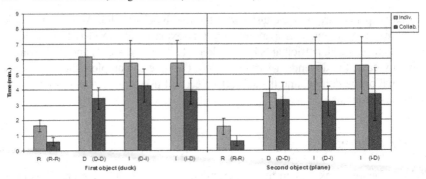

Fig. 4. Mean completion times for duck (left) and the airplane (right).

In order to analyze the data gathered from the usage of the virtual game, different ANOVA (ANalysis Of VAriance) were carried out to confirm if the differences observed in data were significant or not. A first analysis showed no evidence that building the duck was different from one platform to another ($F(4,30) = 1.08$; $p > 0.05$), even though the completion times in collaborative tests were slightly lower. However, this was not the case for the airplane, for which ANOVA revealed a significant difference in time ($F(4,30) = 3.15$; $p < 0.05$). This outcome confirmed our expectations, as the first model –the duck– was supposed to be difficult to split in parts that could be completed in parallel by each participant of a pair, so no significant improvement in time was expected in that case. On the other hand, the airplane was thought to be easier to divide in smaller objects which could be build by a different participant of each pair, and then put them altogether, thus some improvement in time was expected in comparison with single user trials.

Then, the analysis was repeated once again without the completion times from individual tests, so that only collaborative were accounted this time, using ANOVA to check if any particular pair of platforms performed better than the others. This time, the results for the duck model ($F(2,18) = 0.91$; $p > 0.05$) and for the airplane model ($F(2,18) = 0.27$; $p > 0.05$) showed no evidence of significant difference in data gathered for each pair of platforms. This means that performance in collaboration does not depend on platforms but on the models to build, as stated before. However, these results may be a consequence of the presence of the desktop platform in every trial, lacking this study of completion times when performing the tasks in a pair of immersive environments. Better times may be expected if tested with that combination, as a better perception of depth seems to make manipulation easier in comparison to the desktop.

As for the questionnaires, Table 1 shows the frequencies of values given by users as regards to the operation of each platform in particular. In the questionnaire, they were asked to mark, with a value from 1 to 5, the perceived ease of use of the platform, bearing in mind that a value of 1 meant it was easy to use, and a value of 5 meant that it was difficult to use. At the end of each row in the table, the average value for the corresponding setup is shown.

Table 1. Ease of use of each setup, as perceived by participants. The right table gathers, for each couple, the point of view of the user that employed the platform shown in the first column, showing the platform his or her mate was using in the second column.

Single user	Values						In pair		Values					
	1	2	3	4	5	Mean		Mate	1	2	3	4	5	Mean
R	10	7	1			*1,5*	R	R	16	1	1			*1,2*
D	2	5	9	2		2,6	D	D	4	9	4	1		2,1
I	2	2	6	5	3	3,3	D	I	8	1	6	3		2,2
							I	D	3	4	4	7		2,8

As it can be expected, the participants gave better marks to the real game, as it was not hampered by input technology. Surprisingly enough, the desktop is the second most valued system by users, which in turn makes it also the preferred platform when collaborating with other users. This may be caused by the way rotations were performed in the desktop environment, not as smooth as in the immersive environment but in successive amounts of 90 degrees, which was introduced to facilitate the task to users. This finding also stands true for the desktop-immersive combination, as it gives us the perception of the user from the desktop side of the coupled systems, no matter which platform the other participant used. On the other hand, not only the desktop interface was improved, but also the immersive one was, doing our best to adapt the interaction to the platform used. Thus, in the immersive case, the problem found was to correctly align one block with another in order to connect them, and so a kind of magnetic field was added to help the user in this task, connecting the blocks even when they were not totally aligned.

Although it should be noted that a direct comparison of our results with those obtained by other researchers is difficult, due to differences in the devices used or in the concrete tasks carried out, there are some works [8, 9] that are similar enough to our experiment, at least as regards the environment and task used, to place such comparison. However, when doing so, the conclusions are not so similar. First, their authors report that the performance obtained by using immersive platforms is better than using the desktop setup. In our case, the results of performance are quite independent of the platform, and so we do not come to the same conclusion. This could be motivated by the fact that those works relied on projection technology, not on head-mounted displays. Even though both systems are referred as immersive ones, each one has its unique characteristics. Second, if we account for the ease of use of each setup as perceived by participants, our conclusion also differs from those authors, because in our study the users valued the desktop platform as being better than the immersive one. This result could be motivated by the previous experience of users, who were more familiar with desktop-based devices than with immersive ones.

Finally, only one of the participants complained about being hindered by the other user, the rest of them simply suggested improvements to the system, and commented about the operation of the input and output devices. Regarding the immersive system, some of the participants complained about the amount of wires around them, as well as the weight of the helmet and the fatigue it caused to them. As for the desktop system, the comments were related to depth perception (moving blocks further or closer), which may be solved by using 3-D stereo graphics, not used here.

6 Conclusions and Future Work

A Collaborative Virtual Environment –CVRPrismaker– that reproduces a block building game has been described in this paper. This CVE has been developed following a novel environment model that takes into account spatial and organizational information when interacting inside the CVE, which made the design easier and also allowed us to adapt interaction to each platform used. This model has been briefly described in this paper, and is currently under development.

Besides, it has also been described an experimental evaluation of the CVE in different setups, real and virtual, individual and collaborative, and the results of that experiment have been presented and analyzed. It this experiment, especial attention is given to the task to be developed, since users have to build different objects, designed having collaboration details in mind.

As the most important conclusion, this evaluation has showed that, even though the collaborative task completion time were lower than the individual one, there is no significant evidence that collaborative work is better than individual work in every situation. According to the factors evaluated in this paper, we try to explain it focusing on the platform used and the task performed.

Regarding the platform used, with a study and an adaptation of the interaction to the capabilities of the platform used, the CVE can be experienced using immersive devices as well as conventional desktop-based devices, resulting in similar performance outcomes.

The bigger impact is then due to the task performed. Thus, designers should take into account the study of the suitability of the tasks performed in their system for a collaborative approach before choosing these kinds of systems.

Another conclusion of the evaluation is that users preferred the use of desktop platforms. This can be explained having a look at the description of the participants, being all of them used to working with desktop computers, but not with VE systems. Besides, some of them complained about the use of the VR devices (wires and helmet), what might have a great influence in their decision.

As a future work, it is planned to carry out a new evaluation using immersive systems at both ends of the collaborative system, and also study collaboration on the Internet as opposed to a local network. Both issues are currently under development.

Acknowledgments. The authors thank the subjects in the experiment for their time and effort. This work has been partially supported by MEC CICYT TIN2004-08000-C03-01 and JCCM PAI06-0093 projects.

References

1. Caligary TrueSpace 7. http://www.caligari.com/
2. Figueroa, P., Green, M., Hoover, H.J. (2002) InTml: a description language for VR applications. In: 7th international Conference on 3D Web Technology. Web3D '02. ACM Press, pp 53-58.
3. Frécon, E., Stenius, M. (1998) Dive: A scalable network architecture for distributed virtual environments. Distributed Systems Engineering Journal, 5(3), pp 91-100.
4. García, A.S., Molina, J.P., González, P. (2005) Aproximación a la evaluación de interfaces de Realidad Virtual. In: VI Congreso de Interacción Persona-Ordenador (AIPO).
5. Greenhalgh, C., Benford, S. (1995) MASSIVE: a collaborative virtual environment for teleconferencing. In: ACM Trans. Comput.-Hum. Interact. 2, 3 (Sep. 1995), pp 239-261.
6. Greenhalgh, C., Vaghi, I. (1998) Demanding the Impossible: Data Consistency in Collaborative Virtual Environments. (Technical Report version 1.2, Department of Computer Science, University of Nottingham UK)
7. Grudin, J.: CSCW: History and Focus. University of California. IEEE Computer, pp 19-26. (1994)
8. Heldal I, Steed A, Schroeder R (2005) Evaluating Collaboration in Distributed Virtual Environments for a Puzzle-solving Task. In: HCI International 2005, the 11th International Conference on Human Computer Interaction. Las Vegas
9. Heldal, I., Spante, M., Connel, M.: Are Two Heads Better than One? Object-focused Work in Physical and in Virtual Environments. In: 13th ACM Symposium on Virtual Reality Software and Technology, Cyprus. (2006)
10. Kiyokawa, K., Takemura, H., Katayma, Y., Iawasa, H., Yokoya, N. (1997) VLEGO: A Simple Two-Handed Modelling Environment Based on Toy Blocks. In: ACM Virtual Reality Software and Technology, pp 27-34.
11. Martin, D., Sommerville, I. (2004) Patterns of cooperative interaction: Linking ethnomethodology and design. In: ACM Trans. on Computer-Human Interaction , pp 58-89.
12. Martínez, D., García, A.S., Molina, J.P., González, P. (2007) Towards an interaction model for CVEs. In: 12th International Conference on Human-Computer Interaction, Beijing, China.
13. Molina, J.P., García, A.S., Martínez, D., Manjavacas, F.J., Blasco, V., López, V., González, P. (2006) The development of glove-based interfaces with the TRES-D methodology. In: 13th ACM Symposium on Virtual Reality Software and Technology. Cyprus, pp 216-219.
14. OpenSceneGraph. http://www.openscenegraph.com/
15. Ogre3D. http://www.ogre3d.org/
16. Rakkarsoft: Raknet. www.rakkarsoft.com/
17. Roberts, D., Wolff, R. (2004) Controlling Consistency within Collaborative Virtual Environments. In: 8th IEEE International Symposium on Distributed Simulation and Real Time Applications DS-RT, Budapest.
18. Roberts, D., Wolff, R., Otto, O., Steed, A. (2003) Constructing a Gazebo: Supporting Teamwork in a Tightly Coupled, Distributed Task in Virtual Reality. Presence: Teleoperators and Virtual Environments, 16 (6), pp 644-657.
19. Ruddle, R.A., Savage, J.C.D., Jones. D.M. (2002) Symmetric and Asymmetric Action Integration During Cooperative Object Manipulation in VE. In: ACM Transactions on Computer-Human Interaction, Vol. 9, No. 4, pp 285–308.

20. Singhal, S., Zyda, M.(1999) Networked Virtual Environments: Design and Implementation, Addison Wesley.
21. VR Juggler. http://www.vrjuggler.org/
22. VRML. http://www.web3d.org/x3d/specifications/#vrml97

Presentation Adaptation: Results from a Case Study

A. Pedrero, V. Alonso, M.A. Villarroel, P. de la Fuente, A.S. Cabaco

Computer Science School. Pontifical University of Salamanca, 37002 Salamanca, Spain
{apedreroes, valonsose} @upsa.es

Computer Science Department. University of Valladolid, 47011 Valladolid, Spain
{miguelv, pfuente}@infor.uva.es

Psychology Department. Pontifical University of Salamanca, 37002 Salamanca, Spain
asanchezca@upsa.es

Abstract   This work presents some of the results from a study analyzing the effects of interface customization on user tasks. The study was developed in the context of an interface developed for specialists visiting a Virtual Museum. The information about the time used to complete a task has been collected to acquire quantitative data. The observations were developed both before and after the adaptation of the interface. The way in which the users interact with the customization system was also analyzed, paying special attention to the effects that the customization process has on the interaction with the main system. To acquire qualitative and subjective data, the users were asked to fill out a questionnaire to find out their opinion about the interface adaptation.

1 Introduction

The customization of everyday things has become usual in our lives. For example, when we want to buy a new car, we are used to choosing the exterior colour, the interior or other accessories according to our preferences or needs. From a technological point of view, today it is common practice to change the melody of our mobile phone or even have separate melodies depending on the identity of the caller. Working with computers, many users know how to personalize the Microsoft Work icon bar by adding or removing icons based on the task they are doing.

Apart from aesthetic questions, is it useful for the user to spend time personalizing a computer program according to his/her needs? This work aims to answer this question. To do so, we have studied presentation adaptation in a hypermedia system. We look at the users' subjective opinion about the adaptation, and we also look at more objective results to evaluate it. The rest of this work is organized as

M. Redondo et al. (eds.), *Engineering the User Interface*,
DOI: 10.1007/978-1-84800-136-7_15, © Springer-Verlag London Limited 2009

follows: Firstly, we introduce the Iconographic Programme of St. Ignatius Loyola, the hypermedia system used to make the tests with the users. Then, we present the two tests carried out with the users and the results of these tests. After a description of related work, we end with some conclusions and future work.

2 About the Iconographic Programme

In 1566 St. Francis Borgia commissioned Ribadeneria to write the biography of Saint Ignatius. In 1572 "*Life of the Blessed Father Saint Ignatius Loyola*" was first published in Latin. This biography would form the literary source that formed the basis for the "*Life*" of the Saint in engravings.

The sketches and drawings of this biography were produced by Petrus Paulus Rubens (around 1605-1606). The engraver Jean Baptiste Barbé then reproduced these drawings in a collection of 80 prints that illustrated the life of St. Ignatius. These prints were produced in Rome in 1609 as "*Vita Beati P. Ignatii Loiolae*". Inspired in these prints, Sebastian Conca (1680-1764) made 28 canvases to show the life and most important acts of the Saint. For the majority of the sequences, Conca followed the dictates of Barbé's prints almost literally. This 28 canvas collection, unique in the world (it represents the only complete iconographic sequence on the life of the Saint) is dated before 1755 and is located at the Pontifical University of Salamanca. All the canvases are double-framed in the Baroque style with a tightly angled edge contour against the canvas. At the bottom of each item (both prints and canvases) there is a legend that aims to describe the illustration belonging to an event of his life.

With all this material, we have built a digital library that we have used in the work. So, each of the 28 elements that make up the digital library is composed of a text passage of St. Ignatius' life, the print and the canvas, both print and canvas legends and a fragment of text containing a deeper study that compares the illustrations. The images (print and canvas) can be shown larger (by clicking on them with the mouse). In figure 1 there is a screenshot of a canvas beside its legend and the biographic text of St. Ignatius' life. Also shown are the buttons used to navigate through the different elements of the library and to return to the main index.

This system will be used as the main teaching material in a degree subject (Theology) at the University. This subject is based on the study of the Saint's life. The students, separated in groups, will work on distinct elements of the iconographic programme (sometimes legends, or prints, other times legends and canvases, ...).

3 Related Work

There are different terms to describe systems that are changeable in the context of use: "adaptable", "customizable", "tailorable", "malleable" [19].

There are also different adaptive hypermedia systems classifications: e.g. [3, 4]. Other works in the literature belongs to the fields of e-commerce [2, 11, 20], e-learning [6, 7, 14, 17] and information retrieval [5]. Just as in [18], in our work, the interface adaptation is applied to each individual user, not to all the users. The methods we have used (questionnaires and time measurement) are not new, and they are common methods in usability studies [10]. Up to the present, we have not found any references of experimental works similar to the one we are presenting now. There are some examples of empirical evaluations of adaptive systems, although it is difficult to value the success of this adaptation because there are no widely accepted measures [9]. In [14] there is an example applied to Athens University Computer Science and Telecommunication second year students.

The aim was to evaluate an educational system and to analyze the students' behavior throughout the study. The most similar experiment to the one we have made is the work of Alpert [1]. In that work they did three tests aimed at seeing how an electronic commerce system adapts itself to the preferences of its visitors. It must be said that they were longer tests (from 2 to 5 hours) in which the participants were paid for their collaboration.

In any case, the specific nature of the evaluated webs (e-commerce 4 sites) is quite different to the one we have used in this work (virtual art museums).

In the case of works related to art museums, [13] proposed a metric to evaluate the quality of web sites and it is applied to a comparative study of four museums (the Louvre, the Prado Museum, the Metropolitan Museum and the National Gallery of Art). There is also a similar work in [8]. Nevertheless, the main aim of both works is to check the sites usability, functionality, reliability and efficiency, but they do not consider any adaptation aspects.

4 Description of our Work

In order to analyze the effects that interface customization has on the user tasks we have done two tests. In the first test, we wanted to assess these effects in an objective manner. To do so, information about the time used to complete a task has been collected to acquire quantitative data. In the second one, the users were asked to customize an interface to visit a virtual museum using an easy tool (similar to a wizard). Then, the different interfaces created by the users were studied to see which interface elements were most frequently added. We also considered the users' degree of satisfaction with the new interface. Another question we asked ourselves at the beginning of the work was related to the users' mental model of the system: do the users need to modify this model after the adaptation process? Do they understand the elements that appear in the new interface and their relations?

4.1 First Test

The main objective of this test was to know if interface adaptation has any influence on the time a user spends doing a task (reducing this time). To do so, we collated information concerning the time users took to complete a task before and after the adaptation of the interface. As a secondary objective, we also considered the users' opinion about the adaptation process.

How we did the test: The test was carried out with three groups of students coming from different degree courses of the Pontifical University of Salamanca. The numbers of the students in each group were as follows:

- 13 students from the 5th year of Theology.
- 28 students from the 5th year of Computer Science.
- 19 students from the 1st year of Speech Therapy.

The difference in the numbers of the students in each group was due to the dissimilarity in the number of students in each degree course and this difference was unavoidable.

All the tests took place on the same date (and using the same computers). First of all, the participants were told why they had been called and the purpose of the study. Then the contents of the virtual museum and the iconographic programme representing St. Ignatius Loyola's life were shown to them. After this explanation they were introduced to the two-part task they had to do:

- Firstly, they had to answer some questions about the different contents they could find in the digital library. Then, they had to fill out a questionnaire related to aspects of using the system (ease of use, ...) but not linked to the contents of the library.
- Secondly, they also had to answer a few questions about the contents of the library but, this time, using a new interface (the meaning of the word interface was explained to the students of Theology and Speech Therapy because some of them did not know the term). Again, they had to fill out another questionnaire to know their opinion of the adaptation process.

As for the students' abilities using Internet, 62% of the Theology students visited the Web more than five times a week. In the case of the Speech Therapy students, the percentage was a bit lower (32%), although 63% of them visited the Web at least four times a week. As expected, all the Computer Science students visited the Web more than 5 times a week.

On the other hand, it must be said that most of the students that collaborated in the test (independently of the degree they were studying) did not use the Web to visit museums frequently (almost 45% of the Theology and Computer Science students had not visited any web museum; this percentage rose to 84% for the Speech Therapy students).

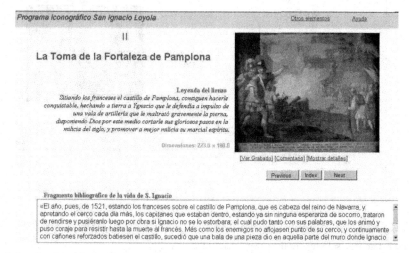

Fig. 1. Interface used in the first part of the test.

In the first part of the test, the students had to answer four questions related to some contents of the digital library. It must be noted that the interface used in this part did not have all the information needed to answer the questions. The interface (Fig.1) included the canvas and its legend, a text with a fragment of St. Ignatius' life, besides a link to the picture, the deeper comments and the details. As all the questions were related to the contents of both the canvas and the picture legends, and due to the absence of the latter legend in the interface, the users had to follow the link labelled as *"View Picture"* to get to the information they needed to answer the questions.

All four questions were related to the first four elements of the library, so the users only had to press the *"Next"* button to reach the contents needed to answer the following questions.

After answering the four questions, the participants filled out a questionnaire to know their opinion of the system, the ease of use, the amount of information on the screen, the user's habits, ... In addition, to evaluate their mental model of the system they were also asked about the position on the screen of some interface elements.

The users then started the second part of the test. They had to answer some questions about the contents of the library (again, all the questions were about consecutive elements of the library, so they only had to press the *"Next"* button to get to the new element).

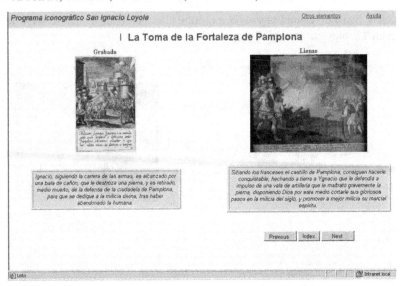

Fig. 2. Interface selected for the second part of the test.

In the second part, the interface had been adapted to the task the user had to do. The interface adaptation was done automatically by the system (without any user intervention). Both the print and its legend were included in the interface. Thus, the users did not have to follow any link to get to this information. In order to keep the interface clean (without too many elements) the biographic fragment of the Saint's life located at the bottom of the interface was removed.

Once more, after answering the questions, the users had to fill out a questionnaire. In this case, its purpose was to know the users' opinion of the second interface and the comparison of both interfaces. There were also questions related to the presence/absence and position of the different elements in the interface.

Results of the first test: As can be seen in Fig. 3, 4 and 5, the average time used to answer the questions of the second task is lower than that of the first task. The results are similar in the three groups. According to the initial hypothesis, the interface adaptation (by including an element needed to complete the task) has allowed a reduction in the time spent by the users to complete the task.

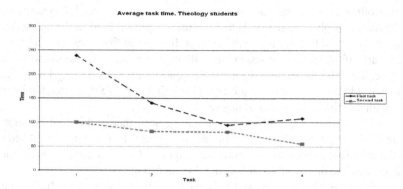

Fig. 3. Average time used to answer each question (Theology students)

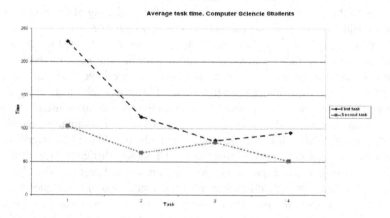

Fig. 4. Average time used to answer each question (Computer Science students)

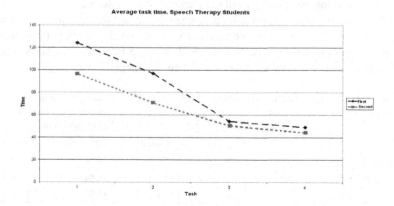

Fig. 5. Average time used to answer each question (Theology students)

In both tests, as the user answers the questions, the time needed to answer them is lower. Probably, one reason is that the user is getting used to the task as she/he does it. To avoid this, we asked the users to fill out the first questionnaire between both parts of the test. In the second test although the user is forced to use a new interface, the time needed to answer the first question is considerably lower that the one needed to answer the first question of the first test. We think that the interface adaptation is the main reason of this reduction of time.

Looking at the results of the test, it can be seen that in the third question the time used is significantly lower. The reason is that this question was related only to the print (not to the canvas). In the second part of the test there is also a notable variation in the time used to answer the third question.

In this case, this is because of the larger size of the legends (more time is needed to read them) and perhaps because of the poor wording of this question. All the results of both tests can be read in [15].

One of the questions we asked ourselves at the beginning of the work was if the user would feel lost when he/she had to use a new interface.

Taking into account the fact that all the users could complete the task correctly with the new interface, we consider that the user has not been forced to re-learn the operation of the system. It must be noted that we have analyzed the system logs; looking at them we can see that none of the users felt "lost" using the new interface (none of them significantly increased the number of mouse clicks needed to look for the answers). The questions of the second questionnaire were aimed at finding out the difficulties the users had when adapting to the new interface. Their answers revealed that many of them did not find any difficulty (see Table 1). In this questionnaire some questions about the presence/absence of the elements in the interface and their position were also included. Two of these questions were: *"Do you remember the position of the canvas in the first/second interface?"* or *"Was the biographic fragment of the Saint's life shown in the second interface?.*

With these questions we wanted to analyze the users' mental model of the system and how the users recognized the elements in the interface.

Based on the results and taking into account the fact that the majority of the users answered these questions correctly, we can conclude that they made a correct mental model of the system. So, we think that the interface adaptation does not modify the users' mental model of the system in a negative way.

Table 1. Users' opinion of the difficulty of adapting themselves to the new interface.

	Did you have any difficulty adapting to the new interface?				
	Much	Regular	Not much	Very little	None
Theology	0 %	15 %	15 %	24 %	46 %
Computer Science	0 %	0 %	14 %	14 %	72 %
Speech Therapy	0 %	0 %	11 %	11 %	78 %

Table 2. Question about the position of the engraving in the second interface?

	Which position was the engraving in?		
	Correct	Wrong	Don't remember
Theology	77 %	23 %	0 %
Computer Science	89 %	11 %	0 %
Speech Therapy	89 %	11 %	0 %

4.2 Second Test

The main aim of the second test was to know which interface the users prefer when they have the possibility of choosing its content and the layout of elements on the screen. We also wanted to know the users' opinion of the functionality of selecting the interface elements and whether they consider interface adaptation to be a waste of time.

How we did the test: The test was done with two student groups coming from different degrees of the Pontifical University of Salamanca.

- 38 students from the 2nd year of Computer Science.
- 32 students from the 4th year of Educational Psychology.

As for the frequency of Internet use by the participants, 71% of the Computer Science students visited the Web more than five times a week (the percentage was lower than that of the first test, perhaps because of the level of the students -2nd year in this test as compared to 5th level in the first-). The frequency of Internet use by the Educational Psychology students is notably lower: only 24% used the Web more than five times a week and 44% used the Web less than once a week. As in the first test, the majority of the students did not visit web museums frequently (71% and 91% of the students had not visited an on-line web museum).

As we did in the first test, the participants were told why they had been called, the purpose of the study and the tasks they had to do. Then, they had to answer some questions about the contents of the digital library (four questions) using the interface in Figure 1. After that, they had to run a wizard to make a new interface according to their needs and preferences.

Using the wizard [16] users could select the content and the layout of the interface: for example they could choose whether the interface included both the prints and the canvases, their legends ... Through 5 steps, the tool asked the users about the presence/absence of the different elements of the library. In relation to the legends, they could be directly shown on the screen or they could be shown when the user moved the mouse over a link labelled "*Legend*". The wizard uses a grid layout: from a template it lays out the different interface elements selected by the user.

The number of rows depends on the number of interface elements selected by the user to be included in the interface. The wizard does not allow certain combinations of elements: that is, a canvas legend cannot be chosen to be in the interface if the corresponding print or canvas is not also selected.

The layout also considers other questions: the legend is near the corresponding image, if the number of elements is high, the image size is shrunk, ... The new interface is saved as part of the user profile and is not modified unless the user runs the wizard again. Saving each interface allows us to compare them and look for similar interface patterns, as has been done in this work. The study of these interfaces would allow the interface shown to new users of the system to be modified: the "default" interface could be modified using the elements included by other users in their interfaces as the basis.

After the interface adaptation, the participants had to resume the test, using the new interface to look for the information and to answer the four remaining questions. Finally, the users had to fill out a questionnaire in order to know their opinion about the system, the task done and the interface they had made.

Results of the second test   The analysis of the interfaces made by the users with the assistant has allowed us to see how most of the users included the same library elements in the interface. These elements are mainly those needed to do the task: both images (print and canvas) and their legends. The differences between the interfaces were mainly the position of the elements (image with legend 12 on the right/left) and the presence of the biographic text about the Saint's life. From a correspondence analysis and from a hierarchy agglomerative cluster analysis [12], four main interface groups have been detected:

- A first group with those presentations that include most of the elements (images, legend and the text with a biography fragment). About 33% of the interfaces were in this group.
- The second group has the interfaces with both images (print and canvas) and the legends shown directly on the screen (the interface is very similar to the one shown in Fig. 2). 46% of the interfaces were in this group.
- A third group having the interfaces made up of the images and the legends, the latter being accessed by the user moving the mouse over the link. About 15% of the interfaces where in this group.
- A fourth, very small group (about 6%) where the interfaces were not modified (they were identical to the ones used in the first part of the test).

As we said before, looking at the results, we can see that most of the users included the elements needed to do the task. The biggest group (the second one – near half of all users–) included only the elements needed to do the task. This means that they do not include only the elements they need but also they remove those ones that they do not use in the task. In the case of the fourth group, we cannot conclude if the users wanted to leave the interface unchanged or they did not understand the task (interface construction) they had to do.

When the users were asked for their opinion about the possibility of adapting the interface to the task they were doing, the majority of users evaluated this functionality as quite or very positive. When evaluating the time spent doing the interface adaptation, most of them did not consider the adaptation process as a waste of time. It must be noted that in the second group (Educational Psychology students) this opinion was less generalized, although most of them considered the possibility of choosing the elements' position as positive. As we said before, this group of students uses the Web less frequently. In a deeper analysis of their answers, we have seen that the students who considered this effort as a waste of time were those with a frequency of Web use of less than once a week. Perhaps that is why they considered it to be a waste of time.

The customization facilities could also be useful in those situations where the user works with different elements at different moments, but also in a repetitive way. In order to help the user to customize the interface it is important that the customization tool would be easy. It could also be important that this tool do not take too much time to complete the customization process.

Table 3. Users' opinion about the possibility of adapting the interface.

	Do you think it is positive to control which elements will be in the interface and where they will appear?				
	Not at all	A bit	More or less	Quite	Very
Computer Science	0 %	0 %	2 %	53 %	45 %
Educational Psychology	0 %	6 %	9 %	69 %	16 %

Table 4. Users' opinion about the time spent in the adaptation task

	Do you think personalizing the interface is a waste of time?				
	Certainly	Probably	Perhaps	Probably not	Certainly not
Computer Science	2 %	8 %	11 %	47 %	32 %
Educational Psychology	3 %	19 %	28 %	31 %	19 %

5 Conclusions and Future Work

Starting from the question asked at the beginning of this work about the usefulness of user interface adaptation, we have set about demonstrating, with empirical results obtained from two tests with users, that this adaptation could be positive for the user. The results of both tests have shown that the adaptation is helpful when it aimed to adapt the interface to a concrete task and that the user evaluates this functionality as positive. These results, not only the objective ones (time measurements), but also the subjective ones (the users' personal opinions) lead us to think that the interface adaptation could turn the time spent in that process into a reduction of the total time spent by the user in doing the task (the easier the interface becomes, the less time the users spend doing the task).

We are aware that the task is very specific and the system used to do the tests is not a system widely used by users. Moreover, in the second test, the user was "forced" to run the wizard in order to personalize the interface.

In fact, we know that users do not frequently use the Web to visit museums (in the case of this iconographic programme, as we said before in the 2nd paragraph, it will be used as the basic material of a subject so it is supposed that the number of visits will be higher). Nevertheless, we think that the results of our work can be extrapolated to other kinds of systems, because the repetition of a task over different elements of a hypermedia system [14] is frequent in museums, libraries, etc., especially when we are talking about researchers who need to know in depth specific museum/library contents. The customization facilities could also be useful in those situations where the user works with different elements at different moments, but also in a repetitive way. In these situations, not all the users work in the same way, nor they are interested in the same contents and, so, not all of them would use the same interface. In any case, as we will propose next, it would be interesting to look at the results of a similar test in other kinds of systems.

As future work, we shall consider the following matters:

- To analyze whether the user voluntarily runs the wizard developed for the adaptation purpose (up to now we have asked the user to run the wizard).
- Repeat the tests with non-student users to see if the results are similar or different. It would also be interesting to do the test with other groups of users with different ages (if possible with older people) and compare the results of the tests.
- To attempt to include task detection mechanisms for the system to recommend the inclusion of interface elements and, after that, to value how the user reacts to those recommendations.
- To do the tests using systems with different characteristics (different from museums).

References

1. Alpert S.R., Karat J., Karat C.M., Brodie C., Vergo J.G.: (2003) User attitudes regarding a user-adaptive e-commerce web site. User Modeling and User- Adapted Interaction 13(4): pp. 373-396
2. Ardissono, L., Goy, A., Meo, R. et al.: (1999) A configurable system for the construction of adaptive virtual stores. World Wide Web Journal 2(3): 143-159
3. . de Bra, P.: (1999) Design issues in adaptive web-site development. In: Proceedings of the 2nd Workshop on Adaptive Systems and User Modeling on the WWW
4. Brusilowsky, P.: (2001) Adaptive hypermedia. User Modeling and User Adapted Interaction 11: 81-110
5. Bueno, D., Amos, A.D (2001) .: METIORE: a personalized information retrieval system. In: Bauer M, Gmytrasiewicz PJ, Vassileva J (eds) User Modeling 2001, Proceedings of the 8th International Conference UM 2001, pp 168-177
6. Carmona, C., Bueno, D., Guzmán, E., Conejo, R.: (2002) SIGUE: making web courses adaptive. In: Adaptive Hypermedia and Adaptive Web-Based Systems. Proceedings of the 2nd International Conference AH 2002. Springer, pp 376-379

7. Gonschorel, M., Herzog, C.: (1995) Using hypertext for an adaptive help system in an intelligent tutoring system. In: Proceedings of AI-ED'95, 7th World Conference on Artificial Intelligence in Education. AACE, Washington, pp 351- 358

8. Harms, I., Schweibenz, W.: (2001) Evaluating the usability of a museum web site. In Museums and the Web 2001 Conference Proceedings. Seattle, Washington

9. Höök, K.: (2000) Steps to take before intelligent user interfaces become real. Interacting with computers 12(4):409-426

10. Jordan, P.W.: (1998) Methods for Usability Evaluation. In: An Introduction to Usability. Taylor & Francis. London-Bristol, pp 51-80

11. Karat, C.-M., Blom, J., Karat, J. (eds) (2004) Designing Personalized Users Experiences in eCommerce. Human-Computer Interaction Series 5. Kluwer Academic Publishers, Dordrecht, The Netherlands

12. Lebart, L., Morineau, A., Warwick, J.F.: (1984) Multivariate Descriptive Statistical Analysis. John Wiley, New York

13. Olsina, L.: (1999) Web-site quality evaluation method: a case study on museums. In: 2nd Workshop on Software Engineering over the Internet

14. Papanikolaou, K.A., Grigoriadou, M., Kornilakis, H., Magoulas, G.: (2003) Personalizing the interaction in a web-based educational hypermedia system: the case of INSPIRE. User Modeling and User-Adapted Interaction 13(3):213- 267

15. Pedrero, A.: (2004) Efectos de la adaptación de la presentación en sistemas hipermedia. Ph.D. thesis, Universidad de Valladolid

16. Pedrero, A., Alonso, V., Villarroel, M., de la Fuente, P (2005)..: Two different tools for user interface personalization. In: Iadis International Conference WWW/Internet 2005, Lisbon, pp. 76-80

17. Pérez, T., Gutiérrez, J., Lopistguy, P.: (1995) An adaptive hypermedia system. In: Proceedings of AI-ED'95, 7th World Conference on Artificial Intelligence in Education. AACE, Washington, pp 351-358

18. Perkowitz, M., Etzioni, O.: (1999) Towards Adaptive Web Sites: Conceptual Framework and Case Study. Computer Networks 31(11-16):1245-1258

19. Stevens, G., Quaisser, G., Klann, M. (2006) Breaking It Up: An Industrial Case Study of Component-Based Tailorable Software Design. In: Lieberman H, et al. (eds) End-User Development. Springer, Dordrecht, The Netherlands, pp 269-294

20. Strachan, L., Anderson, J., Sneesby, M., Evans, M.:(1997) Pragmatic User Modelling in a Commercial Software System. In: 6th International Conference on User Modeling (UM-97). Springer, Italy, pp 129–200 16

Improving a Zoom+Pan Interface with Overview+Detail or Focus+Context Features: A Comparative Evaluation

J. Urquiza-Fuentes, C.A. Lázaro-Carrascosa, J.Á. Velázquez-Iturbide

Department of Computer Science Languages and Systems, Rey Juan Carlos University
C/Tulipán s/n, 28933 Móstoles, Spain

{jaime.urquiza, carlos.lazaro, angel.velazquez}@urjc.es

Abstract We present an evaluation of adding Focus+Context vs. Overview+Deatil features to a Zoom+Pan interface. The framework of the evaluation is an interface to deal with large sets of items with specific structural properties (sequential order, heterogeneous sizes), and behavior requirements (flexible interaction, maximizing screen space, minimizing changes in screen). The evaluation involved 43 participants. We studied the effect of three factors (namely, experience with the tasks, size of the sets, and tasks performed with the same set) on effectiveness, efficiency and user's satisfaction. The results show that experienced users of the interface enhanced with the Focus+Context features obtained the best results on effectiveness and efficiency. Furthermore, a satisfaction questionnaire showed that users felt more comfortable with the Focus+Context approach.

1 Introduction

Zoom+Pan (z+p) interfaces represent one of the simplest approaches to cope with large scale workspaces. The user interacts by zooming into items and panning to navigate through the workspace. Although this kind of interfaces has many advantages, also it has an important drawback: the loss of context. In this paper, we investigate possible enhancements to z+p interfaces. We have compared the effect of separately using overview+detail (o+d) or focus+context (f+c) features, within a z+p interface. We implemented both interfaces as a part of an integrated development environment (IDE). The interfaces assist in a novel, effortless approach to the generation and maintenance of program animations [1]. A key feature of the approach is the availability of smaller versions of static visualizations of the execution steps, so that the user can select the most relevant ones. A critical issue here consists in preserving the comprehension of reduced visualizations. Typically, there are a large number of visualizations, so we need some tech-

M. Redondo et al. (eds.), *Engineering the User Interface*,
DOI: 10.1007/978-1-84800-136-7_16, © Springer-Verlag London Limited 2009

nique to cope with them. The rest of the paper is structured as follows. The next section describes the interfaces that we compared. The features and findings of the comparative evaluation are described in sections 3 and 4, respectively. Finally, our conclusions are drawn in section 5.

2 Description of the Interfaces

The original interface was a z+p one. It offered users two independent scrollable views of the items: at their natural size and at reduced size (where the reduction factor was controlled by the user). Fig. 1 shows a snapshot of this interface.

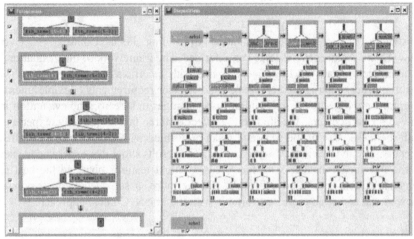

Fig. 1. A snapshot of the original z+p interface.

The view on the left displays items at their natural size, while the view on the right displays the reduced versions. Notice that both views have to be scrollable. Our first approach was to add a detail window to the interface. Therefore, when a reduced item is selected, it is shown at its original size in the detail window. However, in a general usability evaluation [2], we realized that users did not use this interface, even after watching the instructor using it.

We explored alternative ways to enhance the comprehension degree of items [3]. Firstly, we improved the quality of the reduced items by means of the reduction algorithm, by maintaining the aspect ratio and by adding some typographic features. Secondly, we worked on visualization techniques that allow the users to work with global and detailed views of the items. The two following subsections describe both interfaces, they represent respectively enhancements of the z+p interface with o+d and f+c features.

2.1 The Zoom+Pan Interface with Overview+Detail Features

O+d interfaces [4, chapter 4] use two separate windows, one to display the whole workspace and the other for a partial but detailed view of it. The overview window allows the users to navigate through the workspace more efficiently [5], facilitates the user's orientation [6], and gives the user a feeling of control [7]. This kind of interfaces is widely used; for example, most of the operating systems with GUI allow navigating through the file system with an o+d interface.

The result of adding o+d features to our z+p interface is an overview window where reduced items can be amplified (zoom in) and downsized (zoom out). In addition, when the space occupied by the items is larger than the overview window, the scroll (panning) can be used to navigate through the items. Finally, if a reduced item is selected, its original version is shown in the detail window (see Fig. 2).

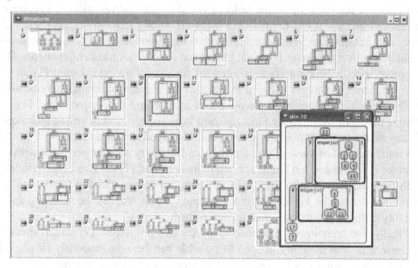

Fig. 2. Z+p interface merged with o+d features. Notice that the quality of the reduced items has been significantly improved

However, we have identified some possible drawbacks in this approach. First, the detailed version occludes some parts of the overview window. We did not allocate any specific area for the detail view because items have different size and shape, so the detail view would change in size (and therefore the size of the overview window) every time a new item was selected, distracting the user's attention. In addition, it has been argued [8] that, in some circumstances, o+d interfaces are slower than zooming ones, probably due to the mental effort required to switch between the detail and the overview windows [9], and to integrate them mentally [4, 10].

2.2 The Zoom+Pan Interface with Focus+Context Features

F+c interfaces [4, section 3.3] also allow accessing global and detailed views of the workspace but in the same window. When an item is selected (focused, in f+c terminology) to display it in detail, the remaining elements are redistributed within the window. These interfaces are supposed to solve the problems of the o+d ones produced by the separation of the overview and detail views.

There exist many interfaces based on the f+c principles. To choose the most appropriate one, we analyzed which interfaces satisfied the requirements imposed by our domain.

2.2.1 Analysis of F+c Techniques Based on the Requirements of our Domain

Our interface has to facilitate the tasks of visual search and selection in a sequence of reduced images. It has to provide a trade-off among space filling, context visibility and images comprehension. It also has to minimize distraction of the user's attention by trying to keep invariant global and relative locations of elements. Being more specific, our interface is intended for the following domain: (1) an ordered sequence of images reduced in size, (2) the number of images may be arbitrarily large, (3) images are heterogeneous in size and proportions, and (4) the relative proportions of reduced images must be preserved. Being an f+c technique, (5) any image can be brought into focus and displayed at a larger size.

From the point of view of user interaction, flexibility must be provided with respect to: (6) the reduction factor applied to images, and (7) the size of the window. Both facilities may lead to the situation where, for some reduction factors, all the miniatures cannot be visible at the same time. Therefore, (8) the scrolling functionality of the z+p interface must be maintained.

Finally, the technique is intended to satisfy two properties: (9) screen space is minimized so that as many images as possible can be simultaneously displayed, and (10) changes in the screen produced by a change of focus are minimized.

Our first requirement states to deal with a sequence of images. Consequently, techniques which do not work with sequences were discarded, such as ConeTrees [11], Tree-maps [12], and Continuous Zoom [13]. We also discarded techniques which work with sequences of elements but unfocused ones are distorted in non-uniform ways (by requirement 4), as Bifocal Lens [14], Perspective Wall [15], or Document Lens [16].

Other f+c techniques exhibit more similarities. Fisheye Views [17, 18] and the Rubber Sheet [19] allows distorting the focused element without distorting the rest. The requirement of keeping as invariable as possible the location of all the elements is (almost) satisfied by Flip Zoom [20], which works with sequences of elements, where non focused elements are uniformly distorted. However, its user interaction facilities are very poor.

We did not find any technique that totally satisfies our requirements. Therefore, we developed a new one, called R-Zoom. It accommodates the facilities of existing f+c techniques that are useful in our domain - Fisheye Views [17, 18], Rubber Sheet [19] and Flip Zoom [20] - as well as some additional ones.

2.2.2 Description of R-Zoom

Here we describe the R-Zoom technique; a preliminary, comparative explanation of the technique can be found elsewhere [21]. Let us call "miniature" to a reduced image and "focus" to a selected image. Ideally, the focus is at its original size. At most, there is one focus at a time, which is highlighted by putting it into a frame. This ensures that it can be distinguished, because it is typical for small images to have the same size both as a miniature and as a focus.

Elements are always placed in left to right and top to bottom order. Each row contains as many miniatures as possible, thus maximizing space filling (see Fig. 3). R-Zoom switches between two states: no-focus state and focus state. The initial state is no-focus, where all the elements are miniatures scaled with the default reduction factor (see Fig. 3a). The focus unselection restores reduced size and location of the focus, as well as the location of the miniatures following the focus.

When a miniature is selected, R-Zoom switches to focus state. Then, the row of the focus is split into two rows, one with the miniatures previous to the focus and other with miniatures after it (R-Zoom stands for Row-splitting Zoom). If the focus fits the first row, it is located there (see Fig. 3b). If it only fits the second row, it is located there (see Fig. 3c). Otherwise, a scaled version of the focus is placed in the row with more free space available. If a second miniature is selected, the operation is equivalent to the unselection of the previous focus followed by the selection of the new one.

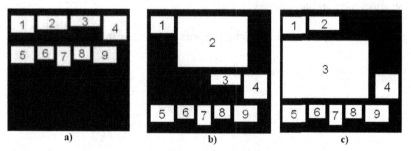

Fig. 3. Distribution of miniatures in: a) no-focus state, b) focus state with the focus located in the first row, ant c) focus state with the focus located in the second row.

Properties (9) and (10) are satisfied by the choices adopted for splitting and laying images out. In summary, these choices split a row into only two rows, use alignment to facilitate user reading, and place images so that changes in focus within a row restrict screen changes to that row.

Miniatures in the first row are aligned to the left and the top, and those in the second row are aligned to the top, maintaining their horizontal location. In addition, a focus placed in a first row is aligned to the top with the miniatures placed before, but a focus placed in a second row is aligned to the bottom with miniatures following it. Screen changes due to focus selection in a row are restricted to the two resulting rows by placing the following row in a vertical location equal to the maximum of:

- The maximum enlarged size of the visualizations at the top row, plus the maximum size of the miniatures at the bottom row.
- The maximum size of the miniatures at the top row plus the maximum enlarged size of the visualizations at the bottom row.

Other possible interactions are: scrolling, change of scale factor, and resize of the window. These interactions affect state transition as summarized in Fig. 4. Scrolling behavior is provided only if all the miniatures do not fit the window. A change in the scale factor produces a new distribution of miniatures in rows, and updates the scrolling properties. A change in the width of the window produces redistribution, and a change of either width or height updates the scrolling properties.

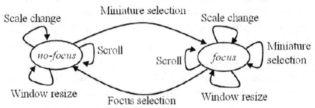

Fig. 4. State transitions and interactions of R-Zoom

A snapshot of the implementation of the R-Zoom technique can be seen in Fig. 5.

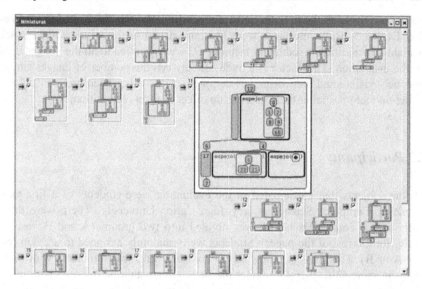

Fig. 5. R-Zoom, the result of improving the z+p interface with f+c features.

3 Description of the Evaluation

We conducted a controlled evaluation where users had to complete a number of visual-search tasks. Visual-search performance of two approaches was compared: R- Zoom (the f+c approach) and the o+d approach. It attempted to find differences in effectiveness, efficiency and the user's satisfaction between both interfaces. We have not found previous evaluations comparing f+c and o+d facilities on z+p interfaces. However, there a number of evaluations showing the advantages of using f+c interfaces [22, 23, 24]. A set of demonstration videos about the evaluation is available via Web: http://www.escet.urjc.es/~jurquiza/rzoom/ demos.htm .

3.1 Apparatus

Computers used in the evaluation were Pentium III 933 MHz processors with 256MB of RAM running Microsoft Windows XP Professional, 17" Hitachi CM620ET monitors at 1024x768 resolution, and Intel 82815 AGP 32MB video cards. We used two applications for the experimental session: the monitor software that was used to time tasks and log users' errors, and the interfaces with which the users worked (i.e. f+c and o+d). Both interfaces were integrated within the same IDE. Both the monitor software and the IDE were developed using Borland Delphi 5. Both interfaces were maximized to use the whole screen space available. In addition, a reduction factor of 50% was applied to all the images used for the evaluation. This factor is a trade off between the number of images simultaneously visible and their degree of comprehension. It has been proved [25] that reduction factors smaller than 50% has no effect in form recognition.

3.2 Participants

All the subjects that participated in the evaluation were students of a first year course of Computer Science at Rey Juan Carlos University. There were three shifts of this course. Each shift was divided into two groups (A and B, respectively, for the rest of the paper). Students were randomly assigned to a group (either A or B). This division allows us to compare tasks measurements with users from the same shift, therefore under the same circumstances, between both interfaces. Participation in the evaluation was voluntary. A total number of 43 students completed the tasks: 17 in A groups and 26 in B groups. All of them had normal or corrected-to-normal vision.

3.3 Method, Procedure and Experimental Design

The participants' tasks involved image magnifying and zooming, and navigating through collections of reduced images seeking specific ones. Target images are cues to the tasks; as they represent execution stages of an algorithm, the user could guess their relative position in the collection. A task was complete when the correct index number of the target image was written in the text box of the monitor software and the user clicked on the "next" button. Then, a new task was presented.

The instructor explained each interface and then the participants trained. Training consisted of one drill-and-practice exercise cued in precisely the same way as the logged tasks. Collections used for both training and logged tasks were visualizations resulting from the execution of different algorithms.

Nine logged tasks were completed with each interface: three different tasks (which had targets at the initial, half and end position, respectively) with three different types of collections: short (one screen), medium (one screen and half), and large (three screens). Participants were not informed that targets were a discrete level of distance away, and the order of exposure was previously fixed for each task. The collection and the target image associated to each task were the same independently from the group the user belonged to. To avoid users getting blocked in tasks, they were allowed to fail four times per task, after which the monitor software noticed the user the correct index number of the target image and continued with the next task.

Participants in group B first completed nine tasks using the o+d interface. Simultaneously, the same tasks were completed by group A using the R-Zoom interface. Then, each group changed the interface and completed nine additional tasks. For the second interface, different images but the same collections were used. Dependent variables of the evaluation are: effectiveness, measured as the number of errors in each task; efficiency, measured as the task completion time related to the effectiveness of the given task; and user's satisfaction.

The maximum number of errors allowed for each task is four; an error occurs when the user types an incorrect index number in the textbox and clicks on the "next" button. Task completion time is the time taken between the beginning of the task (last click on the "next" button of the previous task) and the end (click on the "next" button of the current task with the correct index number in the text box). We compute efficiency as follows: *task_completion_time/(4-number_of_errors)*, so the less the value, the better the efficiency is. We analyzed data using T-student, Willcoxon Signed Ranks, and Mann-Whitney tests, depending on the type of distribution of data, and the comparison being performed.

After completing all the tasks, we measured user's satisfaction. Participants were asked to comment on the interfaces. They filled a questionnaire to rank the interfaces by several subjective measures: overall preference, usefulness, easiness of use, advantages, drawbacks, and the necessity of zooming interfaces in program animation construction.

4 Results

In this section, data are analyzed in two ways: group-interface-based and task-based. In the group-interface-based analysis (GIB, for the rest of the paper), data are referred by the group they belong to, A or B, and the interface used, RZ (R-Zoom) or OD(the o+d interface). Thus, four groups were formed: ARZ, AOD, BOD and BRZ. Within these groups, we also investigated existing dependencies of effectiveness and efficiency, with the size of the collection, and the number of tasks previously performed by the user with the same collection. In the task-based analysis (TB, for the rest of the paper), data are referred by the GIB reference plus a collection index (three collections) and an image index (three images per collection). Thus, task AOD21 is the task where users from group A, using the o+d interface, had to find the first image of the second collection.

In addition to using information on the group and interface used, experience was taken into account. Note that the pair group-interface denotes experience with tasks. Group B firstly used the o+d interface, so BOD denotes no more experience than training (1 task); the same occurs for ARZ. AOD denotes more experience, because they had previously used the R-Zoom interface (1 training task + 9 R-Zoom tasks); the same occurs for BRZ.

Results analyze separately effectiveness and efficiency in target acquisition, and users' satisfaction.

4.1 Verifying Quality of Data

Ideally, subjects in the same group but in different shifts completed the tasks under the same circumstances. Thus, time and error data can be processed independently from the shifts division of participants. Belonging to the same population has been tested for data obtained from participants in the same group but in different shifts. Error data analysis supported this hypothesis, where the minimum value of p was related to ARZ13 ($U=57,000$, $p=0,099$). But significant differences were found in time data for AOD12, BOD22, BRZ11 and BRZ12, see Table 1.

Table 1. Tasks where significant differences exist between users in different shifts

Taks	Significance analysis in time measurements
AOD12	$t(24) = -2,261, p=0,033$
BOD22	$t(15) = 2,722 , p=0,016$
BRZ11	$t(15) = 2,486 , p=0,025$
BRZ12	$t(15) = 2,409 , p=0,029$

Another anomaly was detected in AOD11 and BRZ11. The time spent working with the second interface over the first image of the first collection was considerably greater (over 10 times) than the time for the rest of images of the same collection. Table 2 shows the time in seconds spent by both groups working with the second interface on the first collection, divided by the images found. We conclude that the difference was due to the users having to learn a new interface. Another training task should be included after completing the tasks with the first interface.

Table 2. Average task completion time for each group, in images of the first collection, in the second interface

Group/Image	1st	2nd	3rd
A	482.61 s	34.11 s	42.88 s
B	356.94 s	33.88 s	34.88 s

We have considered both situations: significant differences among the shifts of the same group, and the first image of the first collection in the second interface. For the rest of the analysis we have decided to ignore the time results obtained in the tasks involved: AOD11, AOD12, BOD22, BRZ11, and BRZ12.

4.2 Effectiveness in Target Acquisition

Of the 774 tasks (43 participants using 2 interfaces with 3 collections, and 3 images per collection), 59 failed: 55 one time and 4 two times.

The GIB-analysis found significant differences. Table 3 shows effectiveness data and Table 4 shows the significance difference analysis. For each pair of group-interface, efficiency is measured as: number of errors, error rate (per task) and error probability (computed as the division of the number of errors between the total possible errors, 4 per task). Although both interfaces are highly effective, experienced users with R-Zoom (BRZ) are those who obtained least error rate and error probability.

Significant differences analysis in table 3 shows that adding experience to the use of R-Zoom (ARZ-BRZ) helps users in making 72.0% fewer errors. Note that this is not true for the o+d interface (BOD-AOD). Experienced users also got better error rates and probability: an improvement of 70.8% if they use R-Zoom (BRZ-AOD). Finally, no differences were found for users with little experience (BOD-ARZ).

Table 3. GIB effectiveness data, providing for each pair group-interface: number of errors, errors ratio, and error probability.

Group/Interface	# of errors	Errors / Task	Error prob.
BOD	13	0.085	0.021
ARZ	24	0.102	0.025
BRZ	4	0.026	0.007
AOD	22	0.094	0.024

Table 4. GIB significance differences analysis for effectiveness data, (shadowed cells are no significant differences)

	AOD	BRZ	ARZ
BOD	$U=5910.5, p=0.251$	$p=0.039$	$U=5846.5, p=0.168$
ARZ	$p=0.770$	$U=16835.0, p=0.018$	
BRZ	$U=16607.5, p=0.006$		

In addition, effectiveness is highly independent from both, the size of the collection and the number of previous tasks performed with the same collection, see Table 5. Though slightly (τ-b=0,112), only results from AOD users are dependent from the size of the collection.

Table 5. GIB correlation analysis of effectiveness, with the size of the collection and the number of previous tasks performed with the same collection. Statistical analysis has been performed with the Kendall's Thau-b test (shadowed cells are no significant correlations)

Group/Interface	Size of the collection	Number of previous tasks
BOD	τ-b=0.06 , p=0.228	τ-b=0.029 , p=0.36
ARZ	τ-b=-0.099 , p=0.055	τ-b=-0.082 , p=0.091
BRZ	τ-b=0.028 , p=0.377	τ-b=-0.027 , p=0.379
AOD	τ-b=0,112 , p=0.044	τ-b=0.022 , p=0.367

Results of the TB-analysis were greater than 0.1, so differences in effectiveness come from the whole group of tasks and not from individual ones.

4.3 Efficiency in Target Acquisition

Efficiency is measured as task completion time in seconds related to effectiveness. The GIB-analysis found three significant differences of the six possible comparisons. Table 6 summarizes efficiency measurements together with task completion time, and Table 7 summarizes the significant differences analysis.

Table 6. GIB efficiency data, providing values of both, efficiency & time for each pair group-interface

Group/Interface	Efficiency data	Time data
BOD	M=27.41 , SD=18.680	M=106.8 , SD=71.148
ARZ	M=24.79 , SD=21.609	M=94.31 , SD=78.241
BRZ	M=17.95 , SD=14.712	M=70.93 , SD=57.087
AOD	M=22.26 , SD=16.012	M=85.39 , SD=60.497

Table 7. GIB significance differences analysis for efficiency data, (shadowed cells are no significant differences)

	AOD	BRZ	ARZ
BOD	U=7409, p=0.351	p=0.000	U=12867, p=0.157
ARZ	p=0.430	U=8810.5, p=0.006	
BRZ	U=8956, p=0.011		

Experience has impact on efficiency results for R-Zoom (ARZ-BRZ), the improvement rate is 21.58%; but not for o+d (BOD-AOD). Inexperienced users (BOD-ARZ) got same results, independently of the interface they used. Experienced users (BRZ-AOD) that used R-Zoom got better results (22.64%). Rest of results (BRZ-BOD and ARZ-AOD) support previous ones.

On the contrary to the effectiveness analysis, all but one of the correlations tested in the efficiency analysis were significant, see Table 8. The bigger the collection, the worse the efficiency is, though not very important (τ-b values range between 0.169 and 0.352). And the more tasks previously completed with the same collection, the better the efficiency is. These results were expectable, and the importance of the correlation was similar among the four groups, but the number of previously completed tasks seems to have stronger influence than the size of the collection.

Table 8. GIB correlation analysis of efficiency, with the size of the collection and the number of previous tasks performed with the same collection. Statistical analysis has been performed with the Kendall's Thau-b test (shadowed cells are no significant correlations)

Group/Interface	Size of the collection	Number of previous tasks
BOD	$\tau\text{-}b$=0.169 , p=0.006	$\tau\text{-}b$=-0.537 , p=0.000
ARZ	$\tau\text{-}b$=0.239 , p=0.000	$\tau\text{-}b$=-0.492 , p=0.000
BRZ	$\tau\text{-}b$=0.352 , p=0.000	$\tau\text{-}b$=-0.44 , p=0.000
AOD	$\tau\text{-}b$=0,027 , p=0.31	$\tau\text{-}b$=-0.487 , p=0.000

TB-analysis has been applied to the results of the GIB-analysis, so only the pairs BOD-BRZ, ARZ-BRZ and BRZ-AOD have been taken into account. Of the 20 possible comparisons (3 pairs with 9 tasks per pair, minus 7 ignored tasks), 10 gave significant differences, all of them in favor of the BRZ users. Tables 9, 10 and 11 show the tasks, the significance differences analysis, and the improvement rate.

This analysis evidences that the improvement rate, in average, is bigger in the second and third tasks (36.13% and 36.25%) than in the first task (26.15%). Also, half of the tasks with significant difference are related with the second image. The rationale of this result is the main feature of R-Zoom, it maintains as far as possible the location of context elements. Thus, after locating the first image, the user has had the opportunity of viewing the surrounding context, where the second and the third images could be found, or at least, other images working as cues to locate the target ones.

Table 9. TB-analysis of effic. for BOD-BRZ

Task	Result	Impr.
21	$t(16)$=3.107, p=0.007	28.07%
23	$t(16)$=3.354, p=0.004	40.98%
31	$t(16)$=2.157, p=0.047	22.20%
32	$t(16)$=2.543, p=0.022	39.56%

Table 10. TB-analysis of effic. for ARZ-BRZ

Task	Result	Impr.
21	$t(41)$=2.830, p=0.007	28.17%
22	U=114,000, p=0.008	44.01%
23	$t(41)$=2.276, p=0.028	33.11%
32	$t(41)$=2.322, p=0.025	26.94%

Table 11. TB-analysis of effic. for BRZ-AOD

Task	Result	Impr.
22	$t(38.012)$=2.312, p=0.026	34.04%
23	$t(41)$=2.592, p=0.013	34.67%

4.4 User's Satisfaction

Data about users' satisfaction were collected with a questionnaire. First, we asked about the necessity of zooming interfaces to build algorithm animations with our IDE. 80% of users totally agreed with this need, 18% agreed, see Fig 6a. The second question was about users' preferences. 86% of them preferred R-Zoom, against the 12% who preferred the o+d interface, see Fig 6b.

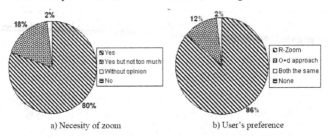

a) Necesity of zoom   b) User's preference

Fig. 6. Users' subjective opinion about the necessity of zoom and interface preferred.

Users' opinion about ease of use was collected in the third question, see Fig 7a. 86% of users thought that R-Zoom is easier, or much easier, to use than o+d, while 6% thought that both interfaces were equally easy to use, and only 8% thought that o+d was easier or much easier to use. The opinion about usefulness was asked in question five, see Fig 7b. 42% of users answered that R-Zoom was much more useful than o+d, 22% answered that R-Zoom was more useful, 34% said that both were equally useful, and 2% said that o+d was much more useful.

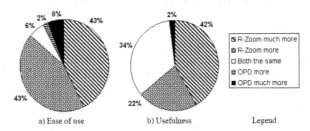

a) Ease of use   b) Usefulness   Legend

Fig. 7. User's subjective opinion about the ease of use and usefulness of both approaches: R-Zoom (the f+c approach) and the o+d approach.

Finally, users were asked to identify advantages and drawbacks in the interfaces they had used. 38 out of 43 users wrote comments. Two common comments were advantages of R-Zoom: 40% said that it offered a global vision of the collection and 24% said that they felt comfortable viewing the focused element and the context ones in the same window. Another common comment is a drawback of o+d: 20% said that they did not feel comfortable viewing the focused element and the context ones in separate windows. Three additional comments were advantages: 17.1% said that it is difficult to get lost with R-Zoom, 17,1% said that o+d offered a global vision of the collection and 14% said that they liked cursor navigation possibilities of R-Zoom. A last comment is a drawback: 11.4% said that is easy to get lost with the o+d interface.

5 Conclusions

Zoom+pan interfaces have many advantages, but their facilities are not enough in some domains. We have studied two ways of augmenting the facilities provided by a zoom+pan interface, by using either an overview+detail or a focus+context approach. The main characteristics of the domain where we carried out the study are to provide the user with a trade-off among space filling, context visibility and images comprehension, and with minimizing the distraction of the user's attention. The starting point was a zoom+pan interface that is a part of an integrated development environment. We developed both approaches by enhancing the zoom+pan interface with overview+detail or focus+context facilities. We had some difficulties to find a proper focus+context technique, so we developed a new one, called R-Zoom, inspired in other existing techniques.

To compare both approaches, we conducted a controlled session. Users worked with both the R-Zoom and the overview+detail interfaces. The evaluation revealed that experienced users using R-Zoom got better results than those using the overview+detail interface. Improvement rates for effectiveness and efficiency were 70.8% and 22.64%, respectively. We also found that experience did not have any impact on users of the overview+detail interface, while it caused improvements in users of R-Zoom. Effectiveness and efficiency improvement rates were 72.0% and 21.58% respectively. Finally, we found that, in both approaches, the number of tasks previously completed with the same collection has stronger influence on efficiency than the collection size.

These measurements were corroborated by users' satisfaction results. 86% of users preferred R-Zoom, 86% thought that R-Zoom was easier or much easier to use than overview+detail, and 64% thought that R-Zoom was more or much more useful. Finally, the two most frequent comments identified to be an advantage the one-window interface of the focus+context approach versus the two-separate-windows interface of the overview+detail approach.

Acknowledgments   This work was supported by project TIN2004-07568 of the Spanish Ministry of Education and Science and by project S-0505/DPI/0235 of the Autonomous Region of Madrid.

References

1. Velázquez-Iturbide, J.Á., Pareja-Flores, C., and Urquiza-Fuentes, J. An approach to effortless construction of program animations, Computers & Education, in press.
2. Medina-Sánchez, M.A., Lázaro-Carrascosa, C.A., Pareja-Flores, C., Urquiza-Fuentes, J., and Velázquez-Iturbide, J.Á. (2004) Empirical evaluation of usability of animations in a functional programming environment, Complutense University of Madrid, Tech. Rep. 141/04.
3. Naharro-Berrocal, F., Pareja-Flores, C., Urquiza-Fuentes, J., and Velázquez-Iturbide, J.Á. (2002) Approaches to comprehension-preserving graphical-reduction of program visualizations, In Proceedings of the 2002 Symposium on Applied Computing, ACM Press, New York, NY, , 771-777.
4. Card, S.K., Mackinlay, J.D., and Shneidermann, B. (1999) Information Visualization. San Francisco, CA: Morgan Kaufmann,.
5. Beard, D.B., and Walker, J.Q. (1990) Navigational techniques to improve the display of large two dimensional spaces. Behaviour and Information Technology, 9(6):451-466
6. Plaisant, C., Carr, D., and Shneiderman, B. (1995) Image-browser taxonomy and guidelines for designers. IEEE Software, 12(2): 21-32,
7. Shneiderman, B. (1998) Designing the User Interface. Reading, MA: Addison-Wesley.
8. Hornbæk, K., Bederson, B.B., and Plaisant, C. (2002) Navigation patterns and usability of zoomable user interfaces with and without an overview, ACM Transactions on Computer-Human Interaction, 9(4), 362-389.
9. Hornbæk, K. (2001) Usability of Information Visualization: Reading and Interaction Processes. PhD thesis, University of Copenhagen. Department of Computing,
10. Spence. R. (2001) Information Visualization. Reading, MA: Addison-Wesley/ACM Press.
11. Robertson, G.G., Mackinlay, J.D., Card, S.K. (1991) Cone Trees: Animated 3D visualizations of hierarchical information, In Proceedings of the SIGCHI Conference on Human factors in Computing Systems '91, ACM Press, New York, NY, 189-194.
12. Johnson B., and Shneiderman, B. (1991) Tree-maps: A space-filling approach to the visualization of hierarchical information structures, In Proceedings of the IEEE Information Visualization Conference (InfoVis'91), IEEE Computer Society Press, Los Alamitos, CA. 284-291.
13. Bartram, L., Ho, A., Dill, J. and Henigman, F. (1995) The continuous zoom: A constrained fisheye technique for viewing and navigating large information spaces, In Proceedings of the 8th annual ACM symposium on User Interface Software and Technology(UIST '95), ACM Press, New York, NY , 207-215.
14. Spence, R., and Apperley, M. (1999) Data base navigation: an office environment for the professional, In: S.K. Card, J.D. Mackinlay and B. Shneidermann (eds.), Information Visualization. San Francisco, CA: Morgan Kaufmann, , 331-340.
15. Mackinlay, J.D., Robertson, G.G., and Card, S.K. (1991) The Perspective Wall: Detail and context smoothly integrated, In Proceedings of the SIGCHI Conference on Human factors in Computing Systems '91, ACM Press, New York, NY, 173-176.
16. Robertson, G.G., and Mackinlay, J.D. (1999) The Document Lens, In S S.K. Card, J.D. Mackinlay and B. Shneidermann (eds.), Information Visualization. San Francisco, CA: Morgan Kaufmann, , 526-569.
17. Furnas, G.W. (1999) The FISHEYE view: A new look at structured files, In: S.K. Card, J.D. Mackinlay and B. Shneidermann (eds.), Information Visualization. San Francisco, CA: Morgan Kaufmann, , 311-330.
18. Sarkar, M., and Brown, M.H. (1992) Graphical fisheye views of graphs. In CHI '92: Proceedings of the SIGCHI Conference on Human Factors in Computing Systems, ACM Press, New York, NY, 83-91.
19. Sarkar, M., Snibbe, S.S., Tversky, O.J., and Reiss, S.P. (1993) Stretching the Rubber Sheet: A metaphor for viewing large layouts on small screens, In: Proceedings of ACM User interface software and technology'93 (UIST '93), New York, NY, 81-91.

20. Björk, S., Holmquist, L.E., and Redström, J. (1999) A framework for focus+context visualizations, In Proceedings of IEEE Symposium on Information Visualization (InfoVis'99), IEEE Computer Society Press, Los Alamitos, CA, 53-56.

21. Urquiza-Fuentes, J., Velázquez-Iturbide, J.Á. (2005) R-Zoom: A visualization technique for algorithm animation construction. In: Proceedings of the IADIS International Conference Applied Computing 2005, IADIS Press, Lisbon, Portugal, 145-152.

22. Shiaw, H., Jacob, R.J.K., and Crane, G.R. (2004) The 3D vase museum: a new approach to context in a digital library. In: Proc. 4th ACM/IEEE-CS Joint Conference on Digital Libraries, New York, NY, 125-134.

23. Bederson, B.B., Clamage, A., Czerwinski, M.P., and Robertson, G.G. (2004) DateLens: A fisheye calendar interface for PDAs, ACM Trans. Comput.-Hum. Interact., 11(1), 90-119.

24. Baudisch, P., Good, N., Bellotti, V., and Schraedley, P. (2002) Keeping things in context: a comparative evaluation of focus plus context screens, overviews, and zooming, Proc. of CHI'02, New York, NY, 259-266.

25. Rensink, R.A. (2004) The invariance of visual search to geometric transformation, Journal of Vision, 4(8), 178.

aCaSo: A Card Sorting Management & Analysis Tool

Elena Lafuente Lapena, Luis Mena Tobar, Pedro M. Latorre Andrés

Departamento de Informática e Ingeniería de Sistemas, Centro Politécnico Superior, C/ María de Luna 1 E-50018 Zaragoza.
elafuente@laboratoriousabilidad.com, luis@menasl.com

Laboratorio Aragonés de Usabilidad, Parque Tecnológico Walqa, Edificio 1 E-22197. Cuarte (Huesca).
platorre@unizar.es,

Abstract The Card Sorting method is widely used to obtain a structure on a group of ideas that are not in order, and it is frequently used to obtain the underlying structure of a set of items for a web menu. The manual analysis of the sessions can result in a tedious job for the moderator. On the other hand, there are a lot of computer applications to obtain the data, but none for the whole data analysis. For these reasons the Usability Laboratory of Walqa decided to develop a tool to automate the whole process as far as possible. This paper explains how aCaSo works, a tool that allows the gathering of information through conducting Card Sorting experiments by the users, the analysis that follows with various existing statistical algorithms, the outlook of results and the creation of reports. Also a typical session, the process of verification of results and the final conclusions are detailed. Beforehand the different existing methods for data analysis are revised and the selection of the ones that are finally implemented is justified.

Keywords: Card Sorting, Usability Engineering, clustering, multidimensional scaling, human computer interaction

1 Introduction

Usability Laboratories need applications that allow managing the evaluation processes and automating as many tasks as possible. With this objective, the Aragonese Usability Laboratory is developing a set of applications named WebA [9,10], which at the present moment permits the management of sessions and the

M. Redondo et al. (eds.), *Engineering the User Interface*,
DOI: 10.1007/978-1-84800-136-7_17, © Springer-Verlag London Limited 2009

carrying out of satisfaction tests from users, the verification of accessibility, and the evaluation of web or applications usability.

In addition, the process of user interface design must be integrated throughout all the software development cycle. One of the most delicate phases is the definition of the conceptual hierarchy, related to the Information Architecture. In this scope, one of the most effective techniques to discover the underlying information structure is Card Sorting [1, 15], which can be developed in two ways (open or closed [1], according to whether the user is allowed to label the group of items or not). Different techniques of analysis are used for the analysis of collected data, of which the most used are clustering and multidimensional scaling [3].

Due to the importance of this analysis in the design phase, the Laboratory decided to implement an application that automates the whole process as far as possible. This paper includes, in the first place, an introduction section which briefly explains the activities and nature of the Aragonese Usability Laboratory, the set of computer applications that have been currently developed, and a state-of-the-art study on the techniques tied to Card Sorting. Then, aCaSo is presented and described, an application which has been developed with the objective to have a tool that allows the evaluator to create and manage the sessions in this method, applying the most adequate analysis techniques and visualizing the results with all of the aforementioned techniques. Finally a set of conclusions are formed and future work is presented.

1.1 The Aragonese Laboratory of Usability

The Aragonese Laboratory of Usability (www.laboratoriousabilidad.com) is an initiative of the General Directorate of Technologies for the Information Society of the Government of Aragon, Spain. Its activities are developed in facilities shared with the Advanced Judicial Applications Laboratory (labje.unizar.es) at Walqa Technological Park, Huesca, (www.ptwalqa.com), with the Faculties of Law and Economics and Business Management and with the Polytechnic Superior Center (of Engineering) of the University of Zaragoza, Spain.

The Aragonese Usability Laboratory is a lab for research and development dedicated to the analysis, implementation and optimization of new techniques for the improvement of human-computer interfaces whose objectives are:

- To collaborate throughout the whole interface applications and websites design cycle to assure their usability and accessibility from the first stages of development
- To check to what extent this design adapts itself to the potential users and its ease in use by those users.
- To check the operation in different applications and websites platforms.
- To carry out accessibility test, based on standards such as those of the W3C.

The Laboratory also develops R & D projects in the field of interfaces usability and accessibility analysis and evaluation such as the investigation of the responses from the consumer to different stimuli, the application of different design techniques, the evaluation of interfaces based on the user's responses and on the heuristic evaluation of experts.

The Laboratory is already carrying out some studies for companies and institutions, such as the projects mentioned in the acknowledgements, among others.

1.2 The group of applications WebA

One of the first necessities of the Laboratory was to have a group of tools – which are called WebA (from Web Analysis) [9] [10], - which allowed managing the processes and evaluation sessions (online and in situ), automating the evaluation processes up to where it could be achieved.

At the moment this online management tool can be used online and in situ (registering the process, the management of evaluators, the selection of methods, the management of the development of sessions, reports). WebA also includes some semi automated web interfaces or applications evaluation tools (testing accessibility following the norms WCAG 1.0, the evaluation of usability adapting ISO 9241 10-17 norms, and the user satisfaction evaluation based on rules of Nielsen [11]).

The last lines of work have been centred on incorporating two new applications into WebA. The first is a tool that allows carrying out studies on the behaviour of consumers and users of a web page through logs analysis, and the second is the one that is presented here: aCaSo, a computer application that permits carrying out open & closed card sorting processes and their analysis following two methods: hierarchical clustering and multidimensional scaling.

2 The Technique of Card Sorting

The technique of Card Sorting [1] –which in its most traditional form consists in presenting a group of labelled cards with the description of the contents from a site to an observer so that he organizes them, from where it takes its name– is a method whose goal is to find the latent structure between a group of ideas or items that are not in order.

Here, these ideas represent the menu labels for the contents of the website which is being studied. In each card the identification name of each of the pages or sections that will form the final design should be written. This previous step of determination of these labels or descriptors is important because depending on the chosen words, the users will be able to locate the information more easily. A correct information architecture design will improve the "findability" of the contents.

In a session of Card Sorting the involvement of users is required. Each participant receives a pile of cards and he/she organizes them in groups according to his/her criteria, which the participant can assign a name to, and the evaluator will keep them in mind when designing the final solution. In this case we are speaking of open Card Sorting. Another option is that the number of groups and their names are already fixed and therefore the user must put each card in the category that he/she considers appropriate. In this case one would be speaking of a closed Card Sorting session.

When all the users have completed their session, the obtained set of data is analyzed with statistical algorithms that will provide a grouping based on the structures proposed by each user. This sorting process and analysis can be carried out in an automated way; at the present time several programs exist that can partially carry out these tasks.

The most used and complete at the moment is CardZort (http://www.cardzort.com/cardzort/index.htm). This program permits recollection of the groupings indicated by the user by means of an interface that simulates the real cards. Later on, the moderator of the session carries out the program that analyzes the data. This program gives a hierarchical structure that, as a result, is not very intuitive. The only algorithm which is used in data analysis is that of hierarchical clustering, which will be described later on.

This program is the most popular due to its simplicity, but as it has been mentioned it only uses one method of analysis. One of the goals of our application aCaSo was that other methods could be used, because on occasions those methods can achieve a better solution.

Other existing program is CardSword (http://cardsword.sourceforge.net/), which consists of two modules that carry out the analysis with algorithms of hierarchical clustering, too.

Only a program exists that uses multidimensional scaling: Concept System (http://www.conceptsystems.com/). This application is much more complex in use, and a bigger learning curve is needed. There are other types of programs that are only used for the gathering of data, such as CardSort (http://www.cardsort.net/).

2.1 Methods of Data Analysis

The data obtained after carrying out the experiment repeatedly with all the users are organized in a proximity matrix, where the element a_{ij} indicates how many times they have grouped element i with element j. Thus, a symmetrical matrix is created in which the algorithms of dimensional reduction are applied like clustering or dimensional scaling; neural networking can also be used.

Almost the entirety of the existing programs analyzes data using clustering. Next, we will see this method along with others.

2.1.1 Methods based on Clustering

The clustering method [2] consists in grouping the elements into subgroups. The grouping is carried out in function of a determined distance; to obtain this parameter the Euclidean distance [2] or the Minkowski one [2] can be used. This is one of the simplest methods that currently exist; this is one of the reasons for its popularity.

Four clustering algorithms exist: Hierarchical Clustering, Exclusive clustering, Overlapping clustering, and Probabilistic Clustering. The most used one for the management of sessions of Card Sorting is hierarchical clustering; therefore the next part continues to explain its operation extensively.

Hierarchical Clustering

This is an iterative method based on the union of the closest two clusters. The process begins grouping the two closest elements, then the two closest previous clusters and so on, according to one of these three criteria for union: simple linkage, complete linkage and average linkage as follows.

In this case (Card Sorting) the parameter distances are associated directly with the values gathered in the proximity matrix. The higher the value of a_{ij}, the higher relationship found among them by the users. The maximum number of each element in the matrix is obviously the number of participants of the session. Hence we look to unite the elements that have been grouped together the most (those of more value), because they are those that are mentally the closest.

Keeping in mind these values, two clusters unite if the distance among them is the maximum existing between two of its elements, the minimum, or the average of all of them, depending on the union criteria [2]:

Simple linkage

$$(D_{sl}(C_i, C_j) = \{\max_{x,y}\{d(x,y) \mid x \in C_i, y \in C_j\})$$

Complete linkage

$$(D_{sl}(C_i, C_j) = \{\min_{x,y}\{d(x,y) \mid x \in C_i, y \in C_j\})$$

Average linkage

$$(D_{sl}(C_i, C_j) = \frac{1}{|C_i||C_j|}\sum_{x_i \in C_i}\sum_{x_j \in C_j}d(x_i, x_j)), \text{ respectively.}$$

We consider D as a group of n points $D=\{x(1),...,x(n)\}$ and $D(Ci,Cj)$ as the function to measure the distance among the cluster C_i and C_j

The generic algorithm is the following [2]

```
For i=1..n let C_i={x(i)}
While there is more than one cluster left do
Let C_i and C_j be the cluster
Minimize the distance D(C_k,C_h) between any two clusters;
C_i= C_iUC_j
Remove C_j
end
```

The result of these algorithms is a dendrogram tree.

The possible advantages of these algorithms against others are that they are easy to implement and that they calculate a hierarchical structure that represents the organization of the thoughts of users. However, to a great extent the results depend on the definition of distance.

There are several disadvantages to this method. In the first place, the dendrogram can be interpreted in different ways, reaching an inadequate solution according to the desired goal. On the other hand the method does not allow that an element appears in two clusters, which could be convenient or necessary in some cases.

2.1.2 Scaling methods or multidimensional scaling (MDS)

Multidimensional scaling (further on referred to as MDS) [3] is a group of methods whose objective is to represent each item included in the session (of Card Sorting here) as points in a space of n dimensions; in which the distances among those points should belong together insofar as possible as their original dissimilitude. These dissimilitudes are represented in the proximity matrix that is calculated starting from the data obtained after the Card Sorting session. The proximity among each idea is therefore represented in a geometric space, usually in a Euclidean space.

To implement an MDS algorithm that analyzes the data obtained with Card Sorting, the classic non-metric multidimensional scaling should be chosen, which follows the Kruskal pattern [3]:

1. Choose the initial configuration
2. Normalize the configuration so that the centroid is in the origin
3. Find $\{d_{rs}\}$ for the normalized configuration
4. Adjust $\{d'_{rs}\}$
5. Find the gradient

being $\{d_{rs}\}$ the distances among each couple of points and $\{d'_{rs}\}$ the disparity in function of d_{rs} ($d'_{rs}=f(d_{rs})$).

The results in this type of algorithms can be represented in three different ways: a Shepard map, a screen plot or a map of points [3].

An important parameter in this technique is the election of the number of dimensions. The more dimensions, the more precision, even though the result is much more difficult to interpret, without taking into account the difficulty added to the calculation. The results are usually represented in two dimensions, as in our case.

The election of the initial configuration of the points also influences the final result. In our algorithm, this configuration is calculated starting from the values and vectors of the matrix.

MDS is more complex in calculation than other methods, but it is the most appropriate to use in order to give a general idea of the grouping. The hierarchical clustering would be more appropriate for a detailed grouping, as with items for submenus, for example.

2.1.3 Other methods for Data Analysis

Two more methods have been proposed to analyze the data: the pathfinder method and the neural networks.

The Pathfinder method [1] uses the proximity matrix as entry, just as in the cases previously mentioned. The representation of the concepts is carried out by means of nets. The items or ideas are the nodes, and the relationships are established between links among those nodes. The longitude of those links determines the closeness of two concepts. The information is not hierarchical. Therefore through these nets one can obtain the relationship among the contents, but not the structure.

A neural network [13] can only be applied to closed Card Sorting, since this method classifies elements in previously configured groups.

Before it could be used, a neural network needs a learning phase that can be very time consuming. In this phase the neuron "learns" what elements belong to one group or another, therefore that number should be fixed ahead of time.

3 The Application aCaSo (application for Card Sorting)

As it has already been explained, the application aCaSo (application for Card Sorting), developed in the Aragonese Laboratory of Usability, has as goal to computerize sessions of Card Sorting.

ACaSo has been integrated with the group of tools WebA. It consists of two parts: one carries out the sessions and collects the data from the part of the users, and the other manages and analyzes the data from the part of a Moderator or Administrator. Since it is a web application, all the tasks can be carried out online.

The elected methods for the analysis, as previously mentioned, are hierarchical clustering and multidimensional scaling. The first one has been chosen because of its acceptance, all or almost all the existent applications have chosen it to treat their data. Also, it is the most convenient method to scale a group and to create different levels of importance.

The second method is the most appropriate to obtain general groups, a first grouping level.

Comparing or combining the results obtained by these methods the analyst can obtain outlines to better reflect reality.

3.1 Types of aCaSo Users

To use the system, a person should belong to one of these three types of users:

1. System Administrator

The Administrator is in charge of registering new users and sessions. Administrator can create, supervise, edit and analyze any session. He is also in charge of assigning moderators for the sessions.

2. Moderator-Evaluator

Moderator is in charge of creating and publishing the "cards". If the session is open card sorting, he/she should also create the name of the groups or categories. It is necessary to keep in mind that he/she only has access to the sessions that the Administrator has assigned to him/her. He/she also has the capacity to analyze sessions.

3. User

Users can only participate in those sessions in which the Administrator has included them. Users group the cards, make comments and, in the case of open card sorting, can suggest names for the groups. Once they have completed the experiment they cannot carry out the experiment again.

3.2 Steps to be Carried out for the Realization of a Session

Several basic steps have to be carried out to complete a session of Card Sorting. Considering that the Moderator already has the cards that will form the experiment, the phases are as follows:

1. Creation of the session and registration of users by the Administrator

The Administrator introduces the data of the new session (name, description, moderator, open/closed) and registers the users that will carry out the experiment or includes the users that have been previously registered in the experiment. At any point in time he or she can include new users, it is not necessary that all are included at this time.

2. Preparing the experience by the Moderator

In this phase the cards to be used in the experiment should be introduced, and also the name of the categories in case of a closed session. The Administrator can add more users, or modify the session data.

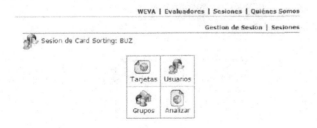

Fig. 5. Screen from where the Moderator selects the action to carry out: managing the cards (Tarjetas or Cards), seeing the users of a session (Usuarios or Users), managing the categories (Grupos or Groups, only for Closed CS), analyzing the session

3. Realization of the experience on the part on the users

In this phase the users will order the cards in the number of groups that they estimate are necessary. If the session is closed, they enter the cards in the appropriate groups.

The user logs in to the system by means of the identification system facilitated by the administrator and he/she chooses the session that he/she wants to participate in. Next the digital board is loaded with the cards to be grouped.

This interface simulates reality as much as possible with pictures of cards. Two areas are noticeable: one for the cards still not grouped (left) and another for the groups already created (right). To label a group it is only necessary to click on the label area and write the name that is in consideration (only in open card sorting).

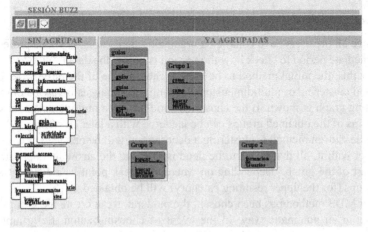

Fig. 2. Screen where a participant visualizes the Card Sorting

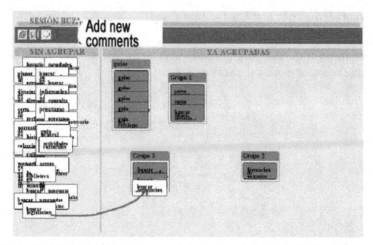

Fig. 3. Screen which shows the entering of comments and how the cards are used by the means of the mouse.

To move the cards on the board you click on the selected one in the left region and drag with the mouse until its final position and then release (click and drag). If the card aligns with a group, it will be included. If the user is participating in an opened Card Sorting session and the card is outside any group, a new group will be created.

At any moment comments can be included, which can be of use to the analyst. It is as easy as clicking on the corresponding icon that will open up a new window where the comments can be made.

As soon as all the cards are in the selected order, the user saves the grouping and returns to the initial screen. Once saved, it cannot be modified. It is preferable that the grouping is not very thought out, but rather that is a first opinion of the users, the most natural one.

4. Analysis of the data (task of the Moderator or of the Administrator)

Once all the users have completed organizing their cards, or if one prefers in an intermediate period to check how the session is going, the data is analyzed.

For this, the initial method to be used is chosen (one of the three types of hierarchical clustering or multidimensional scaling), the analysis is carried out and the resulting graph is shown. If the chosen method has been multidimensional scaling, the items of the obtained groups can be laddered with a later clustering.

If the chosen method is clustering a dendrogram will be obtained as a result. To interact with it, all that needs to be done is to move the arrow that appears in the top part of the graph. Depending on where the break point is, a different amount of groups (for the upper resulting category) will be obtained.

If a MDS method has been chosen, the moderator can create the groups manually or in an automatic way. In the event of choosing automatic grouping, the Moderator can modify the tolerance (a parameter that controls if two points should belong to the same group, therefore controlling the maximum distances allowed) increasing or diminishing the number of created groups.

In both types of algorithms the listing of cards located on the right is upgraded in real-time with the number of groups that are being created, so the analyst has at his/her disposal the items that will form each block through the actual ordering.

The application does not decide which is the best method in each case, it is the experience of the evaluator with the obtained results that will decide which is the most appropriate.

When a structure with several hierarchy (hierarchical MDS or clustering) levels is obtained, a new screen will appear to configure a maximum number of levels that it should have. For example, a site map has been obtained where cards appear in a seventh level. It is possible to configure the tool so that the maximum is four. This way, all the cards that are in lower levels will be grouped in the fourth level.

Once the obtained results have been accepted, the tool generates a report (a pdf file) gathering the most important data: structures obtained, proposed categories (if the session was open), the participants' comments, and problematic cards.

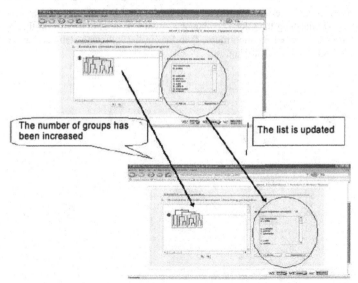

Fig. 4. Screen where the resulting dendrogram is shown. When moving the arrow the final number of groups has increased, as one can observe in the drawing and in the list on the right.

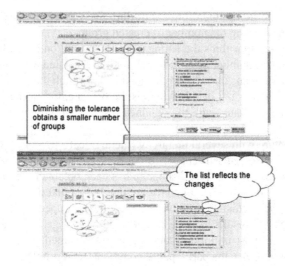

Fig. 5. Screen where the result is shown after the analysis of the data by means of multidimensional scaling. Diminishing the tolerance obtains a smaller number of groups. In this example a hierarchy has been selected for the groups, therefore in the following step each group will be analyzed separately through clustering.

Fig. 6. In this step the maximum depth of our web structure is decided. In this example, the maximum level has been set at 3 so that the page that is that is deeper in the structure would have a route: Start > Category i > Level 1 > Level 2 > Page (three clicks to arrive)

4 Validation of the Analysis Methods

To check the reliability of all the calculations and results, some set of obtained data were compared with those obtained with other tools using the same algorithms.

To test the *clustering* algorithm results were compared with the ones obtained with CardSword. The same groupings were provided to both applications as input, and the same results were achieved.

The validation of the algorithm of multidimensional scaling was carried out comparing results with an available library for Matlab created by Mark Steyvers [14] and with the statistical program SPSS.

As example, a session was analyzed with aCaSo and SPSS and two point maps where obtained (in the case of SPSS it was necessary to introduce the proximity matrix created with our tool). Both results are seen in figures 7 and 8.

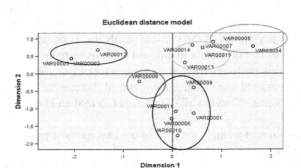

Fig. 7. Results of SPSS

Fig. 8. Results of aCaSo

As it can be observed the same groups were created with both applications.

5 A Real Case of Study

As a final test, aCaSo was used in a real case. The tool helped to generate the web map of the new Web of the University of Zaragoza Library (http://biblioteca.unizar.es). With the classification of 76 participants and taking into account their comments, a structure was obtained that reflects how the potential users organize the resources of a library. The results obtained from aCaSo needed only slight modifications to become the final solution for this complex web structure; a final user satisfaction test is in progress.

6 Conclusions and Future Work

The application aCaSo has been implemented as a solution to the necessity of tools that assist in the design of websites by part of the usability laboratories. aCaSo has been developed with the objective of having an application that allows managing and carrying out of the sessions, analyzing data, and visualizing results through Card Sorting with all the mentioned analysis techniques.

The use of this tool simplifies the management of the sessions avoiding the problems of traditional card management and of the presence of user-volunteers, with the added value of having all the data memorized and being the analysis immediate.

aCaSo combines in a single tool the whole management process and the analysis of data and presentation of results and reports.

The application has been checked by generating several experiments that were analyzed by means of other applications or different libraries, being the results perfectly acceptable.

Its utility has been proven by carrying out the study for the new Web of the Library of the University of Zaragoza, obtaining a web map resulting from the analysis of the data of a large number of card sorting sessions.

As for future work, the possibility of implementing some additional analysis method will be studied, as for example superimposed clustering, to study the contents that could go in two categories. It is also sought to include a method to guide the analyst during the whole process.

Another improvement is to soften the barrier among closed Card Sorting and open Card Sorting. In a closed session category creation by the users can be permitted if the Moderator considers it appropriate. Therefore, this option needs to be reflected in the tool.

Also it is sought that the user can create new cards because he/she considers that some web content is missing.

On the other hand, it is certain that one of the disadvantages of carrying out the sessions in a remote way is that the Moderator does not get the reactions and the users' first impressions are lost, as well as the Moderator's initial introduction and the resolution of doubts. The contact with the end users is of vital importance for usability studies, and a possible solution would be the use of webcams, the inclusion of a chat with the moderator, etc.

Acknowledgments   This paper have been partially financed from the R&D project of multidiscipline character "Analysis of the influence of the usability of the interface in the response of consumers" (PM 034) and from the agreement WALQA (ref. 2004/04/86) Dept. of Science, Technology and University of the Government of Aragon, and from the actions of improvement of the University Library of Zaragoza.

References

1. Bajo Molina, M. T., Cañas Delgado, J. J. (2001) Métodos indirectos de adquisición del conocimiento. P. Adarraga, J.L. Zaccagnini (Ed.) Psicología e Inteligencia Artificial. Editorial Trotta
2. Hand, D.J., Mannila, H., and Smyth, P.: Principles of Data Mining. MIT Press
3. Cox, T. F., & Cox, M. A. A. (1994) Multidimensional scaling. London: Chapman & Hall.
4. .Young, F. W. (1985) Multidimensional Scaling. Kotz-Johnson (Ed.) Encyclopedia of Statistical Sciences, Volume 5, John Wiley & Sons, Inc
5. Kruskal, J.B., Wish, M. (1981) Multidimensional scaling. Beverly Hills; London : Sage Publications,
6. Wickelmaier, F. (2003) An Introduction to MDS Sound Quality Research Unit, Aalborg University, Denmark May 4.
7. Jain A, Dubes R., (1988) Algorithms for clustering data, Prentice Hall
8. Schvaneveldt, R.W., Durso, F.T., Dearholt, D.W. (1985) Pathfinder: Scaling with network structures (Memorandum in Computer and Cognitive Science, MCCS-85-9). Las Cruces, NM: Computing Research Laboratory, New Mexico State University.
9. Mena, L., Latorre, P. (2004) WEVA: Herramienta semiautomática de evaluación de websites. V Congreso Interacción Persona – Ordenador Interacción, Lleida, 3-7 de Mayo 2004. Libro de Actas, pp. 322-325. ISBN 84-609-1266-3
10. WebA (Web Análisis) Herramienta de ayuda para el diseño y para la evaluación de la usabilidad y accesibilidad de sitios web Diseño de la Interacción Persona- Ordenador: Tendencias y Desafíos VII Congreso Internacional de Interacción Persona-Ordenador. Puertollano (Ciudad Real), 13 a 17 de noviembre de 2006. I.S.B.N.: 84-690-1613-X
11. Nielsen, J., and Molich, R. (1990) Heuristic evaluation of user interfaces, Proc. ACM CHI'90 Conf. (Seattle, WA, 1-5 April), 249-256.
12. Jain ANil K. Dubes Richard C. ALgorithms for Clustering data. Michigan State University Prentice Hall
13. Hilera, J. R., Martinez, V. J. (1995) Redes neuronales artificiales. Fundamentos, modelos y aplicaciones. Ed. RA-MA.
14. http://psiexp.ss.uci.edu/research/software.htm
15. Rosenfeld, L. and Morville, P. (2002) Information Architecture for the World Wide Web: Designing Large Scale Web Sites. O'Reilly & Associates

Intelligent User Interfaces: Past, Present and Future

V. López Jaquero, F. Montero, J.P. Molina, P. González

Laboratory of User Interfaces and Software Engineering (LoUISE) Instituto de Investigación en Informática (I3A) Universidad de Castilla-La Mancha, 02071 – Albacete (SPAIN)
{victor | fmontero | jpmolina | pgonzalez }@dsi.uclm.es

1 Introduction

Artificial Intelligence tries to simulate humans' capabilities by means of machines. This challenge, pushed in the world-famous Dartmouth conference in 1956, has focused an enormous amount of interest and effort of the research community in the last 50 years. Although after all these years the community has not been able to achieve to euphoric predictions enunciated at that conference, a good number of milestones in this simulation of human capabilities with machines have been achieved, endorsing the evolution of the Artificial Intelligence field.

Beyond any doubt, one of the cornerstones of simulating human capabilities is communication. Communication in this situation can be realized between humans, between machines or between humans and machines. Communication between humans has been studied for many years in communication theory, and communication between machines is still today a hot topic in conferences, with especial emphasis on ontologies and communication acts. Finally, communication between humans and machines is studied in Human-Computer Interaction discipline. This discipline deals with the design, implementation and evaluation of user interfaces.

The short, but incredibly active, history of computer science have witnessed a complete revolution of user interfaces, from the first command-based user interfaces to the most sophisticated graphical ones. Nowadays, the balance in computation is leaning towards interaction, fostering a growing interest in user interfaces. At the same time, the increasing complexity and sophistication of user interfaces is promoting the development of interaction techniques and modalities closer to the cognitive models of human beings. In the pursue of these goals, during the last fifty years, many different Artificial Intelligence techniques have been embedded into user interfaces to provide a more natural and productive human-computer interaction.

User interface is one of the main parts in an application. If it is properly designed it will make the user feel comfortable when interacting with the machine. On the other hand, even though if an application is able to perform the tasks it was designed for, the application will not be satisfactory to the users unless it is able to communicate with the user in an intelligible and usable manner. There is a real in-

M. Redondo et al. (eds.), *Engineering the User Interface*,
DOI: 10.1007/978-1-84800-136-7_18, © Springer-Verlag London Limited 2009

terest within Human-Computer Interaction community to improve the communication between the user and the machine, endorsed by the vast amount of researchers devoted to the study of techniques aimed at improving usability [16] in a user interface.

In the quest to create user interfaces with a high degree of usability, the Human-Computer Interaction research community is searching how to improve the feeling the user gets from the user interface. In this quest one key issue to be addressed is to make the interaction much more natural. This growing interest in making the interaction much more natural involves raising the quality of the communication between humans and machines. The underlying principles in a natural interaction have led to the consideration and adoption of a great amount of techniques coming from Artificial Intelligence in interaction design, allowing, among many other things, more accurate answers to users' actions. This integration of Artificial Intelligence techniques within Human-Interaction Techniques has coined the term Intelligent User Interfaces, where this work is immersed.

In this paper the evolution of those user interfaces with some degree of intelligence are analyzed, where the machines are supposed to communicate the relevant information in the most appropriate manner by applying one or several techniques based on Artificial Intelligence. Moreover, in this paper the current trends in Artificial Intelligence discipline applied to Human-Computer Interaction are reviewed too, foreseeing where the current paths the community is walking through, in these research lines, are leading us to.

The paper has been structured according to the following sections. First, the composing elements of regular user interfaces are described. Next, the historic evolution of the term intelligent user interface is reviewed, while showing the contributions from Artificial Intelligence. Finally, a general overview of an intelligent user interface runtime architecture is described in depth. The paper ends envisioning which are the current and future trends in the creation intelligent user interfaces.

2 The Different Facets of a User Interface

An interesting definition of user interface was provided by Negroponte [28] defining a user interface as the place where bits and people meet. In this sense, the user interface is the image the user perceives of the application, and the channel the user has to establish a communication with the machine.

In the interaction between users and machines different interaction styles have been used. The most successful of those interaction styles has been *direct manipulation* (see Fig. 1a). This kind of manipulation provides the user with the artifacts to directly manipulate a graphical representation of an application. Some typical examples of direct manipulation applications are most text editors, spreadsheets or video games.

The success of direct manipulation is the constant feedback provided on the task the user is performing at any moment. That continuous feedback on the manipulated objects implies the user is allowed to realize changes or corrections in the operations being executed immediately. Nevertheless, some the main problems in direct manipulation are that every task cannot be described by concrete objects, and not all the actions can be directly performed. Furthermore, in direct manipulation the user is required to perform every task and to control all the events arising from interaction. This requirement in complex applications can lead to cognitive overcharge, and therefore to a reduction of the usability of the system.

Because of the limitations of direct manipulation previously discussed, a new interaction style is emerging in the last years that tries to decrease those drawbacks: *indirect manipulation* [23] (see Fig. 1b). In this paradigm a new metaphor is used where some agents collaborate with the user in the same working environment. In this kind of interaction the user, instead of just manipulating the user interface, is involved in a collaborative environment in which both the user and the agents communicate, control events and perform tasks to achieve common goals. Indirect manipulation is closely related to interface agents.

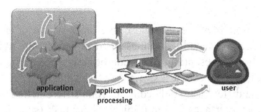

(a) Interaction by using direct manipulation.

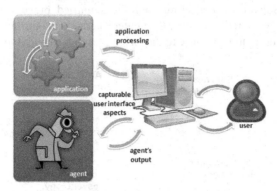

(b) Interaction by using indirect manipulation.

Fig. 1. Direct manipulation vs. indirect manipulation.

An interface agent [19] is similar to a program, which is allowed to manipulate the user interface, but it does not always require explicit user commands. Thus, it can take a proactive behavior performing certain tasks it thinks will help the user to complete his/her tasks. The interface agent reads the input the user transmits to the interface, and it is able to modify the objects shown in the screen (see Fig. 1b). User interface agents are different to simple wizards or assistants. These agents work in the background and take the initiative by themselves when they detect those situations they think are relevant to the user. For instance, if the interface agents are able to find out which task the user is currently carrying on, the agents can decide to hide those objects in the user interface which are not actually useful for the current task. Nevertheless, indirect manipulation is not free of problems [23]. One usual issue related with this type of manipulation is that the user might feel a sense of loss of control. Furthermore, some users dislike the idea of delegating tasks to agents, because some users prefer doing the jobs themselves. Unfortunately, one of the common, and most widely extended, misleading concepts in indirect manipulation is that any agent is anthropomorphic, which is not usually the case.

3 Intelligent User Interfaces

The Intelligent User Interfaces are those interfaces whose objective is improving the efficiency, affectivity and naturalness, and in general the usability, of human-machine interaction representing, reasoning or acting according to a set of models (user, domain, dialog, speech, tasks, …).

Because of the different models coming from differentiated disciplines, the development of user interfaces is a multidisciplinary task (see Fig. 2). Artificial Intelligence contributes the intelligence simulation techniques to improve the communication, Software Engineering contributes unified processes, notations and formal languages. Finally, Human-Computer Interaction contributes to the consideration of the user, and therefore to the techniques to create usable user interfaces.

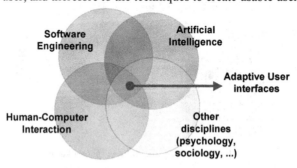

Fig. 2. Different disciplines involved in the development of intelligent user interfaces.

To achieve the main goal of intelligent user interfaces, and to support it in different contexts, they must be able to represent the knowledge they have about the users, the tasks they are allowed to perform through the user interface, the context of use where the user will interact with the application and have the ability to ana-lyze the inputs and generate the outputs in a proper manner [24] according to all the data collected and the knowledge they have.

The context of use is usually described by providing a model of the capabili-ties, skills and preferences of the users of the application, the platforms where those users will interact with the application (both the hardware and the software platform), and the physical environment where the interaction takes place (lumi-nosity, noise level, ...). In [22] the task the user is currently carrying out is also included in the context of use as a first order entity. Because the current task is included in the context of use, it is possible to better describe the reactions the sys-tem will issue given a concrete context of use. For instance, it can be used to eas-ily create context-sensitive help systems. Including the task in the context of use is really useful. However, it is not always possible to have a high degree of certainty about what is the task the user is currently performing. To find out which task is being currently performed, the authors apply some heuristics on a task model ac-cording to the interaction data received from the user. The heuristics work on the basis that at every time just the set of tasks "enabled" [29] in the current presenta-tion the user is interacting with are the potential tasks the user is conducting at a given time.

3.1 Intelligent User Interfaces Goals

In Fig. 3 some of the most relevant challenges found in intelligent user interfaces are shown [41]. These challenges are aimed at achieving the final goal pursued by intelligent user interfaces: improving system overall usability.

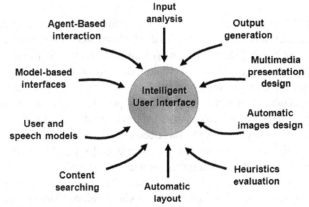

Fig. 3. Most usual goals found in intelligent user interfaces.

In Fig. 3 the reader can observe that some human capabilities such as learning, adaptation, reasoning or world modeling are included. All those capabilities are research lines identified in Artificial Intelligence from the very beginning of this discipline. Lots of Artificial Intelligence research works say that intelligence is a program able to be executed independently of the platform it is executed in, regardless it is a computer or a brain.

When the user interacts with an artifact, two models, the conceptual of the user and the implementation one of the machine must achieve some kind of balance and understanding. The user makes use of a concrete action language determined by the input devices and the metaphor the user interface has been designed with. On the other hand, the artifact must analyze the input, and answer the interaction by conforming the contents, its presentation, and it should also be able to assess the interaction process itself to draw conclusions about how convenient it is.

In Artificial Intelligence there are many fields that contribute techniques, methods and proposals of great interest to the development of intelligent user interfaces. In Artificial Intelligence it can be found methods to provide learning capabilities (such as neural networks or Bayesian networks), knowledge representation models (such as semantic networks or frames), decision models (such as fuzzy logic, expert systems, case-based reasoning and decision trees), etc.

By applying these contributions in intelligent user interfaces we are able to act on the user interface by supporting adaptation (ConCall [40], Mviews [4]), making its use easier (Déjà Vu [12],   STARZoom [3], VITE [15]), assessing interaction (SmartCanvas [25], TaskTracer [6]), simulating behaviors (Adele [17]), guiding the user (Alife-WebGuide [11]) or helping the user interface designer (Moby-D [33], U-TEL [5], EDEM [13], FUSE [20], SUPPLE [10]).

3.2 Intelligent User Interface Development

In software product development, and user interface is not an exception, the predominant tendency has been model-based user interface development (MB-UID) since the last few years [35, 7]. The main idea underlying this trend is to specify, in a declarative manner, a series of models describing the characteristics of the user, the tasks, the domain, the context of use, and the user interface at different levels of abstraction. A *model* is a simplified representation of a part of the world named the system. All those models are usually stored in an XML-based user interfaces description language. XML has become a de facto *lingua franca* for intelligent user interfaces [24]. Intelligent user interfaces [34] and hypermedia systems [18] are being developed following this approach nowadays.

The information the system has about both the application that is being executed and the context of use is stored in knowledge bases. The information about the application is mostly gathered during the different stages of design. In our case the meta-model used for storing the knowledge is a slightly modified version of the XML-based user interfaces description language usiXML[11]. However, other user interfaces description languages such as XIML[12] or UIML[13] could be used too. The user interface knowledge comprises:

- The *domain model* that stores those objects/data the user interface requires for the user to execute his/her tasks.
- The *task model* that represents those tasks the user will be allowed to perform by using the user interface, and the temporal constraints between these tasks. It is modeled by using a notation based on *ConcurTaskTrees* [29].
- The *abstract user interface model* includes the user interface expressed in terms of abstract interaction objects [39], and it is platform independent (it does not rely on the characteristics of the different types of platforms, such as PC, PDA or smart phone) and modality independent (graphical or vocal). This model is very useful to relate the interaction spaces where the widgets will be finally placed with the objects/data required to perform the tasks in those interaction spaces [21].
- The *concrete user interface model* represents the user interface, but in this case it is composed of concrete interaction objects [39]. In this case user interface representation is platform dependent, and it will be the main model used to generate the final user interface presented the user will actually interact with.
- The *context model* stores all the information regarding the context of use that the system is able to collect or manage. It comprises a user model, a platform model and an environment model.

The user model includes those characteristics of the user relevant to the system (preferences, skills, knowledge). This model is updated by applying user-modeling techniques [9, 14] to the input data collected by the sensors and the information already stored. For instance, the interaction history logs all the actions performed by the user in the user interface, so the system can apply data mining or classification techniques to infer new data about the user to update user model.

The platform model includes the characteristics (both hardware and software) of the potential profiles of platforms where the application can be executed. This model is also updated by processing the input data from sensors. For instance, if the user changes the screen resolution it produces a reduction in the visualization space available to present the contents, and therefore probably the layout of the contents, or even the contents themselves, will change. Thus, when the user changes the screen resolution a software sensor detects the change so the platform model can be updated accordingly.

The environment model includes the information about the physical environment where interaction is carried out. Obviously, the potential amount of information collected from the environment would be enormous, and therefore the de-

---

[11] http://www.usixml.org

[12] http://www.ximl.org

[13] http://www.uiml.org

signer must decide which information is relevant because it has an impact in the use of the application. Again, the information stored in this model is kept up-to-date by the incoming data from sensors.

A good interaction management implies an efficient and effective use of all the information stored in the knowledge bases of the models previously described.

Human-computer interaction leverages the design of intelligent user interfaces contributing to issues about the consideration of usability and quality of use [2] that a user interface should always have. *Usability* refers to the extent to which a product can be used by specific users to achieve specified goals with effectiveness, efficiency and satisfaction in a specified context of use (ISO 9241-11). The metaphors, already discussed, the increasing processing power and the new ways of interacting are enforcing the rising of new methodologies supporting the consideration of interaction objects different to those traditionally considered [26]. Most of these methodologies involve or at least take inspiration from *User-Centered Design* (UCD). *User-Centered Design* (UCD) is a highly structured, comprehensive product development methodology driven by: (1) clearly specified, task-oriented business objectives, and (2) recognition of user needs, limitations and preferences.

4 Envisioning the Future: Current Challenges

Nowadays intelligent user interfaces development presents challenges similar to those found in Artificial Intelligence. In the field of human-computer interaction it is well known that the ideal user interface is the non-existing one. Nevertheless, currently it is essential to have an intermediary between the user's intentions and the execution of those intentions. It does not matter how intuitive a user interface is, it will always be there and will yield a cognitive load to the user.

The computer of the future, according to A. van Dam or T. Furness [44], will be a perfect butler that knows my environment, my tastes and my personality, and in a discreet manner gets ahead of my needs without requiring explicit commands. When the user interacts with this butler, the interaction will be mostly spoken, by gestures, facial expressions [30, 32] and other human communication forms, such as drawing drafts. Being able to provide artifacts supporting learning, creation or communication peer to peer with a person has been an aspiration of Artificial Intelligence since its very beginning, 50 years ago.

To make it come true, some agents will be required to interpret gestures and expressions by applying computer vision techniques, or voice processing to recognize and understand natural language. Artificial Intelligence and knowledge-based systems will be the inference engine for those agents. When those agents communicate with the user they will make it in a polite manner, and probably modulate their voice according to the mood the user has at a given time.

The challenges of this technology can be divided in three areas: input, inference and output, and more concretely in the interpretation of the expression human languages, in the representation and management of the environment knowledge and, finally, in understanding human individuals as social beings.

5 Conclusions

Nowadays software products have the capacity to provide us with information, to make us enjoy or to make our work easier, but they can also slow up our work if the user interface offered is constrained or hard to use. In this paper a vision has been shown of how different techniques coming from different disciplines, namely, Artificial Intelligence, Software Engineering and Computer-Human Interaction, have been added through the years to contribute to a satisfactory interaction experience to the user, increasing the overall usability of the system.

In the future, user interfaces should be as natural as talking to a person. We all should remember that the final goal of Human-Computer Interaction is to decrease the cognitive gap between the user and its tasks, making the interface dim until it becomes invisible. Nevertheless, there is still a long way to go to get to the point where we can provide invisible interfaces to the users.

Acknowledgments   This work is partly supported by the Spanish projects PAI06-0093-8836 and ADACO: ADAptive and COllaborative web based systems (TIN2004-08000-C03-01)

References

1. Benyon, D. and Murray D. (1993) Developing adaptive systems to fit individual aptitudes. In Proc. of the 1st Int. Workshop on Intelligent User Interfaces IWIUI'93 (Orlando, January 4-7, 1993). ACM Press, New York, pp. 115–121.
2. Bevan, N. (1999) Quality in Use: Meeting user needs for quality. Journal of Systems and Software 49(1): 89-96.
3. Bruno, P., Ehrenberg, V., (1998) Holmquist. STARzoom: an interactive visual database interface. Proceedings of the 4th international conference on Intelligent user interfaces. Los Angeles, California, United States, 188.
4. Cheyer, A., Julia, L. (1997) MVIEWS: multimodal tools for the video analyst. Proceedings of the 3rd international conference on Intelligent user interfaces. San Francisco, California, United States. 55 – 62.
5. Chung-Man, R., Maulsby, D., Puerta, A. (1997) U-TEL: a tool for eliciting user task models from domain experts. Proceedings of the 3rd international conference on Intelligent user interfaces. San Francisco, California, United States. 77 – 80.
6. Dragunov, A., Dietterich, T., Johnsrude, K., McLaughlin, M., Li, L., Herlocker, J. (2005) TaskTracer: a desktop environment to support multi-tasking knowledge workers. Proceedings of the 10th international conference on Intelligent user interfaces. San Diego, California, USA. 75 – 82
7. Eisenstein, J., Vanderdonckt, J., Puerta, A. (2001) Applying model-based techniques to the development of UIs for mobile computers. Intelligent User Interfaces: 69-76

8. Fernández-Caballero, A., López Jaquero, V., Montero, F., González, P. (2003) Adaptive Interaction Multi-agent Systems in E-learning/E-teaching on the Web. International Conference on Web Engineering, ICWE 2003. Oviedo, Spain, July 14-18, 2003. Proceedings. Springer Verlag, LNCS 2722, pp. 144-154. ISSN:0302-9743.

9. Fischer, G. (2000) User Modeling in Human-Computer Interaction. User Modeling and User-Adapted Interaction, Kluwer Academic Publishers.

10. Gajos, K., Weld, D. SUPPLE: automatically generating user interfaces. Proceedings of the 9th international conference on Intelligent user interface. Funchal, Madeira, Portugal

11. Gaudiano, P., Kater, K. (2000) ALife-WebGuide: an intelligent user interface for Web site navigation. Proceedings of the 5th international conference on Intelligent user interfaces. New Orleans, Louisiana, United States. 121 – 124.

12. Gordon, A., Domeshek, E. (1997) Deja Vu: a knowledge-rich interface for retrieval in digital libraries. International Conference on Intelligent User Interfaces. Proceedings of the 3rd international conference on Intelligent user interfaces. San Francisco, California, United States. 127 – 134.

13. Hilbert, D., Robbins, J., Redmails, D. (1997) EDEM: intelligent agents for collecting usage data and increasing user involvement in development. Proceedings of the 3rd international conference on Intelligent user interfaces. San Francisco, California, United States. 73 – 76.

14. Horvitz, E., Breese, J., Heckerman, D., Hovel, D., Rommelse, K. (1998) The Lumiere Project: Bayesian User Modeling for Inferring the Goals and Needs of Software Users. Proceedings of the Fourteenth Conference on Uncertainty in Artificial Intelligence, Madison, WI, July 1998, Morgan Kaufmann: San Francisco, pp. 256-265.

15. Hsieh, H., Shipman, F. (2000) VITE: a visual interface supporting the direct manipulation of structured data using two-way mappings. Proceedings of the 5th international conference on Intelligent user interfaces 1998. New Orleans, Louisiana, United States. 141 – 148.

16. ISO 9241-11. Ergonomic requirements for office work with visual display terminals (VDTs) - Part 11: Guidance on usability.

17. Johnson, W. L., Shaw, E. Marshall, A., LaBore, C. (2003) Evolution of user interaction: the case of agent adele. Proceedings of the 8th international conference on Intelligent user interfaces. Miami, Florida, USA. 93 – 100.

18. Lang, M., Fitzgerald, B. (2005) Hypermedia Systems Development Practices: A Survey IEEE Software. Volume 22 , Issue 2 (March 2005). 68 – 75.. IEEE Computer Society Press   Los Alamitos, CA, USA

19. Lieberman, H. (1995) Letizia: An Agent That Assists Web Browsing. In Proceedings of the Fourteenth International Joint Conference on Artificial Intelligence (IJCAI-95), pp. 924-929, Montreal, Canada, Morgan Kaufmann publishers Inc.: San Mateo, CA, USA.

20. Lonczewski, F. (1997) Providing user support for interactive applications with FUSE. Proceedings of the 2nd international conference on Intelligent user interfaces. Orlando, Florida, United States. 253 – 256.

21. López Jaquero, V., Montero, F., Molina, J.P., Fernández-Caballero, A., González, P. (2003) Model-Based Design of Adaptive User Interfaces through Connectors. Design, Specification and Verification of Interactive Systems 2003, DSV-IS 2003. In DSV-IS 2003 : Issues in Designing New-generation Interactive Systems Proceedings of the Tenth Workshop on the Design, Specification and Verification of Interactive Systems. J.A. Jorge, N.J. Nunes, J. F. Cunha (Eds). Springer Verlag, LNCS 2844. Madeira, Portugal June 4-6, 2003.

22. López Jaquero, V., Montero, F., Molina, J.P., González, P. Fernández Caballero, A. (2005) A Seamless Development Process of Adaptive User Interfaces Explicitly Based on Usability Properties. Proc. of 9th IFIP Working Conference on Engineering for Human-Computer Interaction jointly with 11th Int. Workshop on Design, Specification, and Verification of Interactive Systems EHCI-DSVIS'2004 (Hamburg, July 11-13, 2004). LNCS, Vol. 3425, Springer-Verlag, Berlin, Germany.

23. Maes, P., Schneiderman, B. (1997) Direct Manipulation vs. Interface Agents: a Debate. Interactions, 4 , Number 6, ACM Press.

24. Maybury, M. (1999) Intelligent user interfaces: an introduction. In Proceedings of the 4th international Conference on intelligent User interfaces (Los Angeles, California, United States, January 05 - 08, 1999). IUI '99. ACM Press, New York, NY, 3-4.

25. Mo, Z., Lewis, J.P., Neumann, U. (2005) SmartCanvas: a gesture-driven intelligent drawing desk system. International Conference on Intelligent User Interfaces Proceedings of the 10th international conference on Intelligent user interfaces. San Diego, California, USA,.

26. Molina, J. P., García, A.S., López Jaquero, V. and González, P. (2005) Developing VR applications: the TRES-D methodology. First International Workshop on Methods and Tools for Designing VR applications (MeTo-VR), in conjuntion with 11th International Conference on Virtual Systems and Multimedia (VSMM'05), Ghent, Belgium

27. Montero, F., López Jaquero, V., Ramírez, Y., Lozano, M., González. P. (2005) Patrones de Interacción: para usuarios y para diseñadores. VI Congreso de Interacción Persona-Ordenador. 13-16 Septiembre, Granada, España.

28. Negroponte, N. (1994) Being Digital. Vintage books, Nueva York, NY

29. Paternò, F. (1999) Model-Based Design and Evaluation of Interactive Applications. Springer.

30. Picard, R. (1997) Affective Computing, MIT Press.

31. Pinheiro da Silva, P., Griffiths, T., Paton, N. (2000) Generating user interface code in a model based user interface development environment. Proceedings of the working conference on Advanced visual interfaces. Palermo, Italy. 155 – 160.

32. Prendinger, H. and Ishizuka, M. (2005) The Empathic Companion: A Character-Based Interface that Addresses Users' Affective States. In Applied Artificial Intelligence, Vol.19, pp. 267–285.

33. Puerta, A., Maulsby, D. (1997) Management of interface design knowledge with MOBI-D. Proceedings of the 2nd international conference on Intelligent user interfaces. Orlando, Florida, USA. 249 – 252.

34. Puerta, A., Micheletti, M., Mak, A. (2005) The UI pilot: a model-based tool to guide early interface design Full text. Proceedings of the 10th international conference on Intelligent user interfaces. San Diego, California, USA. 215 – 22.

35. Puerta, A.R. (1997) A Model-Based Interface Development Environment. IEEE Software.

36. Rich, C., Lesh, N.B., Rickel, J., and Garland, A. (2002) A Plug-in Architecture for Generating Collaborative Agent Responses. In Proc. Of AAMAS'2002 (Bologna, July 15-19, 2002). ACM Press, New York, 782–789.

37. Szekely, P. (1996) Retrospective and Challenges for Model-Based Interface Development. DSV-IS 1996: 1-27.

38. Vanderdonckt, J. (1999) Advice-giving systems for selecting interaction objects, in Proc. of 1st Int. Workshop on User Interfaces to Data Intensive Systems UIDIS'99 (Edinbourg, 5-6 septembre 1999), IEEE Computer Society Press, Los Alamitos, pp. 152-157.

39. Vanderdonckt, J., Bodart, F. (1993) Encapsulating Knowledge for Intelligent Automatic Interaction Objects Selection. In ACM Proc. of the Conf. On Human Factors in Computing Systems INTERCHI'93 (Amsterdam, 24-29 April 1993), S. Ashlund, K. Mullet, A. Henderson, E. Hollnagel & T. White (Eds.), ACM Press, New York.

40. Waern, A., Tierney, M., Rudsstrom, A., Laaksolahti, J. (1998) ConCall: edited and adaptive information filtering. Proceedings of the 4th international conference on Intelligent user interfaces. Los Angeles, California, United States 185.

41. Wahlster, W., Maybury, M. (1998) An Introduction to Intelligent User Interfaces. In: RUIU, San Francisco: Morgan Kaufmann, pp. 1- 13.

42. Wooldridge, M., Jennings, N.R. Agent Theories, Architectures, and Languages: A Survey, Proc. ECAI-Workshop on Agent Theories, Architectures and Languages (eds. M.J. Wooldridge and N.R. Jennings), Amsterdam, The Netherlands, pp. 1-32, 1994.

43. Limbourg, Q., Vanderdonckt, J., Michotte, B., Bouillon, L., López Jaquero, V. (2005) UsiXML: a Language Supporting Multi-Path Development of User Interfaces, Proc. of 9th IFIP Working Conference on Engineering for Human-Computer Interaction jointly with 11th Int. Workshop on Design, Specification, and Verification of Interactive Systems EHCI-

DSVIS'2004 (Hamburg, July 11-13, 2004). LNCS, Vol. 3425, Springer-Verlag, Berlin, Germany.

44. Earnshaw, R., Guedj, R., van Dam, A. and Vince, J. (2001) Frontiers in Human-Centred Computing, Online Communities and Virtual Environment. Springer-Verlag.

Author Index

Subject Index